VISUAL COMMUNICATION ON THE WEB

This book is more than the typical web design manual. *Visual Communication on the Web* integrates practice with theory, providing technical how-to alongside the theoretical, aesthetic, and historical framework you'll need to create thoughtful, functional, and beautifully designed web pages. While interactive exercises in the book explore the technical side of design, concise introductions relate history, design principles, and visual communication theories to the practice of designing for the web. Videos and links embedded in the accompanying Interactive eTextbook will give you additional hands-on web design experience.

By working your way through this text from start to finish, you will learn how to think visually about communicating online and also how to think analytically about assembling code to display your message. Over the course of 14 chapters, a series of exercises helps you create and revise one dynamic web page while learning new coding and tools. Predictable mistakes are purposely included, so you'll learn how to "fix" the project while working on it—a crucial skill for anyone working with code. By the end of this course-in-a-book, you will have created a web page with a centered container div, a Lightbox image gallery, and an external style sheet using HTML, CSS, and copy-pasted and modified code.

The Interactive eTextbook provides concise videos of burrough detailing some of the more complex step-by-step instructions and original chapter introductions by Lester. Users of the eTextbook may also engage in a traditional assessment exercise to test their knowledge of new material. For those who aren't reading electronically, many of these resources are freely available on the blog, viscommontheweb.wordpress.com.

With easy-to-follow instruction and lucid theoretical introductions, *Visual Communication on the Web* makes an excellent companion to xtine burrough's *Digital Foundations* and *Net Works* as well as Paul Martin Lester's *Visual Communication: Images with Messages*.

xtine burrough is Associate Professor in the Department of Communications at California State University, Fullerton. She is the co-author of *Digital Foundations*, editor of *Net Works*, and author of *Foundations of Digital Art and Design*.

Paul Martin Lester is Professor in the Department of Communications at California State University, Fullerton. He is the author of *The Ethics of Photojournalism*, *Visual Communication: Images with Messages*, *Visual Journalism: A Guide for New Media Professionals*, and other titles.

D1318412

VISUAL COMMUNICATION ON THE WEB

PRINCIPLES AND PRACTICES

xtine burrough and Paul Martin Lester

Routledge
Taylor & Francis Group

NEW YORK AND LONDON

First published 2013
by Routledge
711 Third Avenue, New York, NY 10017

Simultaneously published in the UK
by Routledge
2 Park Square, Milton Park, Abingdon, Oxon OX14 4RN

Routledge is an imprint of the Taylor & Francis Group, an informa business

Library of Congress Cataloging-in-Publication Data
burrough, xtine.
  Visual communication on the web / xtine burrough, Paul Martin Lester.
     p. cm.
  Includes bibliographical references and index.
  1. Web sites—Design.   2. Visual communication.   I. Lester, Paul Martin.   II. Title.
  TK5105.888.B85575 2013
  006.7—dc23
                                                                        2012023502

ISBN: 978-0-415-52148-2 (pbk)

Typeset in GaramondThree
by diacriTech

Printed and bound in the United States of America
by Edwards Brothers, Inc.

The authors of this book would like to ~~dedicate it to~~ recognize their nostalgia for Anna Atkins, cyanotype prints, and deprecated tags.

CONTENTS

5 Overview of Styles   71

6 Transferring Files   95

7 Web Typography   111

PREFACE

During the following 14 chapters Paul Martin Lester and I have taken a vow to remember that even the most technical aspects of creating visual media for display on the web can be inspired by design principles that relate to all areas of history.

I'm not a fan of prefaces, the first day of school, or first dates, so here's what you need to know before you begin:

You will need to use Adobe Dreamweaver (versions 5.5 or 6) or an application for writing code. In Chapter 2 you will need to edit an image (I demonstrate this using Adobe Photoshop in versions 5.5 and 6). You can work on a Macintosh or a PC. Since this book was written from the perspective of a Mac user, PC users should translate any instance of the words "Command key" with "Control key." The Options key rarely comes into play, but when it does, you will use the Alt key on a PC.

The exercises in Chapter 1 start at the most basic, beginner level. By the time you complete the exercises in Chapter 14, you will probably be writing code without using the panels and dialog boxes in Dreamweaver. To help you achieve this goal, I have shared fewer images of my Dreamweaver panels and more code that you will need to implement as you progress through the book. Almost every chapter builds upon the previous ones. If you don't want to work through every exercise, you can download the files that I created while completing the exercises from the blog produced in the demonstration of scheduling posts and other activities in Chapter 4. [http://viscommontheweb.wordpress.com/downloads/] There are also a few files on the blog that you will need to download in order to complete Chapters 2 and 10.

If you work your way through this text from start to finish, you will learn how to think visually about assembling messages for the web, as well as how to think analytically about how to assemble the code that makes the web page display your message. We focus on one or two topics in each chapter, so we will build and revisit parts of the page repeatedly until it is finished. Yes, it really does take reading and completing the exercises in 14 chapters to learn how to build a single web page.

Sometimes the code won't work. Sometimes we'll (purposefully, of course) *forget* about elements that snuck into the wrong parts of the code. Together we will hit many of the pitfalls that you are bound to find when working on a creative web project yourself. You will see that code can be fixed just as easily as it can be broken.

To help you focus on important parts of the code, HTML tags, CSS selectors, properties and values are all set in a typographic style to remind you that these words are proper names. For instance, if I write about the **body** tag it would look as so, or maybe like this: **<body>**. Sometimes I share a block of code, as follows:

```
<html>
  <head>
      <body>
          Hi there. You look nice.
      </body>
  </head>
</html>
```

Some exercises call for the addition or subtraction of code. To make this clear, new code is set in black text next to the old code in gray. If you need to delete code, it will have a strike through it, like this set of code from Chapter 8:

Remove excess tags in the HTML code	
`<div><span class="header">Anna Atkins</span></div>`	The original code includes the **div** and **span** tags.
`<div class="header"><span class="header">Anna Atkins</span></div>`	Remove the **span** tag and assign the class to the **div** tag.
`<div class="header">Anna Atkins</div>`	The modified code is simpler, more efficient, and results in a smaller file size.

I am forever indebted to Christopher James, who taught me how to make a cyanotype print when I was a photography student at the Art Institute of Boston in the early 1990s. I still make cyanotype prints and will always feel a connection to and nostalgia for Anna Atkins' mysterious images of British algae. Atkins was among the first photographers to publish a book illustrated with photographs (Fox Talbot's *Pencil of Nature* was published shortly after Atkins' privately published *Photographs of British Algae: Cyanotype Impressions*). The web page that we will wrestle with throughout this text is in homage to Atkins. You will need some images of her work and information for your web page, which you will be advised to download later in this text from the New York Public Library Flickr set and Wikipedia.

Finally, I would like to extend my gratitude to Dr. Les (less formally, my partner in all things) for agreeing to embark upon this project with me. This has been the most fun I have ever had writing a textbook.

Yours truly dear reader,
xtine

ACKNOWLEDGMENTS

It has been an absolute pleasure to work (again!) with Erica Wetter, Margo Irvin, and the Routledge team. Ewan Stevenson showed us a nice time around a "bunch of old buildings" in Oxford (his words). His dedication to the electronic book is greatly appreciated.

We are grateful for our supportive colleagues in the Department of Communications at California State University, Fullerton. A special thank you must be expressed toward those students who used this book in draft format as we worked the kinks out of the exercises that appear in each chapter.

Thank you, always, from xtine to Christopher James at The Art Institute of Boston at Lesley University and from Paul to JB Colson at The University of Texas, Austin for showing us what a passion for photography (whether printed in blue or not) looks like and to be observant in our careers as visual communicators.

VISUAL TOUR

Access your Interactive eTextbook at home, on campus or on the move*, online or offline. Your eTextbook offers note sharing and highlighting functionality, as well as exclusive interactive content to enhance your learning experience. The notes you make on your Interactive eTextbook will synchronise with all other versions, creating a personalised version that you can access wherever and whenever you need it.

Throughout the text you will see icons in the margin where further multimedia resources are available via your Interactive eTextbook. These include:

 offline materials   audio and video

 online resources curated by the author

Unique to *Visual Communication on the Web*...

- A video introduction to the book and author team

---

*BookShelf will provide access to your eTextbook either online or as a download via your PC, Mac (OS X 10.6>), iPad, iPhone, iPod Touch (iOS 3.2>), Android app or Amazon Kindle Fire.

- Screencasts from xtine to walk you through the more complicated steps in the design process

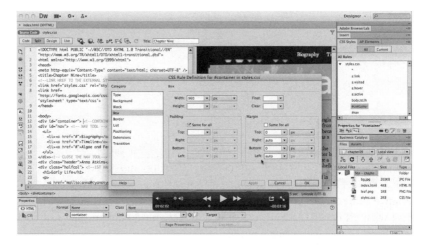

- Videos from Paul expanding upon the different concepts

- Interactive exercises to test your knowledge
- Color versions of the print book's black and white figures
- Screenshots from Dreamweaver CS5, to accompany those in CS6, for those users yet to update
- All of the files to build the website embedded within the Interactive eTextbook for offline use

You can also find the files to build the website at http://viscommontheweb.wordpress.com/

1   GETTING STARTED

VIDEO
INTRODUCTION

Principles, History, Theory

A Brief History of the Web

Which came first—the chicken or the egg?

Although often asked as a joke or, more seriously, as an introduction to a discussion of the nature of evolution, moral philosophy, or between two grocery store clerks, the answer shouldn't be controversial. A recent study suggests the chicken came first. A protein within a chicken's ovaries helps form the egg. Likewise, questions about media technology are also easily put to rest through historical research: paper or the printing press? Paper. Film or cameras? Cameras. Internet or the World Wide Web? Internet.

After the United States was close to its first all-out, scorched-earth, duck-under-your-desk-and-die thermal nuclear war with the Union of Soviet Socialist Republics (USSR) during the 1962 Cuban missile crisis, U.S. military officials who thought they might survive the apocalypse in their secret underground bunkers realized they would need to communicate with others. However, there was a significant challenge: how to chat on the phone with your friends after most of the telephone wires in the country melted. As a result, the Advanced Research Projects Agency (**ARPA**) started to discuss a communications network via computers with a young program manager, Vint Cerf. The Internet was born as a communication technology that could send parts of text messages in separate packets that traveled various routes to be reassembled into a coherent whole message at the destination. In 1969 the first e-mail message was sent between the University of California at Los Angeles (UCLA) and the Stanford Research Institute using a computer network called ARPANet (Figure 1.1). The choice of these two educational institutions was not a coincidence—Cerf received an undergraduate degree in mathematics from Stanford University and a master's and PhD from UCLA. The first text must have been a bit of a disappointment, as the student programmer typing in the command "login" got as far as the "l" and the "o" before the system crashed. Nevertheless, after more computer users started using the ARPANet for work-related and personal messages, the system became so popular that in 1983 it was divided in half—the original ARPANet for university use and MILNet for the military. When satellite links were added to the system, worldwide communication became possible. ARPANet's name was changed to the International Network, now simply referred to as the Internet.

As a result of their work, Cerf, along with his colleague, Robert Kahn, are considered the founders of the Internet. The two received the National Medal of Technology from President Clinton and the Presidential Medal of Freedom from President George W. Bush. Since 2005, Cerf has been a vice president with the title "Chief Internet Evangelist" for the search engine company Google, and reportedly enjoys fine wines, cooking gourmet meals, and reading science fiction.

Figure 1.1 According to the *CIA Fact Book*, the number of Internet hosts within North America far exceeds those in Africa. *Courtesy of Roke (WikiCommons).*

A *net* is useful for catching fish, stopping a soccer ball, and keeping hair out of a customer's food, but as a metaphor for communications, it cannot compete with a *web*, an organic entity that continually grows and shimmers with internal energy when illuminated. Chatting over e-mail and transferring files with a net is all well and good, but the enduring capability of the Internet would soon reveal itself, not through green text messages on a black background, but by the graphically robust World Wide Web.

In the 1950s, Conway Berners-Lee met his future wife, Mary Lee Woods, when they were both programmers who helped produce the first commercial computer, the British Ferranti Mark 1. Eleven months after their wedding, they celebrated the birth of their son, Tim Berners-Lee—no doubt born with a silver mouse. Naturally, he became a scientist, graduating with a physics degree from Oxford University. In 1990, Berners-Lee was working for the Geneva-based European Particle Physics Laboratory, known as CERN, a workplace for more than 10,000 scientists, engineers, professors, and students throughout the world who study high-energy physics using its atomic particle accelerators. Berners-Lee, along with collaborator Robert Cailliau, developed a way to transfer large files between researchers in the tradition of Vint Cerf and his fellow Internet creators. Originally named the Enquire Project, the result was a program named the World Wide Web, with the now familiar acronyms HTTP (Hypertext Transfer Protocol), HTML (Hypertext Markup Language), and URL (Uniform Resource Locator). Ordinary words in a word processing file become *hypertext*, with links to additional materials. In a speech Berners-Lee later made to the International World Wide Web Conference in Budapest, he realized the link between work and play when he said, "Your data is a web, and your life is a web." For his innovations in mass communications, *Time* magazine in 1999 listed him as one of the most influential persons of the 20th century. In 2004 the Queen of England knighted him.

Sir Berners-Lee's program was fine for computer geeks, but it wasn't, would later become a tired and overworked phrase, user-friendly. It took a University of Illinois college student from Iowa and a programmer for the National Center for Supercomputing Applications (NCSA) located on the University of Illinois at Urbana-Champaign campus to create the first killer app, a web browser for the rest of us. Marc Andreessen and Eric

Bina, whose names are engraved on a plaque in front of the NCSA building, developed the code that became the first browser, *Mosaic* (Figure 1.2). Andreessen left the university for California to form Netscape Communications in 1993, which was purchased by America Online six years later for $4.2 billion. He used his wealth to help finance the social media websites Digg and Twitter, launched a new browser, RockMelt, in 2010 that effortlessly links users with Facebook, and is married to Laura Arrillaga, the daughter of the Basque real estate billionaire John Arrillaga. Bina stayed with NCSA, helped license the Mosaic source code to Microsoft, which was used as the basis for its Internet Explorer browser, and had the phrase "Unsung Hero" printed on his business cards.

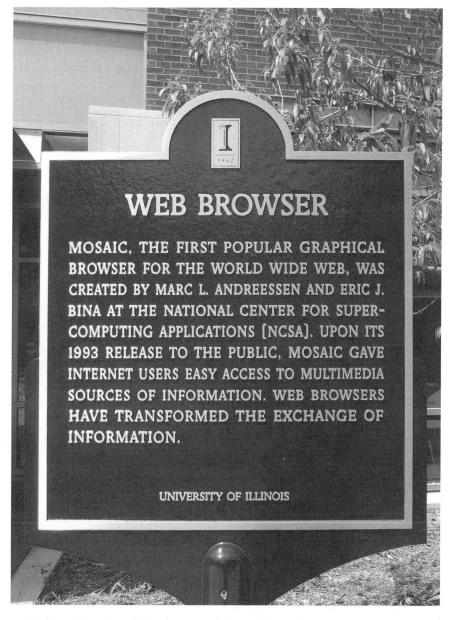

Figure 1.2 The University of Illinois hosts this historical marker that indicates where the first web browser was created. *Courtesy of Ragib Hasan.*

When Andreessen left Illinois, the Internet had about 15 million users worldwide. Today it is estimated that there are two billion users, or about 30% of the Earth's population. The tremendous growth is directly attributable to the ease of use and graphical interface that is the Web. As a medium of communication, it is a dominating force that combines and makes better all other previously known technologies.

Practice

HTML and CSS

HTML is an acronym for Hypertext Markup Language. Hypertext supports links between pages or other types of references, while the markup language represented by tags in the HTML document instructs the browser to display content such as text, images, video, animation, and audio. *CSS* stands for Cascading Style Sheets. Styles or style sheets are used in combination with the markup tags in HTML pages to separate the design of the page from the content. This code is used to instruct the browser how content on a web page should appear. Chapters 5, 7, 8, 9, 10, 11, and 12 focus on combining HTML markup with CSS code. In Chapters 13 and 14 you will learn to validate your code and consider issues related to browser compatibility.

Results of Chapter 1 Exercises

In the following exercises you will create an HTML document in TextEdit, and then modify it in Dreamweaver. You will view your offline work in a web browser (Figure 1.3).

Download Materials for Chapter 1 Exercises

No files are required to begin the exercises in Chapter 1. However, you may download my Chapter 1 results files from the website to see the page that you will make in the following

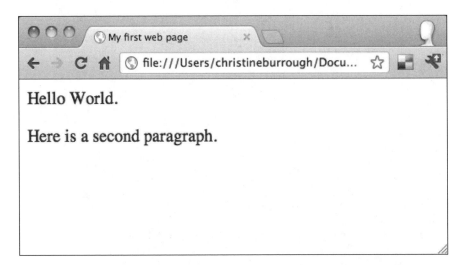

Figure 1.3 When all Chapter 1 exercises are complete, the resulting file is an HTML document that can be previewed in a web browser. Two sentences appear on separate lines as a result of the paragraph tag, <p>.

exercises or to check your work when you are finished. Double-click the ZIP file to decompress the archived folder, *chapter01-results*. Inside the ZIP folder you will find my HTML file, *index.html*. [http://viscommontheweb.wordpress.com/downloads/]

Exercise 1: Creating an HTML File in a Text Editor

While working on the exercises in this chapter, commit to saving everything that you make in one folder saved on your computer. It is recommended that students save to the Desktop and then copy their files to an external hard drive when they are finished with the lesson. Do not make subfolders. Do not make more than one folder. The folder for this chapter is named *chapter01*. While working on the exercises in this book you will create a new folder for each chapter.

> ### Watch Out
> It is absolutely essential that you are aware of the location where your files are saved when you are working with code. For beginners, files often appear "broken" when they are not saved consistently in the same location.

> ### Note
> For most of the following chapters you will copy and paste your files to a single new folder in order to continue to build upon what you learned in the previous chapters.

When you view a web page in a browser, what you are seeing is the browser's interpretation of the code that the web designer or programmer created and uploaded to a server. Most browsers include a View Menu with an option to see the page source code. Some even have an "Inspect Element" feature that allows you to see pieces of the code by clicking on an area of the page. By viewing the source code, you can see how a web page was assembled with HTML, CSS, or other coding languages. While designing content for the Web is an analytical process of writing code that instructs the browser how to display your design, it is simultaneously a practice in visual communication.

1. Open a text editing application, such as TextEdit, TextWrangler, NotePad, or BBEdit. For this exercise, TextEdit will be used. In order to create an HTML document, you will need to save the document with the file extension .html (or .htm). For TextEdit users, this means that the format of the TextEdit application must be plain text. Open the TextEdit Menu and choose Preferences. There are two dialog boxes stored in this screen—*New Document* and *Open and Save*. In the first box, be sure to check the radio button next to "Plain Text." This will ensure that you will be able to save a new file with the extension, ".html." Click the *Open and Save* button and check the radio button next to "Ignore rich text commands in HTML files" as well as "Delete the automatic backup file" (this Delete button for the automatic backup file is not included in TextEdit version 1.7). Make sure that "Add .txt extension to plain text files" is not checked. When you have modified your preferences, you are ready to create a new HTML file.

The new preferences will take place when you create a new document. Close the Preferences window, and then close any open documents and choose File > New (Figures 1.4 and 1.5).

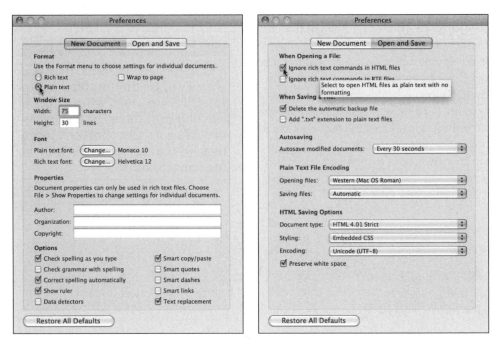

Figures 1.4 and 1.5 Set the Plain Text preferences in TextEdit so that we can create an HTML file.

> **Note**
>
> If TextEdit is set to Rich Text formatting, you will see rulers along the top of new documents. This is an indication that you need to make changes in the Preferences dialog window.

2. Every HTML document opens with the **<html>** tag ("html tag") and closes with the **</html>** tag ("close html tag"). These tags tell the browser that the document has been coded in the HTML language. In turn, the browser displays the content of the page on the Web. The slash (/) is used to close a tag. It is a general rule that tags are deliberately opened and then closed in an HTML file. Start your new document with this code (Figure 1.6).

3. The two distinct parts of an HTML document that appear between the open and close HTML tags are named "head" and "body." The **head** area is used to contain meta-information about the web page (for instance, the title that appears in the browser title bar, keywords associated with the page to influence search engine findings, the language that was used to code the page, and so on). The browser will display visual media that has been coded in the **body**, or the main content area of

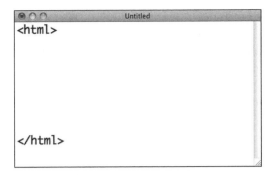

```
<html>




</html>
```

Figure 1.6 The beginnings of an HTML file in a simple text-editing program are seen here. The HTML document always begins with the HTML tag, **<html>**, and always ends with a closed HTML tag, **</html>**.

the HTML document. Add the **<head>** and **</head>** tags and the **<body>** and **</body>** tags to your code between the opening and closing html tags.

The basic structure of an HTML document:	

``html
<html>
    <head>
    </head>
 	
    <body>
    </body>
</html>
``
	Tip: Throughout this book, you will see code demonstrated in the bold font-face Courier as it appears here. Gray lines of code have already been created in previous steps. Black lines of code are new to the current step in the exercise. For instance, in this block of code, we added the head and body tags. The HTML opening and closing tags were already created in Step 2, so they appear in gray.

4. In the head area, add the **<title>** tag, insert a title for the web page, and then close the tag using **</title>**. In the body area (between the open and close body tags), type a message you want to see "printed" in the browser.

``html
<html>
    <head>
    <title>My first web page</title>
    </head>
 	
    <body>
    Hello World.
    </body>
</html>
``
	Note: White space added to the HTML code will not affect the display of the content in the browser. Indentation keeps the code organized for readers who view it. You can use the Tab key or the Return key to keep your code organized. Remember, the resulting white space will not appear in the browser.

5. Choose File > Save As and name the file *index.html*. Make sure that you add the "html" extension to the end of the file name, as it is an essential part of communicating the type of file to the browser. The file name "index" tells the browser that this is the first page to display in any root directory (or first-level folder). Another basic rule of coding for the Web is that the home page is always named "index" (Figure 1.7).

Note

Web file-naming conventions include the following rules: Do not use capital letters, do not include spaces, and do not include reserved characters. Dashes or underscores are appropriate for visually separating words in a file name.

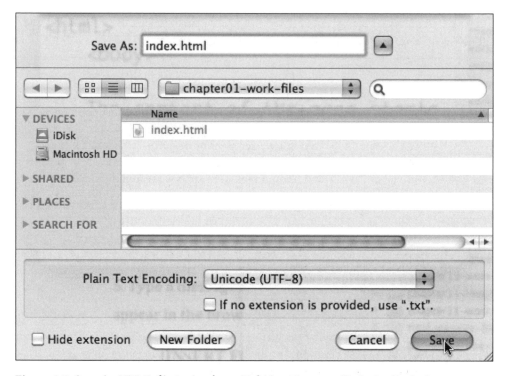

Figure 1.7 Save the HTML file in the *chapter01* folder. The name "index" tells the browser to open this page first when it looks inside the folder named *chapter01*.

Note

Always be aware of the location where you have saved your files.

6. Open a web browser and press Command+O or File > Open to open the *index.html* file you just created. For instance, in the Chrome browser, click File > Open File… and browse to the *index.html* file. Notice that the message you typed between the open and close body tags is displayed in the browser. The tab at the top of the browser displays the title of the web page. The address bar reveals the file path, so you can see exactly where you have saved (and opened) the file (Figure 1.8).

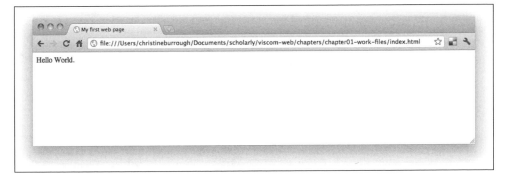

Figure 1.8 Preview the HTML file in a web browser. In the URL address bar you can see the file path to your document.

Exercise 2: Creating a New HTML File in Dreamweaver

While you could write the code for an entire website in a text editing application, it is more common for visual communicators and web designers to use a WYSIWYG (what you see is what you get) application such as Dreamweaver. You should understand the syntax of the programming language. However, you needn't memorize every detail, as Dreamweaver will assist you with code hints.

We will continue to save on top of the file we created in Exercise 1 in the following steps. When you are finished with the exercises in this chapter, you will have just one file, named *index.html*, in your *chapter01* folder.

1. Open Dreamweaver and choose File > Open, or press the Open… button on the Welcome Screen and open *index.html* (Figure 1.9).
2. Click the Split button in the top-left area of the document. Dreamweaver will show you both the code that you are writing in code view *and* what that code would (presumably) look like in the browser in design view (Figure 1.10).

Note

Throughout the exercises in this book you will write your code in Dreamweaver and preview your work in a browser. You should be comfortable toggling between the two applications and refreshing the browser with Command+R (Control+R on a PC).

Figure 1.9 Open the *index.html* document from the Welcome screen in Dreamweaver. You can also choose the File menu > Open.

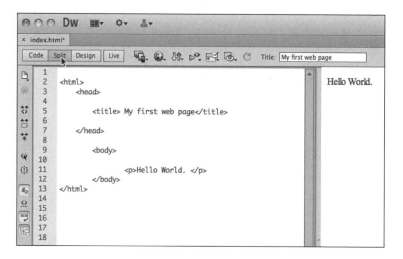

Figure 1.10 Preview the *index.html* document in Dreamweaver's *split view*.

> **Note**
>
> The design view in Dreamweaver can be inaccurate. You should always preview your work in a browser.

3. In split view you can edit your code on the left side (or top) of the page, or your content on the half of the page that appears in the design window. To add a paragraph break and another sentence to your page, place your cursor at the end of your first message in design view. Press the Return key and then add a sentence. Press Command+S to save your file (Figure 1.11).

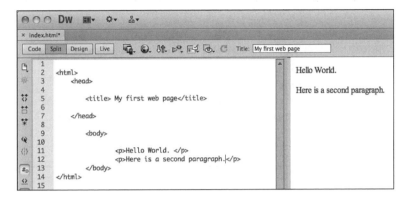

Figure 1.11 When you add a second paragraph to your document in the design view, you will see the code that is added to the file in the code view window.

4. Toggle to your browser and refresh your page, or press the Preview In Browser button in Dreamweaver to open your file in a browser (Figure 1.12).

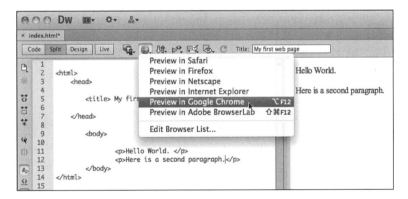

Figure 1.12 You should always preview your work in a web browser. From the globe icon, you can select the browser in which you would like to preview your work.

Note

Command+Tab is a Mac shortcut for toggling between applications. While holding the Command key, press Tab to move through the list of open applications. Release the mouse when the application you want to view is highlighted.

5. Return to Dreamweaver and look in the code that you created for your page. Notice how Dreamweaver changes the code for you. Tags are printed in blue, while the text that displays in the browser is black. The code includes a new tag, **\<p>** and **\</p>**, which creates (and closes) a paragraph break for the new line of text you wrote.

6. Finally, notice the order of the tags in your HTML code.

```
<html>
    <head>
        <title>My first web page</title>
    </head>
    <body>
        <p>Hello World. </p>
        <p>Here is a second paragraph. </p>
    </body>
</html>
```

A translation of the tags would read as follows:

The **HTML** tag is opened, the **head** tag is opened, the **title** tag is opened—the content of the title is "My first web page," after which the **title** tag is closed. The **head** tag is then closed. The **body** tag is opened, then the **paragraph** tag is opened, followed by the first line of textual content. That **paragraph** tag is then closed. A new **paragraph** tag is opened, followed by the second **paragraph**. At the end of the text, the second **paragraph** tag is closed. This is the end of the content on the page, so the **body** tag is closed. Finally, the last tag to close is the **HTML** tag.

The **HTML** tag is the root element, meaning that it is the parent of all other elements. In our example **\<body>** is a parent to **\<p>** because the paragraph tag is nested between the open and close **body** tags. *Nesting* is an important component of proper HTML syntax. Tags must be opened and closed in proper order. For instance, if the **\<body>** tag is opened before **\<html>**, the browser might not understand the instructions in the *index. html* document.

Reference

See the Webmonkey HTML Cheatsheet to learn new tags or refresh your HTML knowledge as you use this book. [http://www.webmonkey.com/2010/02/html_cheatsheet/]

The Art and Craft of Code

The Internet was initially developed during the Cold War era. HTML and other programming languages familiar to the Web now were developed later, after the Internet became the user-friendly Web. Artists and experimental visual communicators have reflected on the syntax of these languages and developed web projects that critique the rigid rules of the coded Web. In the mid-1990s Jodi (a collective of two artists, Joan Heemskerk from The Netherlands and Dirk Paesmans from Belgium) pioneered net.art with the subversive "bomb" in the code of their web page, http://wwwwwwwww.jodi.org.

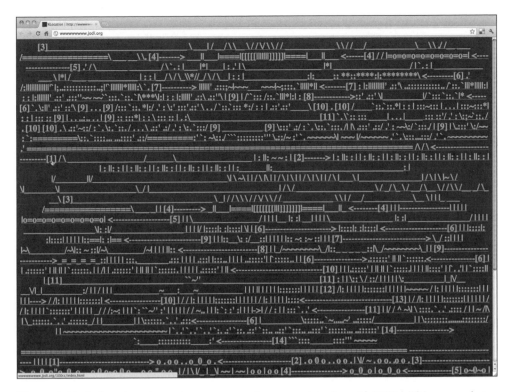

Figure 1.13 *Jodi.org* is an important net.art project created in the mid-1990s. This screen shot is a point of reference, but it is much more fun to explore the website and find the ascii-text/art bomb in the code.

Create, Reflect, Critique

Open a new HTML document in Dreamweaver (File > New > HTML). Notice the extra code that has already been added to the **head** area for you by Dreamweaver. Search the Web to learn what these new tags mean for the web page. Title the new web page "My Computing History." In the body area of your document, add several new paragraphs to the page explaining your personal history of learning to use the computer. Try adding some of your page elements in code view rather than relying on the ease of design view. In later chapter exercises, you will more often be directly modifying the code. Can you remember to use the paragraph tag around your paragraphs? When you go to close the tag, did Dreamweaver "help" you with its *tool tip*? Did you learn any new tags while assembling your personal page? Save the file as *computing.html* in your *chapter01* folder and view it in a browser.

VIDEO
WALKTHROUGH

Glossary Words

ARPA; **<body>**; CSS; HTML; **<html>**; **<head>**; Mosaic; **<p>**; **<title>**; and tool tip

2 PREPARING GRAPHICS

VIDEO
INTRODUCTION

Principles, History, Theory

Using Contrast to See and Perceive

Should graphic designs engage our brains or our minds?

At a minimum, sight requires our eyes to be able to sense light, but if that were all that mattered, we would be the functioning equivalent of earthworms. For perception to proceed, the process is a bit more complicated than being able to notice if it's dark outside or light. The eyes' irises regulate the amount of electromagnetic energy that enters the gooey orbs. The lenses focus the images on the retinas. The photoreceptors transform light into chemical impulses and transfer it to nerve cells in the visual cortex of the brain that process images into four major categories, or *visual cues*—color, form, depth, and movement. It is these four visual cues that the brain sees. And so, yes, we see with our brains. But there is one slight problem—all of this seeing happens unconsciously.

Consequently, our brains notice the visual cues before we become aware of what it is we're looking at. Blame the four cues on our ancient, prehistoric animal selves when it was important to know if a fruit's color meant poison, a shape was familiar or new and thus friendly or threatening, objects were near or far and could be grasped, and whether another animal was running toward or away from us. Although the brain's sense of perception began as an elaborate defense mechanism, it has evolved into a precise message decoder. Good graphic artists realize that they can make designs that exploit the visual cues to attract and communicate with a fellow human.

However, it's not enough to stimulate brains. If you want users to notice your website, their minds must be intrigued. Your design becomes a part of their long-term memory. You don't want someone to simply see your work. You want your work to be remembered. *Perception* is the process from the eye to the brain, while *perceiving* is reserved for the mind where understanding and meaning happen. The German philosopher and writer Johann Wolfgang von Goethe once wrote, "The hardest thing to see is what is in front of your eyes." As a result, many designs are ignored or easily forgotten because they do not engage the mind. But if you can spark interest in a viewer's mind, your work can become a permanent addition to that person's visual memory. And so, yes, we see with our minds too.

One of the first and most respected proponents of the brain-mind connection related to the visual arts was the German gestalt psychologist Rudolf Arnheim. He was in his twenties when he fled Nazi Germany for Fascist Italy and then left for London and eventually America where he taught at Harvard University, Sarah Lawrence College, and the University of Michigan until his death at age 102. His German heritage and the collective nightmare of Nazism no doubt influenced his choice of what must be considered one of the most memorable trademarks in the history of graphic design—the swastika—within his seminal 1969 work concerned with the understanding of visual messages, *Visual Thinking*.

15

Although the swastika design had been used for centuries as a symbol of strength by cultures throughout the world, Adolf Hitler, a former painter, usurped the simplified and abstract shape. He described it in *Mein Kampf*:

> I myself, meanwhile, after innumerable attempts, had laid down a final form; a flag with a red background, a white disk, and a black swastika in the middle. After long trials I also found a definite proportion between the size of the flag and the size of the white disk, as well as the shape and thickness of the swastika.

Hitler's account described the process of getting the brain to notice the design. But Arnheim's description acknowledges that it also engages the mind of the reader. He begins with a simple, yet powerfully touching observation: "I remember that when Hitler visited Mussolini's Rome and the whole city was suddenly covered with Nazi flags an Italian girl exclaimed in horror: 'Rome is crawling with black spiders.'" He goes on to admit that the design was "well chosen," meeting the requirements of distinctiveness and striking simplicity. It conveyed the dynamics of the "Movement" by its tilted orientation in space. The black figure in a white and red setting helped revive the colors of the German Empire and thereby appealed to nationalism. In the Nazi flag, red became the color of revolution, and the black was frightening like the storm-troopers' shirts.

Despite their differences on the emphasis of brain versus mind, Hitler and Arnheim would agree that the one design element of the Nazi trademark that stands out is its reliance on **contrast** (Figure 2.1). Contrast in colors, sizes, shapes, thicknesses, and symbolism make a design noticeable and memorable. Along with balance, rhythm, and

Figure 2.1 Named after the color of the shirts made popular by the Nazi Party, this 1930 meeting in Munich in the "Brown House" between Adolf Hitler and members of the National Socialist German Workers' Party shows the use of the swastika in flags and armbands. *Courtesy of the German Federal Archive.*

unity (discussed in Chapter 9), the design principle of contrast should be a key consideration for any web layout. When used traditionally, these design elements can result in clear, noticeable, pleasing, and useful visual messages. But at the same time, when the rules are bent or broken, exciting results can happen.

A lot of contrast among elements signifies a busy and youthful design (Figure 2.2). Little contrast usually indicates a no-nonsense and conservative approach. The size of the graphic elements should vary but be proportional to the overall frame of the design. *Proportion*, or scale, refers to the spatial relationship between design elements and the size of the page or frame. Sometimes a small element within a large frame has more visual impact than a large element that fills the frame. Space is related to size because the scale of

Figure 2.2 Created by poster artist Estelle Levine in 1936, this WPA (Works Progress Administration) poster for a children's piano competition shows youthful playfulness in the tilted orientation, the gap between the two text columns, and the contrast between the players' hairstyles. *Courtesy of the Library of Congress.*

the elements determines how much space is available. As a general rule, space should be present around the edges of a frame and not trapped in the center. A design with a lot of space is considered modern or classy, whereas a crowded design with little space is viewed as traditional and serious (Figure 2.3).

Figure 2.3 With a frame filled with art and copy, the serious tone is enhanced in a World War I poster attempting to recruit men to join the U.S. Army Tank Corps. *Courtesy of the Library of Congress.*

Practice

How Big Is the Web?

The Internet can be exciting and frustrating for designers because of the flexibility of the *viewport* (what we often think of as the browser—the word viewport refers to any screen on which the Internet is viewed). The size of your user's viewing experience is determined by screen *resolution* (standard preferences within an operating system) and monitor size (hardware). On top of that, the browser window will range in size as the user pushes and pulls its edges to fit it on her screen. This reliance on personal preference allows flexibility for the user—which is helpful for her reading experience and the accessibility of online materials, but it hinders the web designer from knowing just how large the viewing platform will be when the user experiences it. One user may be viewing a website on a relatively large monitor, with a screen resolution of 1920 by 1200 pixels, while another may be viewing a website on a cell phone at just 320 by 480 pixels.

> **Common Viewport Pixel Dimensions (at the Time of Writing)**
> - Computer Screens:
>   800 by 600 pixels
>   1024 by 768 pixels
>   1920 by 1200 pixels
> - Mobile Devices:
>   128 by 160 pixels
>   176 by 220 pixels
>   240 by 320 pixels
>   320 by 480 pixels
> - See Google's lab page on browser sizes. [http://browsersize.googlelabs.com]

The W3 School's website claims that 76% of users view the Web on a screen resolution higher than 1024 by 768. [http://www.w3schools.com/browsers/browsers_display.asp] However, this data was culled from Internet users interested in web development and design. In effect, those providing information were early adopters who often had larger monitors and/or pricey computing equipment. Due to the amount of netbooks, tablets, and other small devices today, there will continue to be a gap between small and large viewport resolutions.

All of these dimensions are important because you will want to size images for the Web appropriately. For instance, if you want to create a background image for your website you might consider a large image dimension, such as 1024 pixels wide. If you resize a logo for placement on a website, you will want to know how the size of the logo relates to the size of everything else on the website. Incidentally, the W3 School's logo is currently sized at 336 by 69 pixels, while Amazon.com's logo is 180 by 45 pixels.

Resolution

VIDEO WALKTHROUGH

At this time of writing, 72 DPI (or dots per inch) is the file resolution most commonly saved in graphic files for viewing on the Web on a commercial desktop or laptop computer. However, monitors display at a variety of resolutions. For instance, if you know you are preparing graphics for an iPad application, you would save the files at 132 DPI (or 264 DPI for a third-generation iPad). We will work with graphics saved at 72 DPI.

> **Reference**
>
> View the Wikipedia page for a list of displays by pixel density for a thorough list of devices and their resolutions. [http://en.wikipedia.org/wiki/List_of_displays_by_pixel_density]

File Formats

In addition to dealing with screen resolutions and image sizes, you need to consider your file format. Currently, images are most often saved for the Web in JPG, PNG, and less frequently, GIF formats.

Comparison of JPG Pros and Cons

JPG Pros:
- You can save up to 16.7 million colors in a single JPG file.
- Images will display a continuous tonal range.

JPG Cons:
- JPG does not support transparency or animation.
- The image compression is **lossy**, meaning you will lose colors that you cannot select or control when you save a JPEG. Also, due to the lossy compression, each time you open and resave a JPG file (which is not recommended), you will lose more image data. The file just continues to become compressed and loses pixel information until it loses its integrity.

Note

Another acronym people remember with regard to PNG is **PNG Not GIF!**

Comparison of PNG Pros and Cons

PNG Pros:
- You can save up to 16.7 million colors in a single PNG file.
- Images will display a continuous tonal range.
- PNG supports an alpha channel (that is, transparency).
- PNG compression is **lossless**— saved files do not lose image data.

PNG Cons:
- What's not to love? Well, PNG does not support animation.

JPG

JPG (or JPEG) stands for Joint Photographic Experts Group. The clue is in the word "photographic." This file is the best choice for photographs or images of continuous tone, such as illustrations with gradients.

PNG

PNG is an acronym for Portable Network Graphics. It is the best compressor to use on typography (when saved as an image), logos, or graphics that use a minimal palette of flat colors. Since the PNG format will save 16.7 million colors, you can also see a continual tonal gradation in a PNG file. The biggest advantage to a PNG file is that it can be saved with a transparent alpha channel. This means two things: You can save an image with transparency for the Web without worrying about setting a matte color around those transparent pixels, and you can save an image with partial transparency. While PNG sometimes seems like the superior format for images you will save for the Web, be advised that the JPG compressor will usually create a smaller file size when you are compressing a photographic image.

GIF

GIF stands for Graphics Interchange Format. This format is not used as frequently now as it was before PNG became so widely supported by various web browsers (around late 2006). Much like the PNG format, GIF is best used for typography, logos, or images that use a minimal palette of flat colors. GIF files can include animation settings (though most contemporary web animations are created with Adobe Flash or using HTML5). Unlike PNG, GIF files can only save up to 256 colors—a quite drastic difference from the millions of colors we have become used to seeing in PNG and JPG.

Native file formats such as Photoshop Document format (PSD) or Adobe Illustrator format (AI), are not viewable in a web browser. Remember, web browsers read a set of instructions (code) to display the markup on the page (the layout and content). If you told the web browser to display a PSD file in your code, the browser would return a broken image link because it simply does not understand this file format. All images saved for the Web are compressed. This means the native files are always compromised for viewing on the Web. You should always save your native or original files in addition to the JPEG, PNG, or GIF images you save for uploading to the Web.

> ## Comparison of GIF Pros and Cons:
>
> GIF Pros:
> - GIF supports animation—if you want to animate a construction worker digging your "under construction" website, this is the format for you. In case you didn't catch the sarcasm: GIF animation is no longer widely used.
> - The GIF file compression is lossless, meaning you can choose exactly which colors you want to save within the file.
> - You can save with transparency; however, you would have to matte the transparent pixels. (This seems like a lost art.)
>
> GIF Cons:
> - You can only save up to 256 colors in GIF format.

Results of Chapter 2 Exercises

In the first two of the following exercises you will save a photograph and decorative type element for the Web using JPG and PNG compressions. In the third and fourth exercises you will add these elements to a new HTML document (Figure 2.4).

Download Materials for Chapter 2 Exercises

You will need the Chapter 2 background photograph file, *bg-start.psd*, which you can download as a ZIP or a PSD file from the website for the following exercises. You only need to download one of the files. [http://viscommontheweb.wordpress.com/downloads]

Exercise 1: Resizing and Saving a Photograph with JPG Compression

The image that we will save as a JPG will later be used as the background image on our website. Any element that you add to a web page must be considered as a visual element in relationship with all other elements on the page. Contrast will be created between the background image and the typography set on top of it in terms of its texture, value, and saturation. Notice how layers have been added to create a desaturated light value throughout the majority of the image area. This overall light gray tone will accommodate legibility when it is coupled with contrasting dark typography. In our final website design, we will see a contrast in the middle of the page among light and dark values, colors, sizes, and texture (the grain of a photographic background as compared to the crispness at the edges of the text).

Figure 2.4 When all Chapter 2 exercises are complete, the resulting files are an HTML document, a background JPG image, and a decorative PNG image. In the Web browser, the HTML document references the JPG and PNG, so all files are seen by following the HTML file path in the URL address bar. The heading tag, **`<h1>`** is used to establish the first heading on the page followed by body copy. Contrast between the background image and the text is achieved through color and value. Contrast between the headline and body copy is achieved through size. In later chapters we will redefine the color and font-face properties of the type on the page and the positioning of all page elements.

1. **Set up your workspace:** Create a folder on your hard drive named *chapter02*. Save the photograph and the resulting JPG and PNG files from the first two exercises in this folder.

2. Open *bg-start.psd* in Photoshop (see the "Download Materials for Chapter 2 Exercises" section if you did not already download this file).

3. View the Image Size dialog box (Image > Image Size from the top menu bar) to see the resolution of this image (Figure 2.5). The image is not terribly large for printing purposes, but it is too large for the Web. If you know how to scale the image using the Image Size dialog, do that now by constraining the proportions and setting the width to 960 pixels. To demonstrate an alternative method, we will use the Crop tool in the next two steps. Click the OK or Cancel button to exit the dialog box.

   a. Select the Crop tool from the Tools panel. Type 960px in the Width Options field (Figure 2.6). At the time of writing, it is common for websites to be designed for a centered box that is 960 pixels wide.

**VIDEO
WALKTHROUGH**

Note

You can use any of the Photoshop units of measurement in the Crop tool, regardless of what your default settings indicate. Be sure to type the numeric value, 960, and add the units of measurement in the Width Options field as stated in Step 3a (960 px).

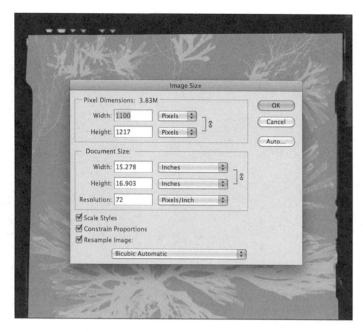

Figure 2.5 You can see the image pixel dimensions in Photoshop's Image Size dialog box. While the top area (Pixel Dimensions) is concerned with pixel dimensions, the lower area of the dialog box (Document Size) is a reference for printing. We are mainly interested in the top set of boxes.

Figures 2.6 and 2.7 (Continued)

Figures 2.6 and 2.7 Use the Crop tool to adjust pixel dimensions.

b. By default, the entire work area will be highlighted (Photoshop users prior to CS6 will need to drag the Crop tool over the entire image, starting and ending in opposite corners). If you wanted to crop something out of the image, you could modify the edges of the framed area, but we simply want to resize our image. Press the Return key on your keypad or click the checkmark icon in the Options bar to commit to the crop (Figure 2.7). Your image will become 960 by 1062 pixels.

Note

It is always safe to resample an image to a smaller size in Photoshop. However, you should never increase the image size by adding pixels to the document.

4. Now that the image has been resized, choose File > Save for Web and Devices to save the image for display on the Web.

Note

This image will be used as the background for a web page in later chapters.

5. Use the pull-down menus on the right side to save the image with JPEG compression. The Quality slider can be used to change the amount of compression applied to the image (Figure 2.8). Your goal is to apply as much compression as you can (the lowest possible quality) without compromising the appearance of the image. In other words, if you start to see pixelization or blurry image areas, you should choose a smaller rate of compression or a higher quality setting.

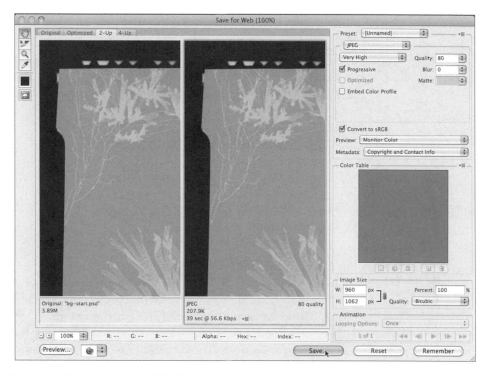

Figure 2.8 Use the Save for Web dialog box to create a JPG image.

Note

The Progressive button can be used to save web images in a format that opens in stages in the web browser. This means that a user with a slow connection to the Internet will see the image as it is downloading, decreasing the time that a user sees a blank space on the page where an image should be loaded.

---

6. Click the Save button and name the image *bg.jpg*. You do not need to save the original Photoshop file (PSD document) when you close it.

Exercise 2: Saving a Decorative-type Element as a PNG File with Transparency

The PNG and GIF file formats are best used to compress line art or graphics with large, flat areas of color. Logos, decorative graphics, and typography, especially when created with transparency, are commonly saved as PNG files for display on the Web.

1. Open a new file in Photoshop that is 40 pixels wide by 25 pixels in height at 72 DPI (screen resolution). Make sure the color mode is RGB (red, green, blue), as this is the color spectrum common to monitors, projectors, mobile devices, and so on. Set the background contents to Transparent (Figure 2.9).

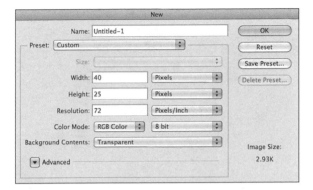

Figure 2.9 Create a new document in Photoshop.

2. If you don't see the Color panel in the top-right area of the Photoshop workspace, choose Window > Color. Use the pull-down menu in the top-right corner of the Color panel to view the Web Color sliders (Figure 2.10). Now when you use the sliders you will produce a color that can be assigned HTML hex color codes (a topic we will return to in Exercises 3 and 4). Enter the values 00, 00, and 99 into the Red, Green, and Blue (RGB) fields, respectively. The foreground color chip will become a dark shade of blue, with no amount of red or green added to the hue.

Figure 2.10 Change Photoshop Color Sliders to display the web palette.

Note

If the new color is assigned to the background color chip (the square on the bottom of the foreground color chip), you can swap the foreground chip with the background chip by pressing the letter *x* on the keypad.

3. Select the Type tool from the Tool panel on the left side of the workspace. Then choose a dingbat font from the Font Family pull-down list in the Options bar. (I used a typeface named "Type Embellishments.") If you can't find the Options bar, choose Window > Character to use the Character panel instead. Set the type color before you click the Type tool in your Photoshop document. Click the Set the Text Color button (it looks like a color chip) in the top Options bar. The Color

Picker window opens. From here, hover the mouse over the foreground color chip. You will notice that the cursor becomes an Eyedropper tool. Click the foreground color chip (Figure 2.11). This loads the color set in the foreground color chip into the Color Picker. Click OK to exit the dialog box and notice the text color chip now assumes the color set in the foreground color chip (#000099 or dark blue).

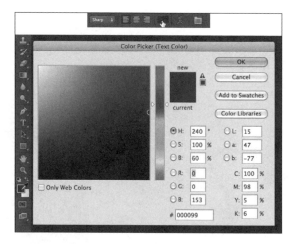

Figure 2.11 First press the Set the Text color button in the Options bar. Then use the Eyedropper tool to load the foreground color chip into the Color Picker. Press OK to exit the dialog box and use the Type tool in the Photoshop document.

4. Click the Type tool in the middle of the Photoshop document, and type a letter. Continue doing this until you find a leaf or plant shape to use on the web page (Figure 2.12). When you are finished, press the Enter key on your keypad, or click the checkmark icon in the top-right corner of the Options bar to commit your edit. You can press the Escape key to start over.

Reference

There are many free "Nature" dingbats you can download on the Dafont.com website. [http://www.dafont.com/theme.php?cat=712]

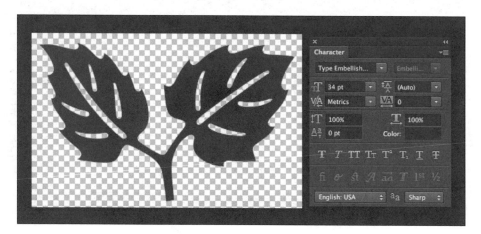

Figure 2.12 Create a decorative graphic with the Type tool in Photoshop.

5. In the Layers panel, set the opacity of the type layer to 80 percent (Figure 2.13). Our file will not only have transparency around the organic shape of the dingbat, but the graphic itself will include transparency. Since we will use this dingbat as a decorative element on paragraph headings, we do not want it to read as a primary figure in terms of hierarchy. Blending the shape slightly into the background will integrate it into the design as a nonessential or decorative component.

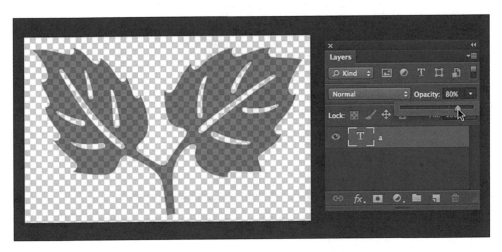

Figure 2.13 Set the layer to 80% opacity.

6. Zoom in by using the Zoom tool or the Command key with the plus sign on a Mac, ⌘+. On a PC the keyboard shortcut is the Control key with the plus sign. Adjust the size of your type/shape so that it fills most of the space in the document. I set the font that I used at 34 points. Yours may be different. You may notice a little extra transparent space near the edges of the Photoshop document. We will remove all of the "extra" parts of the document now using the Trim command.

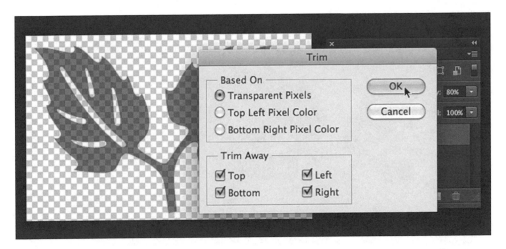

Figure 2.14 Trim an image to remove excessive document space and create a smaller file size.

From the top menu bar, select Image > Trim. Trim the file based on transparent pixels all the way around—on the top, bottom, left, and right (Figure 2.14).

7. Choose File > Save As to save the native file in PSD format before saving the file for the Web. It is a good idea to keep an original version of the file on your hard drive as well as the compressed version that you saved for the Web. In the last exercise, we started with an original, so we did not have to save the file in Photoshop format. Now we can save the compressed version of the file. Choose File > Save for Web and Devices. Click the compressor format pull-down menu and select PNG-24 (Figure 2.15). Since we want to save this graphic at 80% opacity, we need to use the alpha channel available to us in 24-bit (16.7 million colors) mode. PNG-8, like the GIF format, will only save 256 colors, and it will not save a percentage of transparency within the graphic (as we have set in this file).

Note

The native file is one that is saved in the format specific to the application where it was made. The PSD format is native to Photoshop, so documents created in Photoshop saved with the .psd extension are native files. Documents created in Microsoft Word are native when they are saved with the .doc or .docx format. JPG, PNG, and GIF are compressors, so they are not native formats.

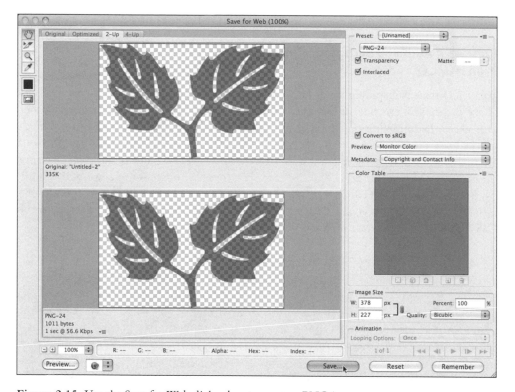

Figure 2.15 Use the Save for Web dialog box to create a PNG image.

Note

When you use the Save for Web and Devices dialog box, the original file you saved from within Photoshop remains open and untouched. The new file is saved to a location on your hard drive that you specified in the saving process. To view the new file, navigate to your hard drive and open the PNG image.

8. Click the Save button and name the file *leaf.png*. Press Command+S (Mac) or Control+S (PC) to save in native format and close the document.

Reference

Image Alpha is a free application that transforms saved PNG files into even smaller files. I used it on the leaf graphic, but since our original was so small (just 749 bytes), the result from Image Alpha (503 bytes) did not provide much of a "wow factor" in size differences. Nonetheless, if you are compressing many graphics for your website, an application like this will result in smaller sizes. My former student, Cory Micek, wrote on his Facebook wall that he "ran comparison tests on three different PNG compressors. Image Alpha works best." He found average savings of Image Alpha to be 73% versus about 23% using PNG Compressor and PNGenie. Download the free application on the PNGMini website. [http://pngmini.com]

Exercise 3: Adding a Background Image as an Attribute of <body> in an HTML Document

When an image is displayed as the background of a web page, it is considered an attribute of the page itself. In code, this means that it is an attribute (or some might say, "property"—see the following note) of **<body>**, the body tag. In Dreamweaver, you can modify the body tag by choosing Modify > Page Properties from the top menu bar. You will see that we can modify these attributes directly in the HTML code of the page or using the language Cascading Style Sheets (CSS). For these exercises (only!), we will modify page properties in the HTML code. In Chapter 5 you will learn how to incorporate CSS into your practice, and you will always add page attributes and other properties to the CSS code that you generate for your Web pages.

Note

There are nit-pickers out there who swear that "properties" must be called "attributes" when we are talking about tag enhancements. I tend to agree, as the World Wide Web Consortium (W3C) defines "attributes" and not "properties." However, Dreamweaver has a useful dialog box named "Page Properties," which does add attributes to **<body>**. For this reason, I will use the words "attribute" and "property" interchangeably.

Before beginning these next two exercises, make sure the *bg.jpg* and *leaf.png* files that you just saved are in one folder (ideally, named *chapter02*).

1. **Set up your workspace:** Once you are sure you know where your files are located, open Dreamweaver and then choose File > New. In the New Document dialog box select Blank Page from the column on the left, then HTML from the Page Type column, and <none> from the Layout column. Click the Create button. (That is, choose File > New > Blank Page > HTML > None and click Create). As soon as it opens, save the document as "index.html" in the *chapter02* folder. Choose Window > Workspace Layout > Designer so that your Dreamweaver workspace is similar to the screen shots demonstrating the exercise steps.

2. View *index.html* in Split view—the design window appears in the right half of the document and the code window is to the left of the design window. Click the design window in the Dreamweaver document.

3. Add a title to the page using the Title bar in the design view or between the title and close-title tags in code view (Figure 2.16). My page is titled, "Chapter Two."

Figure 2.16 Add title content to the HTML document.

4. Add the background image as an attribute of the **body** tag by choosing Modify > Page Properties from the top menu bar. Click Appearance (HTML) in the left column and then click the Browse button next to the Background Image field. Locate your *chapter02* folder and select the *bg.jpg* file you saved in the first exercise (Figure 2.17). Click the OK button to exit the dialog.

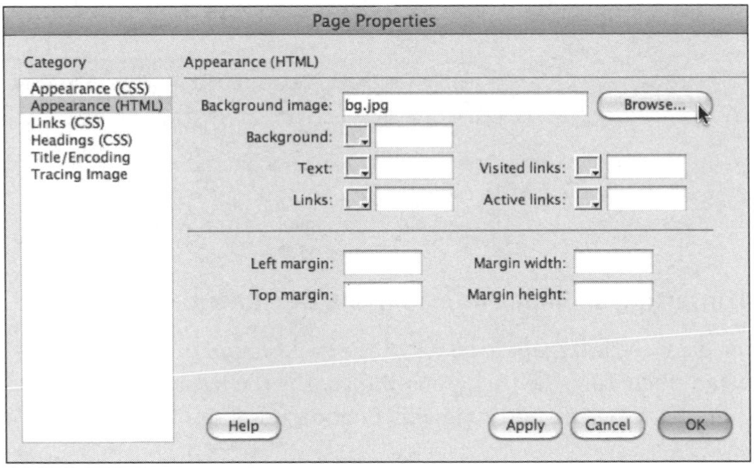

Figure 2.17 Add a background image using the Page Properties dialog box in Dreamweaver.

Figure 2.18 Background images, by default, will tile on a web page. This means they will load repeatedly going across (horizontally) and down (vertically) the page. We will use CSS in a later chapter to control the display of the background image.

5.   Notice that the code view includes the attribution **background="bg.jpg"** inside the **body** tag. Save your page and view it in a browser.

By default, the background image repeats vertically and horizontally, filling the space of the browser (Figure 2.18). There are a variety of methods for treating the background image using HTML and CSS. We will edit the background image with CSS in later chapter exercises.

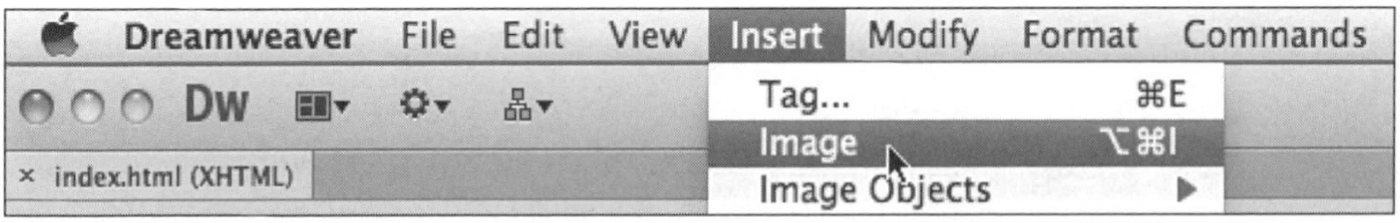

Figure 2.19 Insert an image using Dreamweaver. This action results in the addition of the image source tag in the HTML code.

Exercise 4: Inserting an Image into an HTML Document

We will now place the leaf graphic on top of the background image. You can consider the page properties (including the background image) as the background layer on the page, and everything between the **body** tag and **</body>** as a second layer that floats on the surface of the page.

1. Click one time anywhere inside the design view window. This tells Dreamweaver that we want to add content to the page—in the code, this means we will be adding content between **<body>** and **</body>**. Add the leaf graphic to the page by choosing Insert > Image from the top menu bar, and then browse to *leaf.png* (Figure 2.19).

2. When you add an image to an HTML page, Dreamweaver prompts you for a brief description of the image to be used in the **alt** attribute of the **image** tag. The **alt** attribute is used to assign a textual "alternative" to the visual image. This is an important accessibility feature, as people who view the Web with assistive technology devices (such as a text-to-speech reader) rely on not just being able to see a page, but being able to hear it, too (see Chapter 13). I entered "decorative leaf graphic" as the alternative text for the image. Finally, notice the code added to your HTML page (Figure 2.20). The image tag, **<img>**, is used to refer to images in HTML code. Since the leaf is stored in the root directory, the source attribute **src** of the image tag simply refers to the file name. It is assumed that this file is saved in the same location as *index.html*. See Figure 2.21 for a diagram of the structure of an HTML element (or tag). The image will appear in the top-left corner of the page.

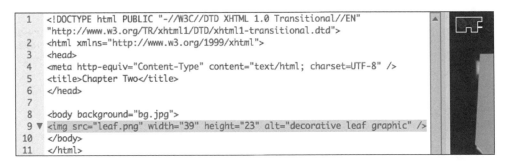

```
1   <!DOCTYPE html PUBLIC "-//W3C//DTD XHTML 1.0 Transitional//EN"
    "http://www.w3.org/TR/xhtml1/DTD/xhtml1-transitional.dtd">
2   <html xmlns="http://www.w3.org/1999/xhtml">
3   <head>
4   <meta http-equiv="Content-Type" content="text/html; charset=UTF-8" />
5   <title>Chapter Two</title>
6   </head>
7
8   <body background="bg.jpg">
9 ▼ <img src="leaf.png" width="39" height="23" alt="decorative leaf graphic" />
10  </body>
11  </html>
```

Figure 2.20 The image source tag in the HTML code embeds the image on the web page.

Note

The browser will add elements to the page from the top-left corner to the bottom-right corner unless it is "told" (or coded) otherwise. For now, we are not concerned with positioning the page content. However, this is an important topic that we will return to in later chapter exercises.

3. Press Command+S (Control+S on a PC) to save the file and view it in a web browser. *Yikes!* The blue leaf nearly blends in with the dark blue background at the edge of the background image. In later chapter exercises we will position the leaf so that it appears on the gray area of the background image for an easier reading of the leaf due to a contrast in values.

4. **Your Turn!** See if you can edit the color of the leaf in Photoshop so that it has a greater amount of contrast with the dark blue background. If you save the file as *leaf.png* (in a different color) on top of the image file we have already saved, you would simply need to refresh your browser to see this change occur on your web page. When you are finished experimenting, set the leaf back to blue (RGB values: #00, #00, #99).

> **Tip:**
>
> You can try out new colors in your graphics by saving on top of the old PNG file (for instance), then reloading the work in the browser. Since you saved the native file (in PSD or AI format) you will always be able to edit the file. Alternatively, you can save a new PNG file (for instance, leaf02.png) then change the code on your web page to reference the new name in the image tag.

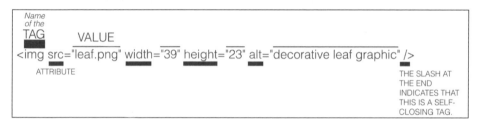

Figure 2.21 The structure of an HTML element, what we will refer to as a tag, can be seen in this diagram of the **img** tag. It includes attributes and values. Since this tag refers to its content as an attribute, it closes itself with the slash before the closing angle bracket. *Diagram courtesy of xtine.*

Exercise 5: Creating Contrast with Page Properties and Text Settings

1. In Dreamweaver, modify the HTML page properties again (Modify > Page Properties) to change the default color of text on the page. I changed mine to bright yellow, #FFFF00 (Figure 2.22). Notice in code view that the body tag now has another property added to it. When we add color to the HTML file we will be using hex values that refer to the amounts of red, green, and blue comprising the color.

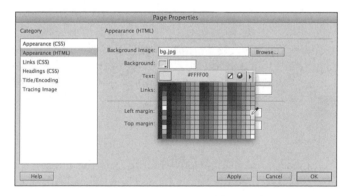

Figure 2.22 Add text color to the web page using the Page Properties dialog box in Dreamweaver.

2. Place your cursor to the right of the leaf image in design view. Add the words "Early Life" to your document. The two words should appear directly next to the leaf on a single line (Figure 2.23).

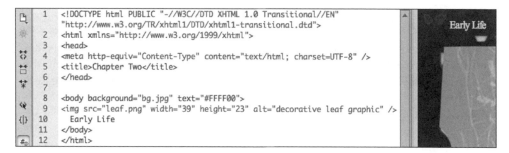

```
1    <!DOCTYPE html PUBLIC "-//W3C//DTD XHTML 1.0 Transitional//EN"
     "http://www.w3.org/TR/xhtml1/DTD/xhtml1-transitional.dtd">
2    <html xmlns="http://www.w3.org/1999/xhtml">
3    <head>
4    <meta http-equiv="Content-Type" content="text/html; charset=UTF-8" />
5    <title>Chapter Two</title>
6    </head>
7
8    <body background="bg.jpg" text="#FFFF00">
9    <img src="leaf.png" width="39" height="23" alt="decorative leaf graphic" />
10     Early Life
11   </body>
12   </html>
```

Figure 2.23 The body tag now includes properties for the background image and page text color. Later we will learn how to add these properties to a CSS file.

Note

We will be using some of the text from the Anna Atkins Wikipedia page to complete the website we are designing in the exercises throughout this book. [http://en.wikipedia.org/wiki/Anna_Atkins]

---

3. Select the words "Early Life" in design view and then apply the **h1** tag, **<h1>**, to set the text as a first-level heading on the page by selecting Heading 1 from the Formatting pull-down menu in the Properties panel (Figure 2.24). Alternatively, you can surround the words with the **<h1>** and **</h1>** tags in code view.

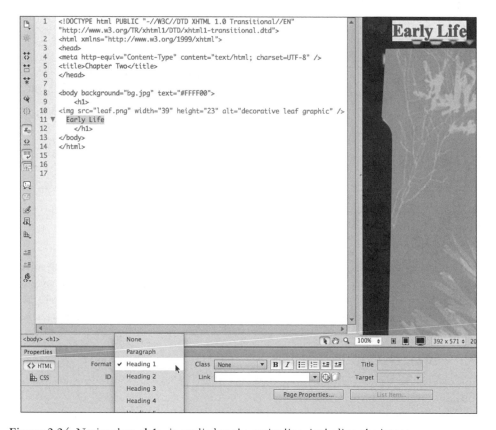

Figure 2.24 Notice that <h1> is applied to the entire line, including the image.

> **Watch out**
>
> If you use the Properties panel, you might notice that you can alter both HTML and CSS properties by selecting the button in the upper-left corner of the panel. For now, we are working on the HTML properties. If CSS is depressed, toggle your properties to the HTML view.

4. From the Wikipedia page describing Anna Atkins, select and copy the first paragraph under the "Early Life" heading. Paste the paragraph to your web page inside the **CODE** view in Dreamweaver, after the tag **</h1>**. Do not paste text into design view, as this will often result in messy code added to your page. Remove all of the bracketed references. Surround your paragraph with the paragraph tag (meaning, put **<p>** at the beginning of the paragraph and **</p>** at the end) and notice the difference in scale between the heading typography and the body copy. The heading tags (varying in levels from 1 to 6) add weight (boldness) and size to what would otherwise be "normal" or paragraph text. Also look in your code. The paragraph tag has been used to identify separate paragraphs, and the heading is surrounded by **<h1>** and **</h1>**. Save your work and view it in the browser (Figure 2.25). [http://en.wikipedia.org/wiki/Anna_Atkins]

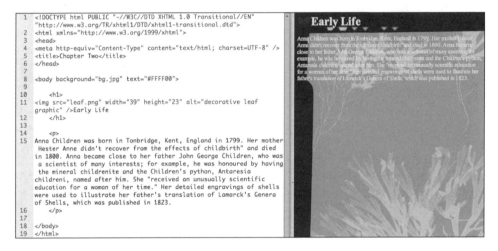

Figure 2.25   Notice the structure of the HTML document, including the properties added to the body tag, and new tags **<img>** and **<h1>**.

Notice that while the heading tag does increase the size and weight of the font, the color is the same as what you have defined as the "text color" on the page. In later chapters we will continue to edit typography and image settings using HTML and CSS, and you will learn how to apply different font faces, sizes, and colors to text elements throughout your web page.

 The Art and Craft of Code

Andrew Venell's Color Field Television Web project is "akin to watching an abstract painting on television, on speed (Figure 2.26). Animated to 12 frames per second, different color sections appear in each frame" (Carolyn Kane for Rhizome). Venell's project reinterprets the "color field" (a style of abstract painting from the mid-twentieth century) as an ever-changing set of possibilities, presented to the viewer not on canvas, or on a television, but in a programmable viewport—the browser. [http://andrewvenell.com/color-field-television/] [http://archive.rhizome.org/exhibition/html_color_codes/]

Figure 2.26 Andrew Venell's *Color Field Television* is best experienced online where you can fall victim to the sway of the animated color fields. *Courtesy of Andrew Venell.*

Create, Reflect, Critique

VIDEO WALKTHROUGH

Browse the Wikimedia Commons Picture of the Day Web page for a photograph to use as a background image in a new web page. [http://commons.wikimedia.org/wiki/Commons:Picture_of_the_day] Search for a static composition (as opposed to a dynamic composition) containing a generous amount of negative space. Open the picture in an image-editing application and resize it (if necessary) for the Web. Modify it to create a low level of contrast (you might create an adjustment layer or simply place a new black or white layer on top of your photograph set at a low or high opacity). Create a new HTML page in Dreamweaver and add your background image to the page. Add typography on top of your image and explore the heading settings (H1, H2, H3, and so on) in the HTML Properties panel. Modify the page settings to create contrast between your background image and the typography layered on top of it. What are some of the challenges you might experience in a browser when a background image has been inserted on the page? How can you be assured that the typography on a page is legible? What elements are at play when you are creating hierarchy in your design by using contrast?

Glossary Words

contrast, GIF, JPG, perception, perceiving, PNG, proportion, resolution, viewport, visual cues, lossy, lossless

3 CREATING LINKS

**VIDEO
INTRODUCTION**

Principles, History, Theory

Constructivism and Eye Tracking: Watching Where We Look for Links

What is a key difference between newspapers and news websites?

The answer seems obvious. A lot.

The glaring disparities are their historical roots, technical elements, workplace practices, writing and graphic styles, cultural impacts, and so on. For example, the first printed newspaper is said to be the *Strasbourg Relation* produced in Germany in 1605, about 40 years after Johannes Gutenberg's game-changing printing press (Figure 3.1). Fast-forward 400 years or so and you could read the "Mercury Center," one of the first newspapers published online. It was available through a telephone modem from AOL when it was a bulletin board and produced by the good folks at the *San Jose Mercury News* (Figure 3.2).

Despite their broad differences, there is one aspect of accessing the news online that stands out among the other features and cannot be duplicated by print on paper: the **hyperlink**. The closest a newspaper story on paper may get to a link is the seldom-used footnote reserved primarily for in-depth, complicated, and educational pieces that require documentation for a reader. And although the footnote has a long and valued place in nonfiction history that gave average readers and academic scholars pleasure through often amusing and thoughtful insights without disturbing the flow of the main text, such an artifact of printing is no match for its excitable and modern cousin.

Tim Berners-Lee, the chief creator of the World Wide Web, felt strongly that words that instantly linked with other databases and related ideas was the key feature of his computer-based system. No wonder he chose "HT" as the first two letters of his Markup Language (HTML) to signify HyperText.

After the practice of accessing interconnected chains of text and illustrations on a website through cursor clicks became common, the word *hypertext* evolved into the more inclusive *hyperlinks*. Finally, the decaffeinated version of the term was introduced: *links*. It is from a website's underlined phrases or bordered pictures, the default style that gives life and substance to an online presentation. As with the corpus callosum that provides communication between the left and right sides of the brain, when links are used thoughtfully and creatively, they combine the best that verbal and visual messages have to offer.

Although today it seems intuitive that links are vital to a web presentation's success, the need and correct placement on a screen was not necessarily obvious to early web producers. However, groundbreaking theoretical work by a cognitive psychologist and two mass media educators not only helped convince web creators that links should be included, but also taught graphic designers where the best location on a page should be to achieve maximum notice from a user.

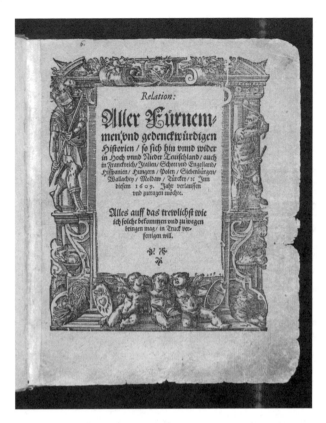

Figure 3.1 The cover page for a 1609 collection of individual issues bound together of the *Strasbourg Relation*, considered to be the first regularly printed newspaper in the world, is a lively array of symbolic images and copy. *Courtesy of the University Library of Heidelberg, Germany.*

Figure 3.2 Teamed with America Online in 1993, the online version of the *San Jose Mercury News* contained daily downloads of news stories accessed through the center menu box while the buttons for major sections remained constant. *Courtesy of the Poynter Institute for Media Studies.*

Julian Hochberg was a professor of psychology at Columbia University in 1970. After closely watching the eyes of student subjects as they looked at a picture involved in one of his experiments, he noticed that they constantly fixated on various elements of an image. He surmised that the brain built a construct of the view by taking quick mental snapshots that became a part of a person's short-term memory. He named his theory of visual communication *constructivism* and wrote of the visual process as an active state of perception.

Hochberg's theory gained popularity after he had his subjects use *eye-tracking* machines in his visual perception experiments. When someone puts on an eye-tracking headset, a researcher can chart accurately the way the viewer looks at a page or a screen. The specific fixation, the length of time spent looking at a specific part of a display, and the path the eyes take between elements can easily be measured.

Twenty years later, two graphic design educators helped make Hochberg's theory practical for visual communicators by showing how viewers notice elements on paper and online.

Drs. Mario García and Pegie Stark Adam of the Poynter Institute of Media Studies used an eye-tracking machine to record on videotape the eye movements of participants as they read different versions of a printed newspaper. Subjects wore special glasses that "contained two small cameras—one that recorded eye movement and another that recorded where the reader looked." The time spent on each element of a page could also be recorded (Figure 3.3). García and Adam found that readers noticed pictures on a page first and then the words. The results indicated how important visual elements are in capturing a reader's attention, but news on paper did not have links.

To study the importance of links in a display, in 2007 a more elaborate study tested readers as they navigated the various elements that make up online pages. The research discovered that readers first seek navigational elements and links when they look at an online news site. It seems we are always surfing for the next big thing.

With links established as vital for a website's make-up, other studies concentrated on where links should be placed. Psychologist Mark C. Russell used undergraduate students in his experiment. He asked them to locate specific links on a web page and discovered that if they were located at the bottom or on multiple locations on a page, they were much easier to locate for the students than if among a menu-type list along the right side

Figure 3.3 In order to conduct research on graphic design attributes for print and online publications, subjects were asked to wear headsets that recorded eye movements and time spent viewing various elements. *Courtesy of the Poynter Institute for Media Studies.*

of a page. Russell concluded that the ease of link use is based on a user's expectations of where a link should be located. This perception is based on a user's prior experience with other websites. Russell's study makes the point that a website might be more favorably rated if its graphic elements are familiar, repeated, and easy to find.

Many years before his death in 2006, the video artist Nam June Paik famously uttered, "Paper is dead—except for toilet paper." The Future Exploration Network in its study of experts determined that news on paper will be an anachronism in the United States by the year 2017. Paper will last longer in other countries (Canada—2020, Germany—2030, Argentina—2040) because of their stronger newspaper readership traditions. Regardless, there will always be a need for news with stories that give quick summaries of events bolstered by user-selected links to more information.

Practice

Local Files and Root Directories

Just as two points are necessary to create a line, you will need two pages to create a basic link (and yes, you will see that you can create a link from a source to a target on a single page later in this chapter). In order to create links, we first need to create the place where the link comes *from* (the hypertext itself) and the place where the link points *to* (the reference).

HTML files are created and saved **locally** (on the author's hard drive) before they are uploaded to a *server*, which distributes files on the Internet. If you include links or images on your web page, then your HTML document references other files (another HTML page or a PNG or JPG file, for instance). The top-level directory (or folder) where you save your *index.html* file is your **root directory**. If *index.html* references "image.png," then *image.png* should be located in the root directory with *index.html*. If *index.html* references "photos/image.png," then there should be a folder (or subdirectory) on your server called "photos" in which *image.png* should be uploaded. In other words, any file referenced in your HTML document must exist on your server; the integrity of the file relationships must be preserved. Your server will be an exact reflection of your *local files*. Dreamweaver is smart enough to understand this "root directory" concept. However, instead of asking where your root directory is located when you open a new file (a better software design suggestion than what happens now—hint, hint Adobe), you will have to know to use the Site menu in order to "define" your site. "Defining your site" is Dreamweaver lingo for naming your root directory. This should always, without hesitation, be the first thing you do when you open Dreamweaver. We'll do this in Exercise 1, and you should do this before every exercise in the rest of this book.

> **Note**
>
> To refer to an image or file in a subdirectory, use the slash. If you want to keep all of your images in a folder named "images," then, for instance, *index.html* should be saved in the root directory and refer to a photo as so: `<img src = "images/photo.png">`. Use Figure 3.13 to determine the syntax of your references.

Where Do the Links Go?

When we saw, "Hello World" on our web page in Chapter 1, we were viewing content that we added to the body section of the HTML document. In Chapter 2, we added images to the body section of the HTML document.

In this chapter we will add links to the body section of the HTML document. There are four types of links that we will create—all of them are references. First we will reference another page, then we will refer to a web page outside of our domain, we will make a reference to an e-mail address or document, and finally we will create a named *anchor* (specify a location) on the page and reference the anchor within a single HTML document (reference Figure 3.13 after you have completed exercises 1, 2, and 3).

What's in a Link?

When you add a link to an HTML document, you have the opportunity to design four distinct "states" of linking: the original link (as it appears in the browser when the viewer first experiences it), the visited link (how a link appears after a viewer clicks a link on a page), the link when the mouse hovers above it (what was once known as the rollover state and is now referred to as the hover state), and the "active" link (what a link looks like when a user clicks it). With CSS, the language we will soon be using to alter the appearance of all of the content in an HTML document, you can dictate the appearance of each of these link states. We will see this by working with the Page Properties dialog box in Exercise 5.

Reference

For an online tutorial about creating links, see Echoecho.com. [http://www.echoecho.com/htmllinks.htm]

Results of Chapter 3 Exercises

In the following exercises, we will create an HTML file that links to a second page (Figure 3.4). We will also create a link to a web page outside of our domain, a link to an e-mail address, and a link to a later section of the page (Figure 3.5). We will modify the

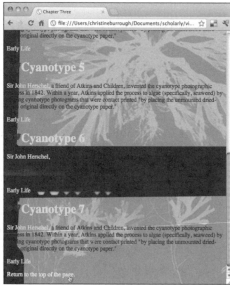

Figures 3.4 and 3.5 When all Chapter 3 exercises are complete, the resulting two HTML files include hyperlinks. You will link from one page to another, to an email address, to a file, and to the top of a document.

properties of our links using the Page Properties dialog and continue to view our work locally. Since we will not upload the files to a server, the work you create in this chapter will only be viewable on the computer where you are saving your files. The final HTML files will not be "live," or online for public viewing, until they have been uploaded to a server (see Chapter 6).

Download Materials for Chapter 3 Exercises

We will modify the *index.html* file created in Chapter 2. You can use the files you created by completing the exercises in Chapter 2 or download the Chapter 2 results files from the website. {http://viscommontheweb.wordpress.com/downloads/}

Exercise 1: Defining Your Site

1. Before you begin working with code, it is imperative to organize your digital files. You should have a plan for where all of your files will be saved, and you should feel comfortable making a commitment to your plan. In other words, you should work in a way that is sustainable for the foreseeable future so that you do not have to move files to other folders or rename working folders. These two actions (moving and renaming) can cause a beginning web designer a lot of unnecessary frustration. Create a folder on your Desktop or hard drive and name it *chapter03*. Copy the files we saved in Chapter 2 to this folder. The new folder, *chapter03*, will be the root directory while you are working on the exercises in this chapter.

> **Note**
>
> You will start nearly all of the remaining exercises in this book by copying your files to a new folder and defining your site.

2. **Set up your workspace:** In Dreamweaver, choose Window > Workspace Layout > Designer so that your Dreamweaver workspace is similar to the screen shots demonstrating the exercise steps. Define your site by choosing Site > New Site from the top menu bar. In the Site Setup dialog box, you will see two fields on the main screen. The first is for the Site Name, or title of the site. You can enter any title in this field that makes sense to you. The second is more important—this is where you are telling Dreamweaver where to save the files associated with your new site. Following the field for Local Site Folder (meaning, the path to the folder on your hard drive), click the folder icon and then navigate to the place on your hard drive where you are saving your files. You might go to Desktop > *chapter03*. Click the Save button (Figure 3.6). The other screens, accessible from the left column of the Site Setup dialog box, contain advanced settings that we will not use in this chapter.
3. Look in the Files panel on the lower-right side of your screen (Window > Files, if you don't see it) and notice that *chapter03* is the site that is accessible from the Files menu (Figure 3.7). Double-click the file *index.html* to open it in Dreamweaver.

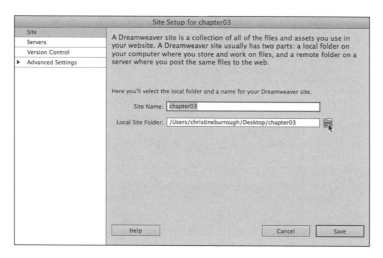

Figure 3.6 When defining your site in Dreamweaver, browse to the folder where you are storing all of your files. This is your offline root directory.

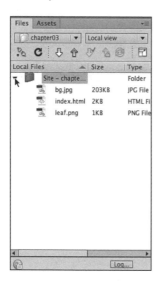

Figure 3.7 The Dreamweaver Files panel lists local files saved in the site that has been defined as the root directory. Once you complete your site setup, you will see the contents of your folder in this panel.

Exercise 2: Creating a Second Page

1. The title appears in the title bar of the web browser. It is highly significant because the word choices you make for the title of the page are the same words that will appear in a user's bookmark list. By default, Dreamweaver titles every page, "Untitled Document." Click in the Title field near the top of your HTML document and rename the title "Chapter Three" (Figure 3.8).

2. When code is highlighted in code or design view, Dreamweaver displays the parent tags for the specified code in the bottom-left corner of the interface. This allows you to easily see and understand the structure of your document. For instance, when "Chapter Three" (the title of my page) is highlighted in the code view, Dreamweaver lists the head and title tags as the elements surrounding (or nesting) this text (Figure 3.9). In other words, "Chapter Three" is surrounded by the **title** tag, which is a child of the **head** tag, which is a child of the **HTML** tag. The **HTML** tag is the root element; therefore, it has no parent.

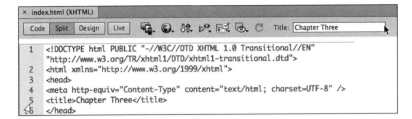

Figure 3.8 Add a title using the Title field in Dreamweaver.

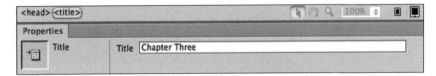

Figure 3.9 You can see how tags are nested in the display near the bottom of the Dreamweaver interface.

3. In Design view press the Return key after the last sentence in the first paragraph. Add the text, "Cyanotype Impressions." We will use this text as a link to a second page that we will create and save in the root directory.

4. Press Command+S (Control+S on the PC) to save the page (you will be saving on top of, or rewriting, *index.html*). Now choose File > Save As and save the page again with the new name *cyanotype.html* inside the root directory. We just made a copy of the index page and called it "cyanotype.html." Both files should be saved in the same folder and both are open in Dreamweaver—notice the tabs that you can use to click between files.

5. In the *cyanotype.html* document, replace the heading "Early Life" with the word "Cyanotype" between the **<h1>** and **</h1>** tags. Then copy and paste the first paragraph (just two sentences) from the "Photographs of British Algae: Cyanotype Impressions" section of the Anna Atkins Wikipedia page [http://en.wikipedia.org/wiki/Anna_Atkins] to replace the paragraph copy on your new page—remember to paste the text into the code view and remove any unnecessary text elements. Replace "Cyanotype" with "Early Life" (Figure 3.10). We will use this text to link from *cyanotype.html* to the index page.

6. Press Command+S to save your work. You can view both files in the browser, but you will have to open one at a time, as the links have not been created.

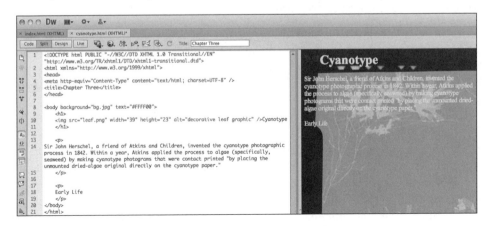

Figure 3.10 Always paste new content to the code view of the file.

Exercise 3: Linking to a Page in Your Root Directory

1. Click the tab to access *index.html* and select the text "Cyanotype Impressions" in design view. The selected text will be clickable in the browser once we add the code that transforms the plain text to a hyperlink.

> **Note**
>
> Elements you add to the design window are simply representations of code. If you highlight the element (in this case, a line of text) in either window, it is automatically highlighted in the other window because the code and the design element both refer to the same content.

2. Use the Properties panel to add a link to *cyanotype.html*. The Properties panel is near the bottom of the screen (you can open and close it by choosing Window > Properties if it is not visible). This panel can be used to add code to the HTML document or to add/modify code in a CSS document. Make sure that the HTML button is selected on the left side of the panel. Click the Browse for File button to the right of the Link field, and select *cyanotype.html* from the *chapter03* folder (Figure 3.11). This is the root directory.

Figure 3.11 Select text and assign a link in the Properties panel.

Take a look at the code view. The **a** tag with the href property, **`<a href>`**, is used to establish the link to the second page. This tag opens before the clickable text and then closes at the end of the sentence with **`</a>`**.

3. Press Command+S to save the file and view it in a web browser. You should be able to click to the second page.

> ### Watch Out
>
> If you open a file in Dreamweaver and use File > Save As to make a copy, or if you save your current file to a new folder, you might end up seeing a Dreamweaver message asking you to "Update Links?" Click the No button, or else Dreamweaver will reroute all of your links to the new folder from the position of where you were saving your file. This can be a hassle and often produces unwanted results.

4. **Your turn!** Return to Dreamweaver and click the tab to access *cyanotype.html*. Add the **a href** tag to the "Early Life" text in order to make a link that returns the viewer to the index page. Save the file and view your work in a browser. You should be able to click back and forth between the index and second page (Figure 3.12).

Figure 3.12 The results of Exercise 3 are a functioning link from the *index* page to the *cyanotype* page.

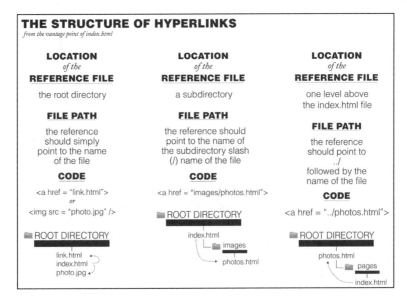

Figure 3.13 The structure of hyperlinks in your files, in the code, and on the server. *Diagram courtesy of xtine.*

Exercise 4: Defining Attributes of Link States

You may have noticed that our links are functioning (yay!), but they appear in ugly shades of blue and purple (boo!). Here we will set the link colors for two of the four link states, the body copy to black, and the heading to yellow.

1. Open Modify > Page Properties from the top menu bar. Choose Links (CSS) from the vertical list of options on the left side.

> **Note**
>
> You could set the link properties in the Appearance (HTML) options, but this would attach your link properties to the **body** tag. We want to begin to see some CSS code because you will want the flexibility afforded by this language in your online documents. Consider this a minor transition to using CSS, which we will explore more thoroughly in Chapters 5 and 7 through 12.

2. Click the Link color chip and select a bright shade of yellow (I selected #FF3). Set the Visited Links and Active Links fields to the same color. Set the Rollover Links field (what we will later refer to as "hover") to white, or #FFF. Also use the pull-down menu to set the underline style to Never Underline (Figure 3.14). When you are finished with your links, choose the category Appearance (CSS) from the top of the list on the left. Set the Text Color field to black (#000) (Figure 3.15). Finally, choose the category Headings (CSS) from the list on the left. Set Heading1 to the same yellow we were using in the color box to the right of the size box. To demonstrate a different method for selecting colors, I placed my cursor over a heading in design view and selected the color from my web page when the cursor changed to an Eyedropper Tool (Figure 3.16). Click OK to exit the dialog.

Figures 3.14, 3.15, and 3.16 (Continued)

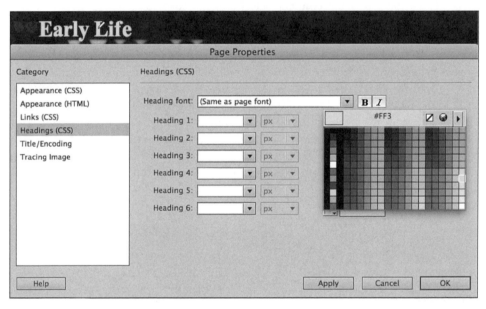

Figures 3.14, 3.15, and 3.16 Assign CSS colors in the Page Properties dialog box (Modify Menu > Page Properties). In Figure 3.16, the Eyedropper tool is used on any part of the web page in design view to select a color (it may be hard to locate, look in the top right corner of the screen shot on the letter "L" in "Life"). Be careful—as you move the tool around the page, it "finds" variations on the hue.

3. View your code (Figure 3.17). The values for each of the link states have been added to a small set of Cascading Style Sheet code that appears in the **head** section of the page. CSS uses a slightly different syntactic format than HTML. Instead of

---

Reference

When colors are defined in CSS, their six-digit alphanumeric hex value may be consolidated to a three-digit value if their digits are repetitive. For instance, #FFFF33 becomes #FF3. #FFFFFF is shortened to #FFF. However, with monitors displaying millions of colors, there are many colors that utilize all six digits. If you search online for "CSS Colors" you will find long lists of colors and their CSS names. The W3Schools' HTML Color Picker is fun to use, as you can select a hue and then alter its value to locate a corresponding hex code. [http://www.w3schools.com/tags/ref_colorpicker.asp]

---

tags, you will see a set of curly brackets, colons, and semicolons. The text color (for the links, body copy, and heading) is defined with the **color** property and the underline is established with a property called **text-decoration**. Save your work and preview it in a browser.

```
3   <head>
4   <meta http-equiv="Content-Type" content="text/html; charset=UTF-8" />
5   <title>Chapter Three</title>
6   <style type="text/css">
7   a:link {
8       color: #FF3;
9       text-decoration: none;
10  }
11  a:visited {
12      text-decoration: none;
13      color: #FF3;
14  }
15  a:hover {
16      text-decoration: none;
17      color: #FFF;
18  }
19  a:active {
20      text-decoration: none;
21      color: #FF3;
22  }
23  h1 {
24      color: #FF3;
25  }
26  </style>
27  </head>
```

Figure 3.17 A view of the CSS code in the **head** section of *index.html*.

Your turn! Click the tab to the second page and insert the code that changes the color of the link states (Figure 3.18). You can use the Page Properties dialog box again, or you can simply copy the code from one document to the other. Since we modified this code within our HTML document, we will have to repeat our steps in every HTML document we create. Soon we will learn how to make global changes to an entire site.

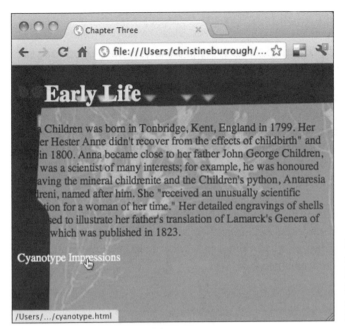

Figure 3.18 The link properties are seen here: no underline is included and a change
has been made to the link
color on the mouse-over, or
hover state.

Note

Just because you *can* change all of the colors and properties of the four link
states, that doesn't mean you *should*. The application of too many colors is a
sure way to disrupt unity on the page. Here we assigned the same link colors
in every state, with the exception of the "hover" state. When a user positions
her mouse over the link, she gets a hint that the link exists. The contrast
between the colors and values of the body copy and the link is another hint
that the text functions as a link. The only trouble with relying on the hover
color for contrast is that, at the time of this writing, users on touchpad devices
do not have access to the "hover" function.

Exercise 5: Linking to Another Website

1. On the *cyanotype.html* page, select the name at the start of the first sentence:
    "Sir John Herschel." By selecting the text, we are indicating that we will use or
    modify it in some way.
2. Use the HTML section of the Properties panel to add the link to the Wikipedia
    page for Sir John Herschel. In the Link field of the Properties panel, paste the
    entire link, starting with http, such as http://en.wikipedia.org/wiki/John_
    Herschel.
3. View your code. The **a href** tag points to the Wikipedia website, and the close
    a tag indicates the end of the hyperlink.

```
Adding the a href tag to link to a page on the Internet

<p>
<a href="http://en.wikipedia.org/wiki/John_Herschel">Sir
John Herschel,</a> a friend of Atkins and Children,
```

Exercise 6: Linking to an E-mail Address

1. Select the first name, "Anna Children," from the body copy on *index.html*. We will use this text as the link to an e-mail address. Either choose Insert > Email Link or place your cursor inside the Link field of the Properties panel to add the link **mailto:anna@cyanotype.com** (Figure 3.19). (Use your own e-mail address to test the link). After you enter the code snippet in the Link field, click anywhere in design or code view. Both views will refresh to display your new line of code (the **a href** tag with mailto).

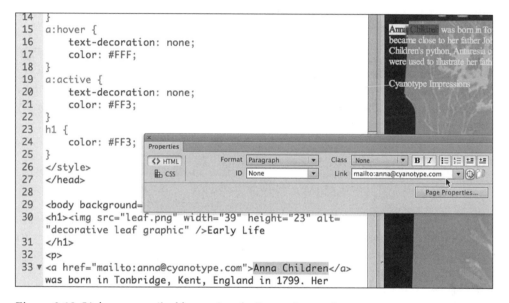

Figure 3.19 Link to an email address using the Properties panel.

2. Save your work and preview it in a browser. The contact link will open in the e-mail application saved in the browser preferences.

Exercise 7: Linking to a Document

You can also link to documents, such as PDF files, DOCX files, and so on. Some of these files might be viewable within the browser, and others will have to be downloaded and opened on the user's computer with another application. There are two things to remember:

1. The file must be saved in your root directory, or else you need to point to the exact file location from the vantage point of where you are saving your HTML page.
2. The code is simply the **a href** tag pointing to the file.

For instance, I downloaded a PDF titled, "Barack Obama: Connecting and Empowering All Americans Through Technology and Innovation," from the website PDFKing. com [http://www.pdfking.com/barack-obama-on-technology-and-innovation/]. The name of the file was "Fact Sheet Innovation and Technology Plan FINAL.pdf" before I renamed it to "obama.pdf" (a much easier file name to remember when writing code). I moved the saved file to my root directory (my *chapter03* folder). Here's how I would link to this file:

A. Insert the text, "Download Obama's Plan for Technology and Innovation" in the *cyanotype.html* document.
B. Highlight the inserted text in design or code view.
C. Either add the **a href** tag in code view or use the Properties panel to point to the file *obama.pdf*.

Creating a link to a file

<a href = "obama.pdf">Download Obama's Plan for Technology and Innovation." **</a>**

Your Turn! Download any PDF, or use one of your own, and create a link to it on the *cyanotype.html* page. Save your work and view it in a browser. Click the link and see how your browser renders the download. Does it open in the browser, or does it automatically save to your Downloads folder or Desktop?

Exercise 8: Linking to an Anchor

At the top of the Wikipedia page for Anna Atkins [http://en.wikipedia.org/wiki/Anna_Atkins] there is an area called "contents" that is similar to a traditional table of contents. The difference is that it links to the contents, and rather than existing on separate pages of a book, all of the contents are "printed" on a single web page. This common way to assist the user in locating information relies on two things: setting up a named anchor with the **a name** tag on the page at the place where the "later" information lives, and using the **a href** tag to reference the named anchor. We will set the named anchor, **<a name>**, using the Insert menu in Dreamweaver, and we will link to it using the Properties panel.

1. Copy all of the code between the body and close body tags on *cyanotype.html* (Figure 3.20). Then paste the code six times to create six new paragraphs before **</body>**. You will have seven copies of the heading, paragraph, and link. Add a

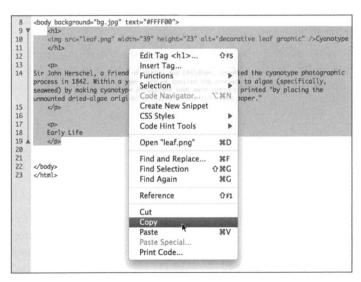

Figure 3.20 Right-click to copy all of the code between the body open and close tags in code view.

number after each heading to be able to identify it (Cyanotype 1, Cyanotype 2... Cyanotype 7). Save the page and view it in the browser (Figure 3.21).

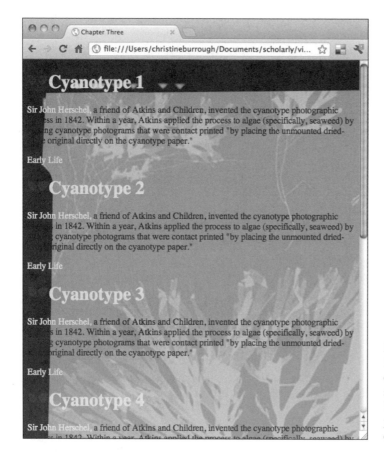

Figure 3.21 Notice that if you shorten the width of your browser window some of the text will fall beneath the "fold" or pre-scroll viewing area on the page.

2. The named anchor is code that points to a specific part of your layout. Add a named anchor called "top" just before the first paragraph. Position the cursor to the left of the leaf before the heading "Cyanotype 1." Choose Insert > Named Anchor from the top menu bar. In the Named Anchor dialog box, name the anchor "top," as this is the top of the page. It is invisible to the user, so the open and close tags, **<a name>** and **</a>**, appear next to each other, with no content between them (Figure 3.22).

Figure 3.22 Set up the anchor in code view.

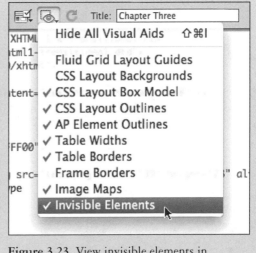

Sidebar: Using Visual Aids

In design view, you will see a yellow shield with an anchor on it holding the place of the named anchor. This is a visual aid that Dreamweaver displays to alert you to invisible code. You can turn off different types of visual aids (in this case, "invisible elements") by using the Visual Aids pull-down menu on the top menu bar.

Figure 3.23 View invisible elements in Dreamweaver's design view.

3. In code view, scroll to the bottom of the page and create a link to the top of the page after the final words in the last paragraph. Add the code **<p>Return to the top of the page.</p>** to create the text that will become a link to the top. Select the sentence and type **#top** in the Link field of the Properties panel. The code **<a href = "#top">** and **</a>** surround the command "Return to the top of the page" (Figure 3.24). Save your work and preview it in a browser.

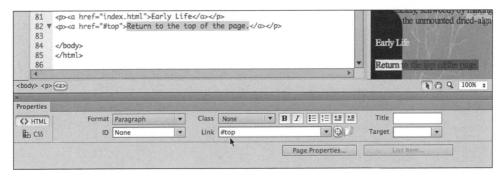

Figure 3.24 To link to an anchor on a page, use the pound sign (#) followed by the name assigned in the **a name** tag.

Note

You can "fake" a link by selecting your link text or image and assigning the pound key as the link in the Link field of the Properties panel or by creating the tag **<a href = "#">** followed by **</a>**. This will create a link that goes nowhere and can be helpful in the design phase of a project.

Note

You can link to a particular place in a separate page by adding a named anchor to one page and linking to it from another. For instance, if I wanted to add a link on *index.html* pointing to the fifth heading on *cyanotype.html* (and let's say, for instance, that my named anchor is called "five"), I would add the tag `<a href = "cyanotype.html#five">`Click here to go to the 5th heading on the Cyanotype page.`</a>`.

Your turn! Repeat Steps 2 and 3 to create a new link *from* the top of the page *to* the beginning of the fifth heading (Cyanotype 5).

The Art and Craft of Code

Don't Click It (Figures 3.25 and 3.26) is an experimental website (also known as the Imaginary Institute for Interactive Research) developed by Alex Frank as a final artwork

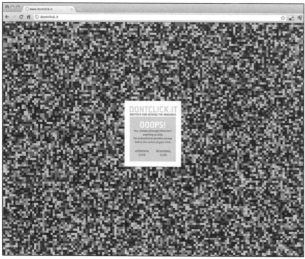

Figures 3.25 and 3.26 Screen shots from DontClick.it by Alex Frank are not the same as interacting with this website to experience how important the click-action is to your sense of navigation. *Courtesy of Alex Frank.*

created for his diploma in communication design at the University Essen-Duisburg, Germany [http://dontclick.it/]. The site challenges users to select links without clicking the button on the mouse or trackpad. By eliminating the single most common mode of functioning online, the website poignantly alludes to the way in which good design (Douglas Engelbart's original idea for the mouse) becomes ubiquitous and relied upon by large groups of users. How would you redesign the method of linking from one page to another? Is it a new way to "click" or prompt the display of selections of content?

Create, Reflect, Critique

Select a timely topic and view its Wikipedia.org page. Create a new HTML page in Dreamweaver and copy/paste some of the Wikipedia page content to the code view of your new document. Format the text using the heading tags and add links to the page where it is appropriate. Don't worry about creating multiple columns on the page. Modify the page settings in order to change the link colors. What are some of the challenges you might experience in a browser when there is so much content on the page? How do viewers know when text is a link? What other visual modifications can you make to a word or a group of words to suggest the idea of linking to new content? In what ways does the page that you made appear similar to the Wikipedia page, and how does it differ?

Glossary Words

`<a>`, `<a href>`, `<a name>`, anchor, constructivism, eye-tracking, hyperlink, local files, root directory, server

---

4 SHARING COLLECTIONS—BLOGS

VIDEO
INTRODUCTION

Principles, History, Theory

Obsession and Cultural Commentaries

What is the one personality trait most useful to a successful blogger?

Tucked innocuously between the Super Flooring Center and the Center for Land Use Interpretation along busy Venice Boulevard in Culver City, California, is one of the most unique tourist attractions in the world—The Museum of Jurassic Technology. Founded by David and Diana Wilson in 1987, a hint to the credibility of the collections found among the dimly lit rooms crowded to the edge of claustrophobia with exhibits on walls and within countless trophy cases can be found in the name itself—dinosaurs never created anything technological during their long Jurassic Era reign. And although many exhibits are actual—micro-miniature sculptures placed within the eye of a needle, trailer park dioramas, paintings of dogs that have flown in space, and eroding dice from the collection of master magician and actor Ricky Jay—overall one should view the museum with the attitude that seeing is not necessarily believing. To prove the point, there are also such pieces as two furry white mice on a piece of toast said to be a cure for stuttering children, evidence of a rare bat that can fly through metal walls, and a reproduction of Noah's Ark—that according to the Old Testament was one of the first repositories for a massive collection of animal pairs (Figure 4.1).

Despite, or because tongue-in-cheek spin on the museum genre, in 2001 David Wilson won a prestigious "Genius Grant" from the MacArthur Foundation fellowship worth $500,000 for his odd collections.

Museums began with wealthy individuals who liked to show off their prized artifacts and artwork brought back from the far corners of the globe, either by themselves or their agents. In what is now known as Iraq, the Ennigaldi-Nanna museum is considered the first in the world, established in 530 BCE by the Princess Ennigaldi located on the palace grounds of her father's kingdom. One of the innovations she used was clay cylinder labels written in three languages that explained many of the estimated 16,000 artifacts in the collection (Figure 4.2). About 2,000 years later, the Vatican, various monarchs, and wealthy donors created museums in numerous European cities. Many of the greatest collections were opened to the public in England (the British Museum) and France (the Louvre). With the advent of online media, virtual museums allow interested patrons to visit remote collections through websites, galleries on Second Life, and even through Twitter. In 2010 the Whitney Museum of American Art in New York City sponsored an "Online Twitter Tour" of its collection. In 2012 Google introduced its Art Project that offers virtual tours of more than 150 collections—from the Acropolis to the Zimmerli. [http://www.googleartproject.com]

Figure 4.1 One of the most popular exhibits within The Museum of Jurassic Technology is the display of mice on toast and mice pie—presumably cures for incontinence and stuttering. *Courtesy of Susan Gerbic.*

Figure 4.2 The clay cylinder found in the ruins of the Ennigaldi-Nanna's museum in the town of Ur, southern Iraq, was the first explanatory label for an exhibit. The innovation was the idea of Princess Ennigaldi. *Courtesy of Sir Leonard Wooley.*

Perhaps inspired by the established and respected works on display in private and public museums throughout history, a current popular genre of cable television—reality shows—often feature troubled individuals who cannot control their compulsive hoarding behaviors. Houses filled with personal objects only the hoarder sees as treasures awe the viewer. Stacks of newspapers are piled to the ceiling so that a simple room becomes a maze. Baby clothes and toys in boxes fill a room and make it unusable. Obscure car parts spill out of garages and into driveways and front yards. These collections cause worried family members to employ hoarding experts to help discard the items.

Writers have been known to collect daily written accounts that have transformed the medium and inspired others. Samuel Pepys would have been a relatively unknown member of Parliament in the 17th century were it not for a daily diary he kept for almost a decade. His personal log detailed insights and slights, accounts of ordinary life in the 1660s, as well as momentous events such as London's Great Plague and Great Fire in which the former caused 100,000 deaths and the latter destroyed more than 70,000 homes and structures. It was through his detailed observations that Pepys was able to include a personal history of the era that was much different from the formal, traditional accounts of the time.

Artists who create works in almost any medium are often known for the found objects they turn into expressive pieces that can clutter workspaces and computer hard drives. French Dadaist Marcel Duchamp, the American photographer Edward Weston, and more recently, the British artist Damien Hirst, all created art from ordinary objects that they took to their studios to transform into cultural commentaries. Noah Kalina, a New York–based advertising photographer with clients that include Motorola, Sony, and Neiman Marcus, decided in 2000 to photograph his face every day (Figure 4.3). His collection consists of thousands of self-portraits staring unemotionally into the camera that continues to this day. A video of the collection was a YouTube favorite and inspired many imitators.

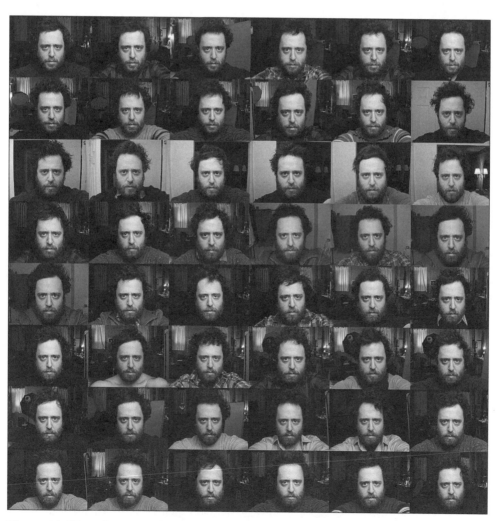

Figure 4.3 "Everyday," detail, 2009 by Noah Kalina. On January 11, 2000, he started to photograph his face every day, a project that continues. *Courtesy of Noah Kalina.*

Obsession. Whether one creates an art project that is a parody of a museum that becomes respected and needs to obtain new acquisitions; a museum curator who must satisfy her patrons, donors, and visitors with constantly updated collections and special shows; a psychologically damaged individual who is sure she can care for one more stray cat even though 71 cats await their supper at home; an amateur writer who must pen personal stories in a journal because of some unseen compulsion; an artist that searches trash dumps for "garbage" that can be transformed into valuable objets d'art; or a photographer who sits in front of a camera to be pictured for more than 2000 days, anyone who is driven to amass observations and objects on a daily basis must be obsessed.

As it turns out, to be a successful blogger, obsession is the one personality trait that is needed in order to include words, pictures, videos, and links of interest on a daily basis to a waiting fan base. American computer programmer Jorn Barger used the title *Robot Wisdom Weblog* for his 1997 daily online updates of his various interests. As one of the first such entities, it received attention from the *Village Voice*, *Wired*, and *Brill's Content*. As weblogs grew in popularity, the name was simplified to *blogs*, with those who commit their daily thoughts to an online audience known as *bloggers*. Once easy-to-use *blogging* software was introduced from such organizations as Moveable Type, Typepad, WordPress, and Blogger, anyone—from a hoarder describing her latest find to a politician explaining her most recent position—could produce daily digital pages for as long as the obsession lasts (Figure 4.4).

Figure 4.4 Dennis Dunleavy teaches photojournalism at Benedictine College in Atchison, Kansas. He has been a blogger since 2003 and updates it about four times a week. With more than 500,000 subscribers, his "Big Picture" blog has been featured in *The New York Times*, *Salon*, *The Digital Journalist*, and *StockPhoto*. Dunleavy admits, "I am obsessed. I don't use drugs, drink or smoke, so blogging is the next best thing." *Courtesy of Dennis Dunleavy.*

Practice

WordPress

Because of its large community of users, great documentation, loads of *themes* and plug-ins, and open-source philosophy (the free source code is available for augmentation and manipulation), we will use WordPress in the following exercises.

WordPress.org is a website where you can find information about installing the WordPress software on your own domain. On WordPress.com you can sign up for a free account and create a new blog within minutes. The distinction between the two sites is significant: the first site contains the blogging software, while the second site contains the blogging service. The software and service are both free, but the service is easier to set up, so we will visit WordPress.com.

Blogs are used to catalog events, activities, images, illustrations, articles, ideas, inspirations, recipes, and more. Most blogs are created around a central theme. For instance, *The Huffington Post* is a news blog, whereas *Lifehacker* is full of "tips for getting things done" (and was purchased by AOL in 2011 for $315 million).

> ### Sidebar: A Note About the Following Exercises in WordPress
>
> Due to the open-source nature of the WordPress software and service, updates occur frequently. Traditional software, such as Adobe's Creative Suite, is typically updated on an 18-month release cycle. That means that a text like this becomes relatively outdated in 18 months and a new edition is printed or uploaded to the e-book server (though I would argue that we are a bit more on the timeline of updates to HTML and CSS than Dreamweaver, as you will find by the end of the text you will be more interested in code than in DW panels, but I digress). I cannot account for the ever-changing nature of WordPress. So here you will find many steps that have been true for at least the past four years at the time of this writing and will likely continue to be more or less accurate. I have included fewer screen shots than usual, as the user interface is more apt to change than the operational features of the WordPress dashboard.

Cataloging is a conceptual activity. The properties of an individual set govern whether or not an item belongs in it. So in order to create a set, you have to define its properties. After completing the exercises in this chapter you will schedule a set of images to post on a new WordPress blog. The technical components to this chapter include creating the blog and scheduling posts, which are fairly simple activities. But one should not underestimate the conceptual challenge of defining a catalog.

Results of Chapter 4 Exercises

In the following exercises you will create a WordPress blog; publish and schedule a new post; and add images, tags, and a category to your post (Figure 4.5).

Download Materials for Chapter 4 Exercises

You will need an image file for the following exercises. I used *leaf.png* from the Chapter 2 and 3 exercises. You can download all of the results files from the website. [http:// viscommontheweb.wordpress.com/downloads/]

Figure 4.5 A Wordpress blog created for *Visual Communication on the Web*.

Exercise 1: Creating a WordPress.com Account

1. Go to Wordpress.com and click the Sign Up Now button to create a new blog using WordPress.com's blogging service. Follow the instructions to set up your blog. You will enter the domain name, title of the blog, and language and privacy specifications. You can change the title of your blog at any time using the WordPress interface. [http://wordpress.com]

> **Note**
>
> You can only set your domain name ONE TIME! The domain name is literally what other viewers will type into their web browsers in order to find your blog. If you are using your name, you will probably choose to leave the blog domain the same as your user name. However, if you choose a user name that is not meaningful to your blog, you may want to set a new domain name in the Blog Domain field.

2. On the next screen, you can fill in your personal information or skip it. More importantly, you will have to verify your new blog by clicking a link sent to the e-mail address you provided in Step 1. Go to your e-mail inbox now and click the link sent to you by WordPress.

3. By following the link from WordPress, you should see a page in your web browser that verifies your active account. Click your domain name to log in and see your new blog.

Exercise 2: Understanding Blog Lingo

You can edit all aspects of your blog, but if you have never created a blog before, begin by looking at the default details associated with the home page of your new blog. The front end of the blog (or what you see at the domain) includes the following:

1. **Header**

   The title of your blog appears in the *header* area of the page, followed by a caption. By default, the caption is "Just another WordPress.com site." You can change this in your settings.

2. **Navigation**

   At the time of this writing, the default theme is the "Twenty Eleven" Word-Press blog, where the navigation buttons appear beneath the header image. The default buttons, which link to **pages**, are "Home" and "About." You can add, edit, or delete pages.

3. **Content**

   a. A blog may be maintained by a single person, a group of people, or an organization. A *post* is created every time the author or administrator of the blog publishes an entry. Posts are displayed in reverse chronological order so that each time a user visits the blog, the newest information is visible beneath the header image.

   b. The *title* of the first post on the default WordPress blog page is "Hello world!" You will see the date of the post and the author (your user name) beneath the title. The content of this first post is text, including a list of items (the **li** tag is in use). Posts can include a variety of content, including text, links, images, and video.

   c. Following the post, you can see how the author categorized it. Blog posts are categorized and tagged to facilitate users in finding the content as the blog becomes a large archive of posts. *Categories* are used to organize posts.

   d. *Comments* or *replies* are created by blog readers. Comments enable users to engage in a dialog with the author of the blog. The blog administrator controls the settings in regard to user comments. You can set up your blog so that users do not have to log in to leave comments, or you can restrict the comments area. You will also see a message bubble at the top-right corner of the post where a number (1, in the default post) represents how many replies have been posted.

4. **Sidebar**

   The default Twenty Eleven WordPress page has the following items in the right *sidebar*: archives and meta, which includes a link to the site administration and to log out.

5. **Footer**

   The *footer* area of the page contains copyright information, including the title of the theme and a link to Wordpress.com.

Exercise 3: Managing Content

1. **Dashboard**

   The *dashboard* is the main area of the WordPress interface on the administrative or content management side of the blog. This is the part of the blog that you need to log in to so you can control posts, pages, and all other settings.

All WordPress.com blogs can be accessed from the domain name of the blog slash (/) wp-admin. That is, I can control a blog named *viscommontheweb* with the URL:

http://viscommontheweb.wordpress.com/wp-admin/

2. **Theme**

The *theme* is used to control the design and style of the blog. By default, your blog will use a WordPress (WP) theme, such as Twenty Eleven or Twenty Twelve (most likely). There are more than a thousand free themes available. Most will include a header area, a content area, a sidebar, and a footer area. Some are designed specifically for photo blogs or video blogs, some are designed in a magazine layout format, and some are designed based on conceptual themes. You will spend a lot of time searching for just the right WP theme. At the time of this writing, you can install a new theme from the dashboard by selecting Appearance > Themes from the side menu bar.

Reference

You can browse all of the free WordPress themes on WordPress.org's Free Themes Directory. [http://wordpress.org/extend/themes/]

---

3. **Widget**

A *widget* is a graphic user interface that visually organizes information. The sidebar usually contains a selection of widgets (every item that appears in the default sidebar is a widget). You can install or remove widgets easily from the dashboard. At the time of this writing, you can modify widgets from the dashboard by selecting Appearance > Widgets.

4. **Settings**

The *settings* area enables you to control the display of many of your blog's features. For instance, we will change the time zone settings in Exercise 4 to see how this will affect publishing a post.

Exercise 4: Setting Up Your Preferences

1. Log in to your blog at **yourdomain.wordpress.com/wp-admin.**
2. Enter the user name and password you established in Exercise 1.
3. Hover over your user name in the top-left corner of the dashboard home page, and then click Edit My Profile. Modify your profile settings. Most people like to alter the Display Name Publicly As field, which assigns the name or nickname of your choice as the author of each post you create. At the time of this writing, the Save button is located at the top of the page called "Update Profile." Click this button, or its equivalent, when you are finished.
4. Click the Settings button and select General from the navigation tool on the left. Here you can change the title, tag line, and time zone associated with your blog. The time zone is set in coordinated universal time (UTC). Since I live on the west coast my UTC is set at −7 during daylight saving time. You can also choose your time zone based on the nearest city if you scroll way, way up (Figure 4.6). Set your local time and click the Save Changes button at the bottom of the page.

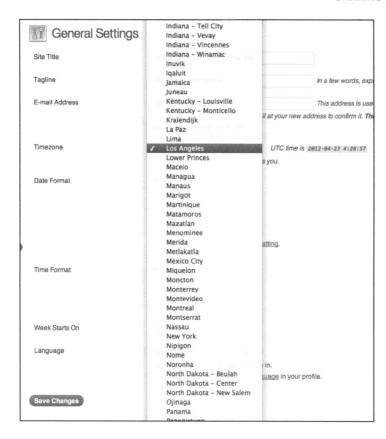

Figure 4.6 It is easy to change the time zone to a city close to you, just scroll up on the Time Zone pull-down menu.

Exercise 5: Editing a Post

1. Now we will edit the default post on the blog, "Hello world!" Click the Posts button and then click All Posts. You will see a listing of all of the posts created on the blog. Hover over the title "Hello world!" and click the Edit link.

2. On the Edit Post page you can see your post in "Visual" mode and you can see the HTML used to create the post. Click the HTML tab to see the HTML code used to format the default post.

3. Modify the post—change the title and the content. If you want to add links, you can write the code in the HTML tab, or you can paste a URL into the field launched when you click the icon of the link in the toolbar. Click the blue Update button, and click the View Post button near the title field.

4. There are a few things you should notice in your new post:
    *   You are viewing just the post, not the entire blog. You may not see widgets or sidebar materials. Notice the URL—it references not just your blog, but the actual link to this post, called the **permalink**.
    *   Also notice that the front end of your post may have opened in a new browser tab. You can use the tab to get back to the dashboard area of your blog. If your post did not open in a new tab, you can use the Edit button near the top left of the title of the post. You can also click the name of your blog in the gray top bar to return to the dashboard. It is important that you know how to get from editing a post to viewing it on your blog and back to editing again.

Exercise 6: Inserting Media and Scheduling a Post

1. Create a new post from your dashboard and add a title. Place your cursor in the Edit Post box.
2. Click the Add Media button next to the Upload/Insert area just above the editing box.
3. In the Add Media window, the first tab allows you to upload files "From Computer." Use this area for uploading *leaf.png* from your hard drive. You can also reference online media from a URL or from a media library that you build within Wordpress.com.
4. Once the file is uploaded, you should enter alternate image information to describe your illustration. You can also enter an image caption that appears beneath the picture in the post, and select the positioning of the image in relationship to text within the post. Click the Insert Into Post button.

Note

Alternate image information is stored in the ALT tag, a property of the image source tag reviewed in Chapter 2.

5. View your post, and then return to editing it. I deleted my caption, as the image is simply too small for a caption. I also added some text to my editing box and realigned *leaf.png* to the left of the text. If you need to edit the image properties, you can click the image in the editing box and then click the icon of a photograph that appears as you hover the mouse over the image.
6. You will also want to add tags and a category to your post. Assume you will have fewer than a dozen categories for the entire site, but you can have an endless number of tags. I added a new category using the link on the right side of the dashboard named "Chapter 4." I added the specific tags, "Exercise 6," "leaf," and "editing."
7. Instead of publishing the post immediately, schedule the post for a later time using the Edit button next to the Publish or Publish Immediately button Figure 4.7. If you already published your post, you can still change its time, or even "unpublish" it, by changing its status.
8. Choose a day and time for your post. If the current time is incorrect, you might need to set your time zone (see Exercise 4).

Figure 4.7 You can edit when a post will be published before or after you press the Publish button. Just be sure to press the **Save** button **and the Schedule** or **Update** button.

9. The post is not scheduled until you click *two* buttons. First, click the OK button to confirm the time of your post. Then click the Schedule button (if it hasn't been published before) or the Update button (if it was previously published).

> **Tip**
>
> Remember, WordPress blogs follow UTC time and follow a 24-hour (not 12-hour) clock. What might be familiar to you as 1:00 p.m. registers on WordPress as 13 o'clock.

10. You can see when a post is scheduled or published by clicking the Posts button or Posts > All Posts.

The Art and Craft of Code

Les Liens Invisibles is an imaginary art group from Italy composed of Clemente Pestelli and Gionatan Quintini. Their work investigates popular online culture, reverse-engineering techniques, social media subverting, and media manipulations. In 2008 they created the blog *A Fake Is a Fake*, which encourages participants to create a WordPress account for the dissemination of fake information (Figure 4.8). They explain, "Rising

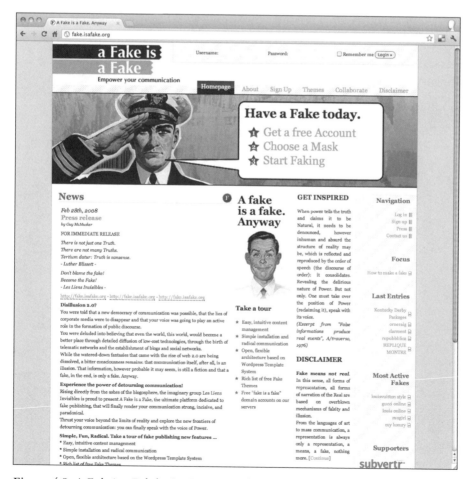

Figure 4.8 *A Fake is a Fake* by Les Liens Invisibles. *Courtesy of Les Liens Invisibles.*

directly from the ashes of the blogosphere, the imaginary group Les Liens Invisibles is proud to present A Fake Is a Fake, the ultimate platform dedicated to fake publishing, that will finally render your communication strong, incisive, and paradoxical." [http://fake.isafake.org/]

Create, Reflect, Critique

Take 26 (or more) photos, one of each letter in the alphabet, by roaming the streets in your neighborhood. Either find the letters A, B, C, D… Z on signs in your community or create letters with your own materials. Each image should include a letter. The word "neighborhood" should be interpreted loosely.

Post an image of each letter to your blog every hour for 26 consecutive hours (schedule those posts—don't stay awake for twenty-six hours). Post the letters in alphabetical order, either A–Z or backwards (Z–A). Add captions for comments to the photographs—where did you find them, what do these images have in common, why do they create a set? Is there something visually cohesive about the letters in your neighborhood, or do they seem to be at odds with each other?

Save your digital images at a screen resolution (72 dots per inch) using compression for the Web. Pictures should be saved as JPG files. Save a set of images with low resolution and no greater than 600 pixels wide.

How does a blog alter the way you think about creating a set of images? What other blogs publish photos or art similar to your creations? Which theme did you choose, and how does it support (or not) your set of posts?

Glossary Words

Blogging: categories, dashboard, header, post, sidebar, theme, widget

5   OVERVIEW OF STYLES

VIDEO
INTRODUCTION

Principles, History, Theory

Freeform and Grid

Is there such a thing as too much style?

Be thankful that written and spoken messages are not burdened with such awkward phrases as "self-contained underwater breathing apparatus," "frequently asked questions," and "Joint Photographic Experts Group." It is so much easier and more efficient to write or say SCUBA, FAQ, and JPEG. Acronyms have simplified and amplified entities and concepts for more than 2000 years, dating from the name of the Roman Republic's form of government, "Senatus Populusque Romanus," or SPQR (Figure 5.1). And so in the 1990s, "Cascading Style Sheets" joined the long and mostly honorable list of commonly known acronyms. Enter CSS.

Figure 5.1 About the size of a penny, one side of a gold coin shows the likeness of Augustus, the first Emperor of Rome who died in the year 14 CE, and on the reverse, the initials of the government, SPQR. *Courtesy of Paul Martin Lester.*

Tim Berners-Lee's Hypertext Markup Language (See? Isn't HTML so much more efficient?) schema for the Web was adequate enough, but after other programmers and graphic designers started to create web pages, a need for a more complex system was realized in which producers and users could control the look and features of the screen presentations without the burden of negotiating the content of the pages. In other words, a system was needed to separate content from style.

To answer this need, Norwegian Håkon Wium Lie and Belgian Bert Bos worked together to develop CSS. With CSS, web programmers could build style sheets that were able to mix their visual choices over as many individual HTML pages as were needed by a website. Users also were given the ability to customize the look of the display. For example, they could control the selection and size of typography or layout divisions.

And yet, knowing the history of acronyms and CSS does not help to answer the question posed at the start of this chapter.

Style is a product of an individual's experiences and willingness to express her unique take on the world verbally and/or visually to others. Style is how much you know and how much others know of you. Style needs to be public so it may influence others. There is no style if your photographs and illustrations are stuck in a box on the floor of a closet.

Web design is no different. As an expression of what you think is a necessary array of visual elements to communicate a message, style dictates the visual appearance a user will appreciate and learn from. Fortunately, you seldom must invent a graphic style from scratch. Most styles are variations of nine graphic arts movements that can be divided into two major groups: freeform and grid.

The *freeform artistic styles* of art nouveau, Dada, art deco, pop art, punk, new wave, and hip-hop are noted for their often playful placement of text and other graphic elements within a design's frame. Originally inspired from ancient Asian paintings, freeform works have a dynamic, internal energy that comes from the use of flowing lines, colors, and typography that attracts the eyes and compels them to follow (Figure 5.2).

Figure 5.2 Czech painter and illustrator Alfons Mucha was one of the most prolific artists of the free form style known as art nouveau. This 1898 lithographic advertisement for F. Champenois, a Parisian printer, shows the flowing lines and delicate colors associated with the graphic design movement. *Courtesy of the Art Renewal Center.*

The grid artistic approach, exemplified by the De Stijl and Bauhaus styles, attempt to give objective, unemotional organization to a work. Designers developed a geometric approach based on horizontal and vertical lines and the basic forms of squares, rectangles, and circles, and usually combined the use of primary colors red, yellow, and blue with black, gray, and white (Figure 5.3). They carefully placed each design element within a frame to ensure unity in the gestalt tradition—individual elements are not as important as the whole.

Figure 5.3 The Dutch architect Gerrit Rietveld designed the "Red and Blue Chair" (with some yellow) in 1917 with simple lines and colors inspired by the grid style known as the De Stijl graphic arts movement. He later rejected De Stijl in favor of a modernistic approach epitomized by the Nieuwe Bouwen or "New Building" architectural style similar to bauhaus. *Courtesy of Elly Waterman.*

Note

The exercises in this book will, for the most part, lead you to design a layout that is truer to the grid than the dynamic features of the Art Nouveau or Dada movements. However, the background images inserted on the page in Chapter 10 suggest an organic break from the grid. Since the **div** tag is nearly always used to organize a web page, it is common for beginners to create designs that are tightly organized in structure. Once you learn to assign styles to your liking, you may feel a sense of freedom or betrayal when you design a website with visual features that are dynamic and unsteady.

Freeform

Freeform styles are characterized by the lack of restrictions in their creation and production. Art nouveau was the first commercial art style intended to make products and their advertisements more beautiful. Art nouveau was influenced by traditional Asian vases, paintings, and screens, particularly from Japan and Korea. Artists of the Dada movement expressed their rage with political leaders during World War I by the use of absurd, asymmetric typography, design layouts, and cut-and-pasted imagery.

Writings and graphics were intended to confuse, educate, and gain attention. The art deco style was noted for its streamlined shapes and curved sans serif typographic lettering that presented a modern graphic look (Figure 5.4).

Figure 5.4 With its sleek lines and curved shapes, the Chrysler Building in New York City is an example of the art deco graphic design movement as an architectural expression. American William Van Alen designed the building that is considered one of the most beloved by residents and tourists alike. *Courtesy of Paul Martin Lester.*

The pop art movement combined the organic vines of art nouveau designs and the rebellious philosophy of Dada. Pop art gets its name from a group of London artists and designers who met in the mid-1950s to graphically express their response to the prevalent and much criticized popular art of the day (Figure 5.5).

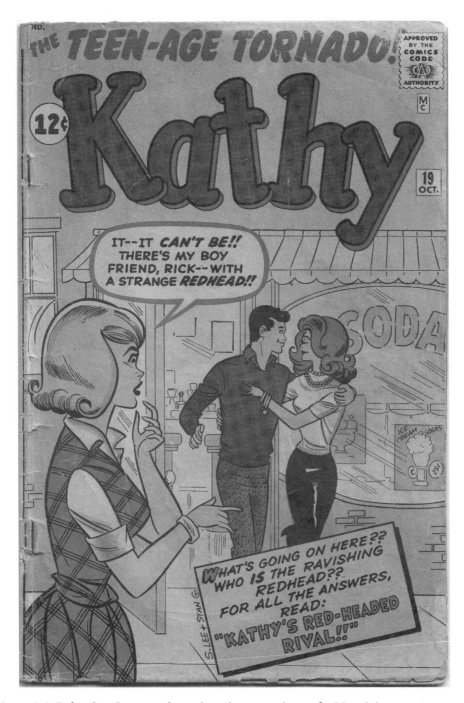

Figure 5.5 Before Stan Lee created popular culture superheroes for Marvel, he was a teen comic book artist. Kathy, "The Teen-Age Tornado," was Lee's foray into the trials and tribulations of well-dressed teens. *Photo courtesy of Paul Martin Lester.*

Punk artists placed typographical and other visual elements on pages in angry, rebellious, and random ways in the style of "ransom note" cutouts. In that way, punk was greatly influenced by the Dada movement. New wave was highly influenced by the ease of typographical and visual manipulations made possible by computer technology. It was connected with a youthful culture that viewed all new technology as exciting. Hip-hop started as a fashion, graphic design, graffiti art, and dance accompaniment to rap music in the 1970s, until it eventually gained mainstream attention (Figure 5.6).

Figure 5.6 A side of a building in the college town of Eugene, Oregon displays the literal message of the art movement known as hip hop as well as its symbolic meaning in the use of spray painted colors and dynamic flowing letters. *Courtesy of Steven Lopez.*

Grid

Grid styles adhere to a strict geometrical approach. De Stijl designers employ an unemotional use of lines, common shapes, and usually the colors of red, yellow, and blue (Figure 5.7). Translated as *the style*, editors have traditionally used a variation of the grid format for newspaper front pages to express a modern look and a sense of objectivity. Bauhaus was originally intended as an architectural school, but grew to include classes in typography, advertising, textiles, painting, and photography. The grid-like look of skyscrapers with their individual cubicles for similarly dressed office workers comes from the spirit of Bauhaus architectural design where "form ever meets function." Art and technology are unified in the De Stijl and Bauhaus philosophies, and are expressed typographically with the ever-popular sans serif font Helvetica.

> **Reference**
>
> View the trailer for the film *Helvetica* directed by Gary Hustwit. [http://www.youtube.com/watch?v=wkoX0pEwSCw&feature=youtu.be]

As a designer, you are responsible for producing web pages that unify the visual and conceptual meaning of the content on the pages for your audience to appreciate. Can you put too much "you" into a design? Can your work be too much about your personal artistic expression and not enough about communicating a message? Is there too much hedonism and too little utilitarianism in your designs? Is De Stijl becoming too shrill?

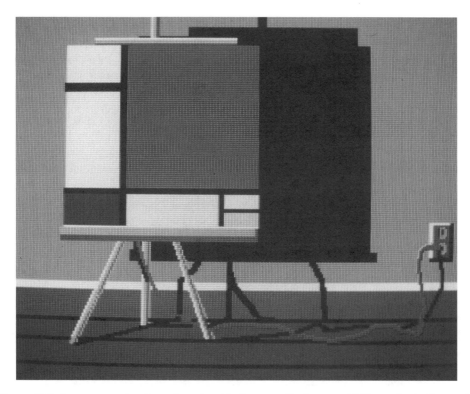

Figure 5.7 A computer drawing of an electrified canvas displays a grid-like style similar to the work of De Stijl and Bauhaus artists. *Courtesy of Paul Martin Lester.*

Relax. Your fan base will let you know when your seesaw moves too high toward form or function. Regardless, you should never be afraid to express your personal style. You should take chances. Create designs that live on the edge and teeter on the brink between your individual approach and the needs of your audience.

Practice

Cascading Style Sheets

Cascading Style Sheets, or CSS, is an essential style sheet language to learn if you are interested in creating content for the Web. Some web designers may sketch their ideas on paper or with Adobe software before coding the design, but eventually, artists and designers should code web layouts in two languages: HTML and CSS.

The CSS code works in tandem with the HTML file. Content items for display on the Web, such as text, images, video, or audio, are coded in the HTML file. CSS is used to manipulate the layout, or "style," of the items on the web page and the page itself (i.e., properties assigned to the **body** tag). You can use CSS to modify something as simple as how a headline is displayed and as complex as the styles mentioned in the introduction.

There are three ways you can use CSS styles to affect your HTML code, as follows. *Internal styles* are saved in the **head** section of the HTML document between the **<style>** and **</style>** tags. *Inline styles* are saved on a single line of HTML code in the **body** section utilizing the **style** attribution of an HTML tag. Finally, external styles are saved in a separate .css style sheet and applied to the HTML document by way of the ***link*** tag in the **head** section.

As a practitioner, I rarely use internal or inline styles. Instead, I save my CSS code to an *external style sheet* because there I can modify one style that is linked to multiple HTML documents. Internal and inline styles are coded within the HTML page. For instance, if you want to make a headline bold and blue across your entire website, it would be repetitive and inefficient to write this code in each HTML document.

We will practice applying styles in each of the three ways; however, we will only be using the external style sheet for CSS code from Chapters 7 through 14.

Results of Chapter 5 Exercises

In the following exercises you will create an HTML page with internal CSS code, inline CSS code, and externally linked CSS code. You will apply a background image to the web page and modify tag elements for display using CSS (Figure 5.8).

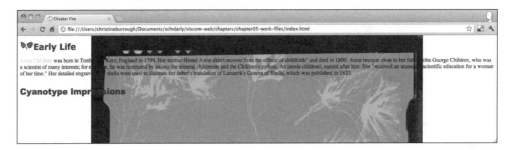

Figure 5.8 As a result of completing exercises in Chapter 5, the web page has typography and a background image all dictated by a cascading style sheet (CSS).

Download Materials for Chapter 5 Exercises

The following exercises expand upon the resulting files created in the Chapter 3 exercises. Use your files, or download Chapter 3 results files from the website. [http://viscommontheweb.wordpress.com/downloads/]

Exercise 1: Style Rules—Internal and Inline

1. **Set up your workspace:** Copy and paste the final Chapter 3 exercise files to a new folder named *chapter05*. Open Dreamweaver and define or edit your site to point to the root directory, *chapter05*. Choose Window > Workspace Layout > Designer. Open *index.html* in Dreamweaver, modify the title tag (I titled my page "Chapter Five") and save your work.

Watch Out

If you choose to open your file in Dreamweaver and use File > Save As to make a copy, you might end up seeing a Dreamweaver message asking you to "Update Links?" Click No.

---

2. We will create or view CSS styles using the two methods—internal and inline— throughout this exercise. First, we will view internal style rules that we have already created in the Chapter 3 exercises (Figure 5.9). In past exercises, we have

```
<head>
<meta http-equiv="Content-Type" content="text/html; charset=UTF-8" />
<title>Chapter Five</title>
<style type="text/css">
a:link {
    color: #FF3;
    text-decoration: none;
}
a:visited {
    text-decoration: none;
    color: #FF3;
}
a:hover {
    text-decoration: none;
    color: #FFF;
}
a:active {
    text-decoration: none;
    color: #FFF;
}
body,td,th {
    color: #000;
}
h1 {
    color: #FF0;
}
</style>
</head>
```

Figure 5.9 Internal styles appear between the **<style>** and **</style>** tags in the **head** section of the HTML file.

selected Modify > Page Properties in order to alter the display of links, font properties, and a background image on the page. In this dialog box you can change how the web page will look using HTML or CSS. In the Chapter 3 exercises we added CSS code to our page in the head area by selecting the CSS properties from the Page Properties dialog box. View the head area of the code—the CSS styles have been added between the style and close style tags, **<style>** and **</style>**.

Note

The **<script>** tag can also be seen in the head section of HTML documents to incorporate JavaScript or other programming languages into a web document.

3. Next we will apply an inline style. Inline styles are inserted directly into an HTML tag to govern how a single element behaves. Highlight the link "Cyanotype Impressions." Remove the link by deleting the reference from the Link box in the Properties panel, or by deleting the **<a href>** tag from the code (remember to also delete the close a tag, **</a>**). The text should remain selected. Click the CSS button in the bottom-left side of the Properties panel. From the Targeted Rule pull-down menu choose New Inline Style (Figure 5.10).

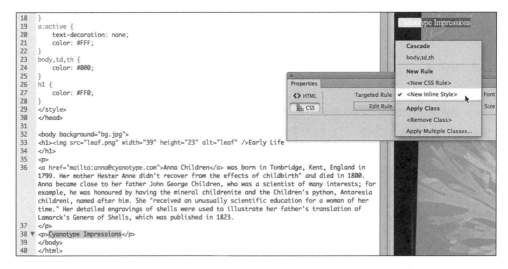

Code View:

```
<p><a href="cyanotype.html">Cyanotype Impressions</a>
</p>
```

Figure 5.10 Create a new inline style using the Dreamweaver Properties panel. Be sure to press the CSS button.

4. Click the Edit Rule button to enter Dreamweaver's CSS Rule Definition dialog box (Figure 5.11). Here you can modify the appearance of nearly anything you

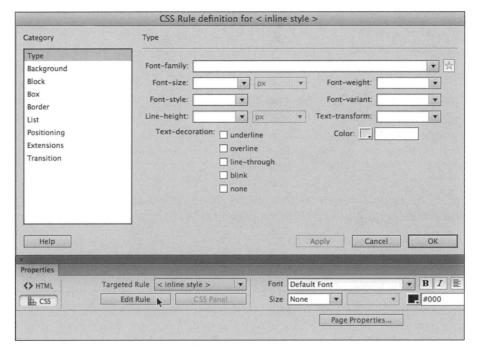

Figure 5.11 The Rule Definition dialog box for the new inline style allows you to select the properties and values for the CSS rule.

place on the HTML page. In this case, the new inline style will be "spanned" across (or placed around) the single line of text that you highlighted in Step 3.

5. Modify the type settings and then click OK to exit the dialog box. We will delete this later, so anything you enter that will make a visible change is acceptable. I selected the font Arial Black, increased the font size to 24 pixels, and changed the font color to dark blue (#009) (Figure 5.12).

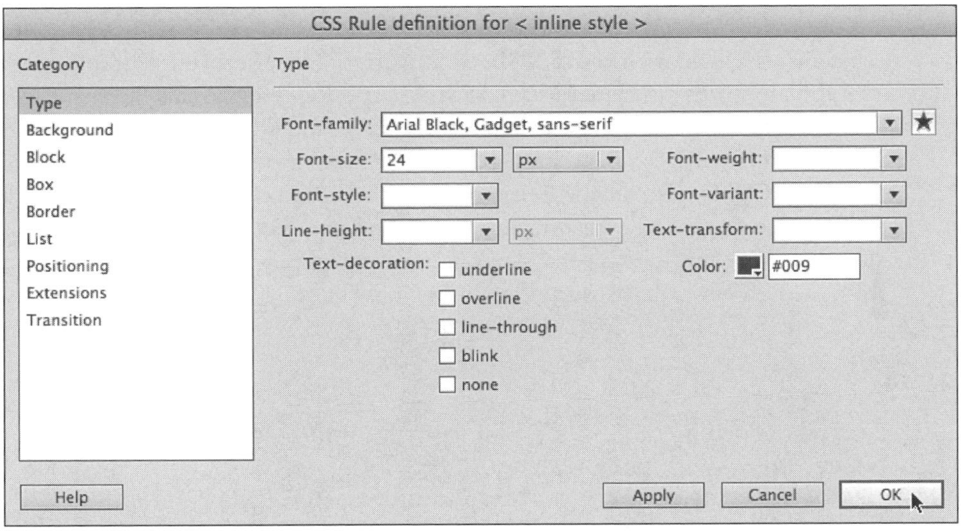

Figure 5.12 The Type category in the Rule Definition Dialog box for the inline style is used to set, among others, the font-family, font-size, and color values.

6. View the HTML code. The style has been attributed to the paragraph tag with CSS syntax for listing properties and values.

Code View:

```
<p style="color: #009; font-size: 24px; font-family: 'Arial
Black', Gadget, sans-serif;">Cyanotype Impressions</p>
```

Note

If we did not use the **p** tag, the style would have been inserted with a separate tag named span, **<span>**. In combination with the attribute "style," **<span style = ...>** the web browser would insert an inline style. By itself, **<span>** simply tells the browser to add a hook to a part of the document. In Chapter 7, Exercise 3, Step 5 we will see **<span>** in use with the class attribute.

While internal and inline styles can be used to modify HTML pages, most web designers choose to keep all CSS styles in one external style sheet.

Exercise 2: External Style Sheets

The most organized way to separate styles from content embedded in the HTML document is to keep the CSS code in an entirely different document and link it to the HTML file. This is easy to accomplish with a single line of code. We will create the external style sheet using Dreamweaver's tools.

1. Start by viewing the CSS Styles panel. The inline styles that we created in previous exercises by using Modify > Page Properties are stored in the **`<style>`** area of the panel. This panel is used to display all inline and externally linked styles that are associated with your HTML document. In Exercise 4 you will learn more vocabulary words associated with CSS styles, and I will define this Dreamweaver panel more accurately. You can modify the CSS properties for any of the listed rules by revisiting the Page Properties dialog box, or by double-clicking a rule from the CSS Styles panel. Alternatively, click once in the CSS Style panel on a *selector* (so far, we have seen tag selectors) and you will see a list of properties associated with it. In this panel you can view and modify ***CSS rules***, and you can also define a new rule, as we will see in the next step.

> **Note**
>
> If you do not see the CSS Styles panel in the top-right area of your screen, either reset your workspace by choosing Window > Workspace Layout > Designer, or open the panel by choosing Window > CSS Styles.

2. In the CSS Styles panel, click the New CSS Rule button (Figure 5.13). Even though we have not yet defined a new style sheet, we can add a rule and choose to create a new external style sheet by using the New CSS Rule dialog box.

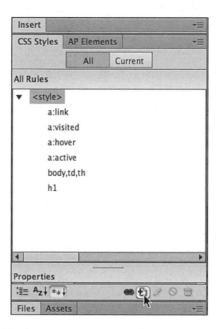

Figure 5.13 Add a new CSS rule using the New Rule button in the CSS Styles panel.

Note

In the CSS Styles panel you may view "All" rules or "Current" rules. Sometimes the Current button is depressed when you view the panel. If you think you should see a bigger list of rules than is displaying in this panel, check to see if you are viewing "All" of your rules or just the "Current" rule.

3. In the New CSS Rule dialog box you will make three choices using pull-down menus. First, choose your selector. You will learn more about the types of selectors in the following chapters. For now, we will simply use the Tag selector, which means that we want to modify the display of an HTML tag (Figure 5.14).

4. Choose the **h1** tag if it is not automatically selected from the second pull-down menu. We will redefine how elements nested in **\<h1\>** appear using our external style sheet. Finally, this is the crucial step: Select New Style Sheet File from the third pull-down menu (Figure 5.15). This indicates you want to create a new CSS style sheet file to link externally with your HTML document.

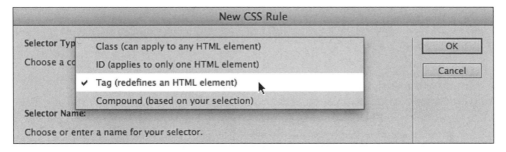

Figure 5.14 Choose a tag selector for the new CSS rule when the style will modify an HTML tag.

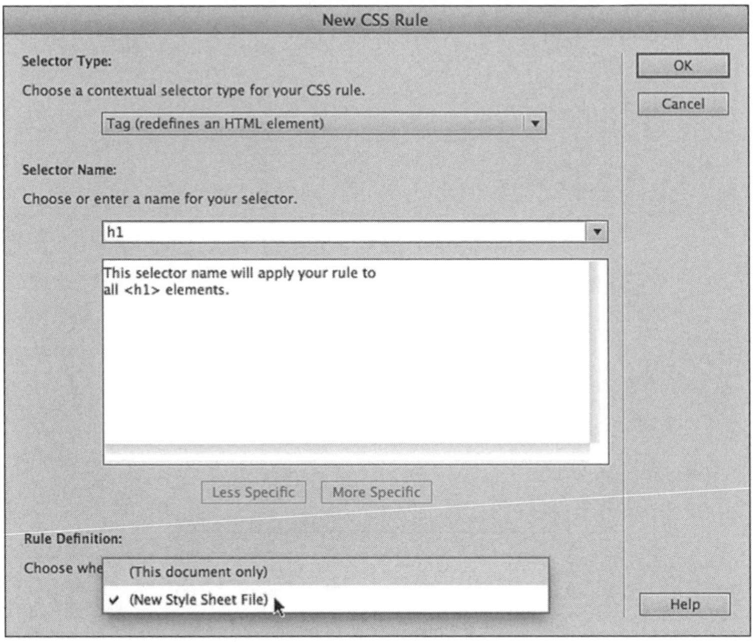

Figure 5.15 Define a CSS rule in a new style sheet via the Dreamweaver New Rule button at the bottom of the CSS Styles panel.

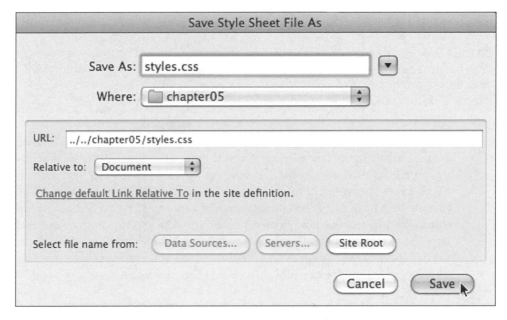

Figure 5.16 Save a new rule in an external CSS style sheet to keep your styles separate from the HTML document.

5. Save the new style sheet in your root directory as *styles.css* (Figure 5.16).
6. As soon as you save the file, Dreamweaver will return you to the CSS Rule Definition dialog box. Here you can make many changes to the **h1** tag. We will first modify the typography as illustrated in the choices I made in Figure 5.17. Click the OK button when you are finished.
7. View your CSS Styles panel. You now have a set of inline styles saved inside a submenu, titled "<style>" and you have an externally linked style sheet, which appears as a submenu titled "styles.css" (Figure 5.18). The information pertaining

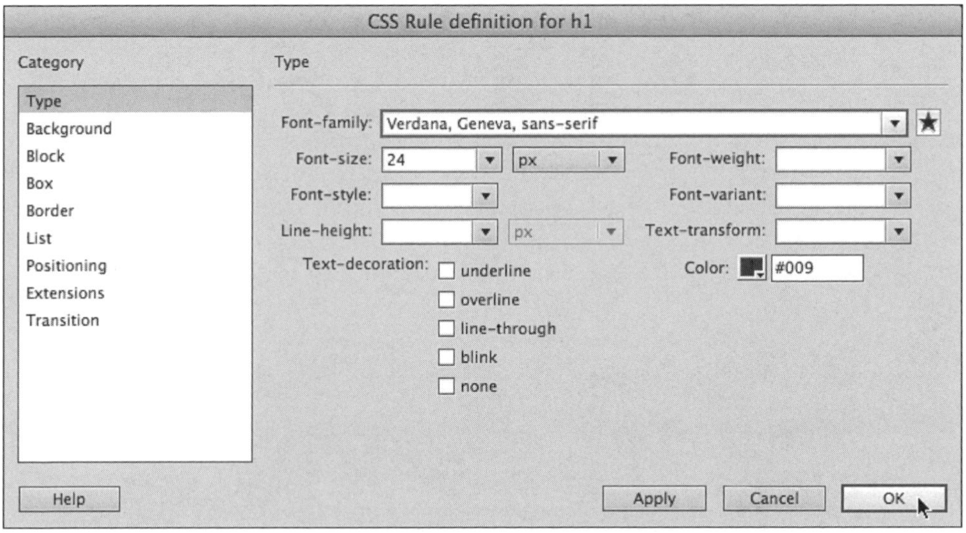

Figure 5.17 Establish the typography display settings for all heading 1 **<h1>** tags.

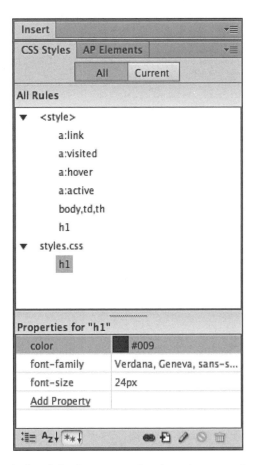

Figure 5.18 The new rule for **\<h1>** is an external style, so it appears in the CSS Styles panel in the category named *styles.css* (the name of style sheet, created in the saving process). All of the internal styles are saved in the category **\<styles>** because the style tag is used to assign styles in the HTML document.

to both **\<style>** and *styles.css* can be viewed and modified or deleted by expanding the name (clicking the triangle next to the name).

8. View the HTML code—one additional line of code has been added to the **head** section of the document:

The **link** tag, with the **href** attribution tells the HTML document that there is a style sheet named "styles.css" saved in the root directory that should be used to attach CSS code to elements in this document. Look at the top bar in Dreamweaver. Next to the Source Code button you will also see a button that opens *styles.css* (Figure 5.19). You can toggle between viewing the HTML source code and the CSS style sheet.

Code View

```
</style>
<link href="styles.css" rel="stylesheet" type="text/css" />
</head>
```

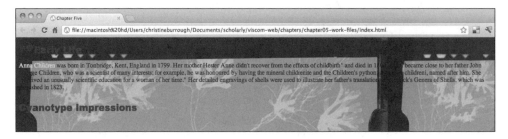

Figure 5.19 Click on *source code* or *styles.css* to view and edit the HTML file or the CSS file.

9. Choose File > Save All to save both the HTML and CSS files. If you notice a small asterisk next to the Source Code or *style.css* button then your document has not been saved with the latest edits.

10. Preview your work in a browser (Figure 5.20). Notice that the heading appears in blue rather than yellow. CSS follows a code of hierarchy (this is the cascading feature in the CSS language). Styles defined in an external style sheet take precedence over those defined as inline or internal styles. Since the **h1** tag was defined with an inline style as yellow and with an external style as blue, you will see that the browser awards priority to the external style sheet: the heading displays in blue.

> **Note**
>
> The design window in Dreamweaver does not always provide an accurate representation of how the design will look in a browser. Add to this the fact that different browsers support different CSS properties (we will explore this in Chapter 14), and you'll find yourself previewing your work in many browsers.

Figure 5.20 The heading is displayed in blue because externally saved styles take precedence over internal or inline styles.

VIDEO WALKTHROUGH

Exercise 3: Copying Inline Styles to an External Style Sheet

1. View the source code (or the HTML document). Select all of the CSS rules between **<style>** and **</style>** that are written in the **head** section of the code. Select Edit > Cut. We are removing these *rule sets* from the HTML document.

Code View:	
Cut the styles out of the **head** section of the HTML document	Results of cutting the code from between the style and close style tags
| ```
<style type="text/css">
a:link {
     color: #FF3;
     text-decoration: none;
}
a:visited {
     text-decoration: none;
     color: #FF3;
}
a:hover {
     text-decoration: none;
     color: #FFF;
}
a:active {
     text-decoration: none;
     color: #FFF;
}
body,td,th {
     color: #000;
}
h1 {
     color: #FF0;
}
</style>
``` | ```
< style type="text/css">
</style>
``` |

2. View *styles.css*. Position the cursor on the line after the closing curly bracket defining the **H1** CSS rule. Choose Edit > Paste. The inline styles are now removed from the HTML document and pasted into the external style sheet.
3. Return to your source code. In code view delete **<style>** and **</style>** as these tags no longer contain any information.

Delete the **style** tags	The **head** section no longer contains **style** tags
| ```
<style type="text/css">
     </style>
``` | ```
<head>
     <meta http-
     equiv="Content-Type"
     content="text/html;
     charset=UTF-8" />
     <title>Chapter
     Five</title>

     <link href="styles.css"
     rel="stylesheet"
     type="text/css" />
</head>
``` |

4. Save your files and preview the web page in a browser. Dreamweaver may ask if you want to save changes to the index page or to "some files," which may have been modified but not saved (this alludes to the CSS file you just edited)—click the Save or Yes button to both.

5. Notice the heading "Early Life" again. This time it is yellow. What happened? View *styles.css*. If you followed all of my steps, then you have two rule definitions for the tag **h1**. The rule that the browser will display is the one that appears last in the document. Since the last rule definition for **h1** is the one that we created as an inline style, this is the one that takes precedence. Let's continue to use the definition we created for the external style sheet (the blue typography). Delete the final **h1** definition from the page. View your work in a browser.

Note

If you save your work and view it in a browser but nothing changes, refresh your browser view. The browser will often save a version of a page that it has displayed before in its cache (a small data repository). When you are browsing the Web, the cache is helpful—for instance, you do not necessarily have to download the same graphics each time you revisit a web page. But when you are designing or developing a new web page this can be a frustrating experience. You actually want to see every minor change on the page. Normally a simple refresh will tell the browser to download all of the code and media again. Sometimes you may have to empty your browser's cache in order to see edits on the page. All browsers are slightly different, but if you search the Web for "empty cache in (name of your favorite browser)" you should be able to find an easy procedure for clearing your cache.

Exercise 4: Understanding CSS Rules

CSS files are simply lists of *rules* (or *rule sets*) saved in a text file that has the extension dot-css (.css). In an external style sheet, a CSS rule consists of a *selector* and a *declaration block* (a list of *declarations* surrounded by curly brackets). Inside the declaration block, each declaration consists of a **property** followed by a colon (:) and this is followed by one or more **values**, finally ending in a semicolon (;).

In the following CSS rule, **h1** is a tag selector. It is defined with a declaration block that includes everything between the curly brackets and the brackets themselves. Each single declaration is a list of properties and values, concluding with the semicolon. For instance, **font-family** is the first property listed, and its values are **Verdana**, **Geneva**, and **sans-serif**. The semicolon indicates the end of the declaration. The next declaration is the property and value pair **font-size** and 24px. The final declaration is for the property **color** (which changes the color of the type) and the value #009 (blue). The closing curly bracket tells us that the CSS rule set for **h1** is complete. White spaces inside the curly brackets are ignored by the browser, so you can list all of the declarations on a single line, or break them up as follows for better legibility:

```
h1 {
  font-family: Verdana, Geneva, sans-serif;
  font-size: 24px;
  color: #009;
}
```

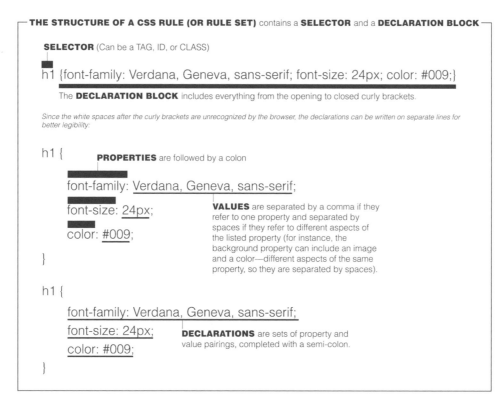

Figure 5.21 The structure of a CSS rule (or rule set) includes a selector (tag, ID, or class) and a declaration block (list of declarations including properties and values). *Diagram courtesy of xtine.*

Assuming this rule set is saved in an external style sheet that is linked to an HTML file, all instances of first-level headings, that is, **<h1>**, would display in Verdana at 24 pixels in the color blue (#009).

Note

It is common for CSS rules to list multiple values for one property on a single line, separated by a comma. In this case, the CSS rule lists the font-family as Verdana (the first choice if it is installed in the browser), Geneva (the second choice), and sans-serif.

With these new vocabulary words in mind, I will now revise my description of the CSS Styles panel in Dreamweaver. Earlier I wrote, "This panel is used to display all inline and externally linked styles that are associated with your HTML document." A more accurate description of this panel is as follows:

In the top window of the CSS Styles panel you will see a list of the names of selectors saved in the HTML document (those saved beneath **<style>**) and in the external style sheet (those saved beneath styles.css). Click once on a selector, and the Properties window (the bottom area of the panel) will display the selector's declaration block (the properties and values associated with that selector). Double-click the selector to access the Rule

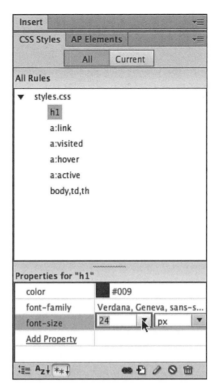

Figure 5.22 Modify a property by using the bottom portion of the CSS Styles panel.

Definition dialog box in order to modify a selector's declaration block. Or, in the Properties window, click once on a value to modify it via a pull-down menu (Figure 5.22).

For instance, if I wanted to change the font size of headings labeled in HTML with **<h1>** to 18 pixels, I could use the pull-down menu in the Properties area of the CSS Styles panel for the **h1** selector. Or, I could double-click the **h1** selector in the CSS Styles panel and set the font size in the Rule Definition box. Finally, another alternative—the method that most practiced users would choose—is to edit the code in the style sheet. Simply view *styles.css* and change the size of the font in that declaration for **h1**. You may work in whatever way is simplest to understand, but you should know that it is most efficient to modify the code directly. Dare to dream big—soon you will be skipping the Dreamweaver panels to create and edit in code view!

Exercise 5: Setting the Background Image on the Page in CSS

1. View the source code (or the HTML page) in Dreamweaver. Notice that the background image displayed on our web page has been added as an attribution to the **body** tag. Our goal is to store as much of the display of the page in the external style sheet as we can. This means removing properties that affect the display of the page from HTML tags when it is possible:

    ```
    <body background="bg.jpg">
    ```

    Select the attribution **background="bg.jpg"** and delete it. The result should simply be the body tag with no spaces:

    ```
    <body>
    ```

2. Your web page will temporarily be a solid color (most likely white). Double-click the **body, td, th** selector from the CSS Styles panel (this is the selector for the body tag and any table data or table heading tags we might use) to enter the Rule Definition dialog box for the **body** tag. Now we will reapply the background using CSS.

3. Click the "Background" category. Then use the Browse button to find the background image (*bg.jpg*) in your root folder (Figure 5.23). Set the Background-repeat to no-repeat and then position it in the top center area of the browser with Background-position (X): center and Background-position (Y): top. Click OK to exit the dialog box. Preview your work in a browser.

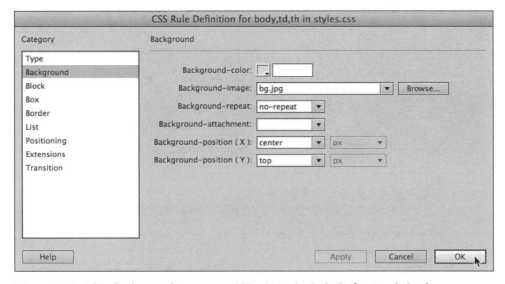

Figure 5.23 Add a background image to a CSS rule in the Rule Definition dialog box.

The Art and Craft of Code

Dave Shea launched the CSS Zen Garden website [http://www.csszengarden.com] in 2003 to encourage designers to show the power of CSS in web design. Participants from around the world created style sheets drastically changing the layout, themes, and design of the same HTML document. For beginning students, viewing just a small selection of works in the "garden" is often a more direct way to showcase the flexibility of designs that are created with CSS code. See Rose Cox's, Eric Stoltz's, and Jon Tan's designs in Figures 5.24, 5.25, and 5.26.

Create, Reflect, Critique

Revisit the Wikipedia page that you created at the end of the exercises in Chapter 3. Create a new HTML page and link a new external style sheet to it. Select the same topic, or a new one, and view its Wikipedia.org page. Copy/paste some of the Wikipedia page content to the code view of your HTML document. Format the text using the **<h1>**, **
** (single line space), and **<p>** (paragraph, or double line space) tags in HTML; then define rules for those tags in your externally linked CSS file. Add links to the page where it is appropriate. Modify the page settings in order to change the link colors, and paste any inline styles to your external style sheet. How does your new knowledge of CSS change

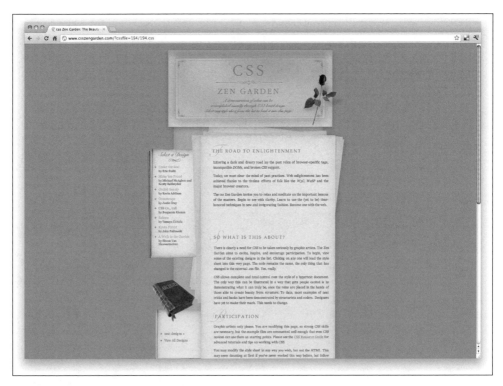

Figure 5.24 *Dark Rose* is a layout created for the CSS Zen Garden by Rose Cox. [http://www.csszengarden.com/?cssfile=194/194.css] *Courtesy of Rose Cox.*

Figure 5.25 *Under the Sea!* is a layout created for the CSS Zen Garden by Eric Stoltz. [http://www.csszengarden.com/?cssfile=/213/213.css] *Courtesy of Eric Stoltz.*

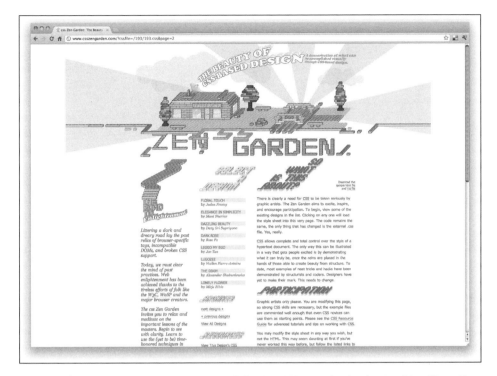

Figure 5.26 *Leggo My Ego* is a layout created for the CSS Zen Garden by Jon Tan. [http://www .csszengarden.com/?cssfile=193/193.css] *Courtesy of Jon Tan.*

the way that you approach designing your second version of the Wikipedia page? Once the page is complete with an external style sheet, change the heading font, add a property not included in this chapter (such as line height or small caps), and notice how the whole page changes after one small modification. Can you explain, from experience, why it is important to save your styles in one file and your content in another?

Glossary Words

CSS: declaration, declaration block, rule or rule set, selector; external style sheets freeform artistic styles, grid, inline CSS styles, internal CSS styles, `<link>`

6 TRANSFERRING FILES

VIDEO
INTRODUCTION

Principles, History, Theory

Classification Systems

In a wide world of webs, how is it possible to find anything?

In an episode of his popular BBC television series, *Connections*, host James Burke, a Northern Irish science historian and television producer, remarked that before Johannes Gutenberg's printing press, palaces and monasteries employed scribes to make copies of all sorts of written materials. But there was a problem. No one had thought to organize the information. That oversight meant that a single leather-bound volume stored on a shelf in a haphazard way with hundreds of others might contain various articles, edicts, census results, local news, and sermons. To make matters worse for those who wanted to find a specific document, the title on the spine might simply refer to the first work in the collection. The only way to know what else was in the book was to view every page.

Likewise, try to find a specific event recorded somewhere on an eight-hour cassette or a DVD in a collection of hundreds and you start to understand why many writings are lost to history (Figure 6.1).

Without a classification system, the only way to know what was recorded was through the tedious process of fast-forwarding through the entire VHS tape.

Scenes From an Uncatalogued VHS Tape

For example, before scenes from movies and television shows were digitized and saved on a computer, I recorded scenes on videotapes, cued each clip, and played them one at a time for an auditorium filled with visual communication students. Over time, hundreds of VHS cassettes filled a bookshelf. One of them was labeled in red uppercase letters, "WEATHER." One might assume that the tape only contains television weather reports to be used as examples during an informational graphics lecture. Wrong. The following is a complete list in order of the content recorded from a television. There were scenes from:

Creature Comforts, Blade Runner, Alanis Morissette music video, Young Frankenstein, Wrong Trousers, Your Face, Citizen Kane, NYPD Blue, Goodfellas, Koyaanisqatsi, Parallax View, Fire Walk with Me, Blue Highway, MTV program, REM music video, Saturday Night Live (SNL), Stop the Church, Jerry Lewis telethon, VW commercial, WGN weather report, ABC7 Los Angeles weather report, NBC4 Los Angeles weather report, A Bug's Life, Rope, AOL's Steve Case interview, Enter the Matrix, NBC news report, President Wilson documentary, LONG SPACE, commercials, ABC news reports, Jurassic Park, commercials, LONG SPACE, The Simpsons, Minority Report, LONG PAUSE, end of tape.

Figure 6.1 Without knowing what is recorded on a DVD, it might as well be used as part of an artistic display next to a record shop that sells music on plastic and vinyl discs. *Courtesy of Paul Martin Lester.*

According to Bob Davis, former CEO of Lycos, an early web search engine, "Search is the ultimate killer app." Why is search so important? Try to find a book somewhere in a city's library without any clue where it might be found. Impossible. Fortunately, for more than 2500 years, systems to classify knowledge have been invented and revised to help the process.

One of the first civilizations to organize writings to make them easier to find was India during the Vedic period (1500–326 BCE). These "Upanishads," or teachers, divided knowledge into four categories: dharma (law, religion, ethics, and sociology), artha (history, politics, economics, and applied sciences), kama (pure science, arts, and literature), and moksha (spirituality and philosophy).

From ancient Greece, Theophrastus, a student of Plato and director of the botanical garden at the Lyceum after Aristotle's tenure, wrote *Enquiry into Plants* that classified over 500 species of vegetation into such characteristics as trees, shrubs, and herbs (Figure 6.2). But it was the son of another gardener, the Swedish scientist and educator Carolus Linnaeus, who is considered the founder of modern *taxonomy*, or the science of classifying organisms. His two-part system, described in his 1735 book *Systema Naturae*, gave general (genus) and specific (species) names in Latin for all living things that are still used today.

Another part of the search story comes from Thomas Jefferson, the third president of the United States. He had a library of about 6700 volumes at his home in Monticello (Figure 6.3).

Figure 6.2 The philosopher and botanist Theophrastus traveled throughout Greece observing and
writing about the plants that he found. For his efforts he is often named the "founder
of botany." The famous Venetian printer, Aldus Manutius, eventually printed his books
in 1495 and inspired others, particularly the Swede Carolus Linnaeus to classify organisms. *Courtesy of Tato Grasso.*

Figure 6.3 Thomas Jefferson, librarian, author, president, and slave owner poses for a portrait while pointing and holding a copy of the *Declaration of Independence*. Perhaps waiting for his portrait to be made is a grumpy Benjamin Franklin who sits in a corner. The engraver Cornelius Tiebout was the creator of the image in 1801. *Courtesy of the Library of Congress.*

Figure 6.4 The Yahoo! listing of categories in 1996 for Los Angeles is simply a collection of topics in alphabetical order. Inspired by a traditional library's card catalog system, this taxonomy became the norm for web masters and their user links until Google broke the mold and popularized a more free form search system. *Reproduced with permission of Yahoo! Inc. ©2012 Yahoo! Inc. YAHOO! and the YAHOO! logo are registered trademarks of Yahoo! Inc.*

With a similar idea as that used by the Vedic culture, he divided his books into three types: memory (history), reason (philosophy and science), and imagination (fine arts). After the British destroyed the U.S. government's library during the burning of Washington, DC in 1812, Jefferson sold his library to Congress for $23,950 (almost $200,000 in today's currency) in 1815. His collection was the start of the Library of Congress. In 1897, Jefferson's simple system was expanded to 21 content categories.

Fast-forward about 100 years when two Stanford University students, David Filo and Jerry Yang, introduced a class project named "Jerry's Guide to the World Wide Web" that became Yahoo! (aka "Yet Another Hierarchical Officious Oracle"), a collection of web pages that were divided into logical categories (Figure 6.4).

As innovative and efficient as Yahoo! was, enter Google, one of the easiest, fastest, and most popular search engines available on the Web. Most searches on Google, no matter how complex, take less than a second to complete as it looks through its database collection of over six billion web pages. The blinding speed, and perhaps more importantly, its accuracy comes from its software that relies on hits from users that constantly improve its performance. With Google (Figure 6.5) and other search engines, the world seems a little closer as knowledge, both factual and dubious, is only a few clicks away.

After a long history of thought and practice behind organizing all types of material for personal and public consumption, it is often vital that the work designers produce can be shared with others. In 1971, Indian Abhay Bhushan, a graduate of the Massachusetts Institute of Technology, combined the features of an e-mail system with digital "folders" into what he named a "file transfer protocol" (**FTP**). With FTP software, others can obtain access to words and pictures on remote hard drives, with password access if needed for security reasons.

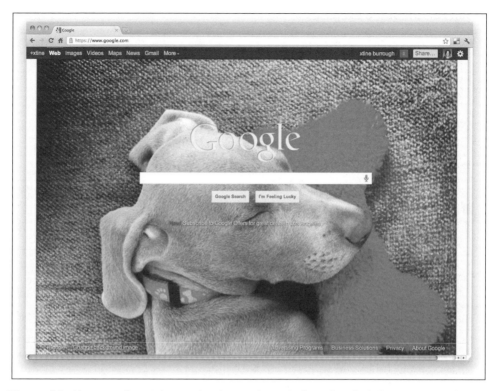

Figure 6.5 Also started as a class project by another pair from Stanford, Sergey Brin and Larry Page moved their operation to a friend's garage in 1998, dropped out of school, and worked for the company full-time. One of the persons who encouraged them was David Filo, of Yahoo! *Courtesy of Google.*

Nevertheless, if a hierarchical system of classifying work is not carefully planned and executed, an important file may be as difficult to find as a weather report on a dusty, obsolete videotape.

Practice

Servers, Domains, and Hosting

In order to see the new web content that you create on a website, you can either view the files locally (as we have been doing so far), or view the files online. If you want to see the files online, you will need to upload your files to a server. Once files are uploaded to a server, they are "live," or viewable from any browser with an Internet connection. If you want to create your own website, you need to make *two* purchases: a **web domain** (that is, a unique Internet Protocol address, which is translated into the name of a website, such as amazon.com or wordpress.org), and *hosting* (server space). If you are purchasing your web domain for the first time, make sure that you also purchase a hosting package.

For most visual communicators, a website will be a place to maintain a professional profile. If you are buying a domain now, consider something as simple as your first name-your last name.com. If you are certain of your industry, you might choose something like yourname-photography.com or yourname-journalist.com. The dot-com extension is used to indicate a professional, commerce-based website. It would also be appropriate to sign up for a dot-net (.net) website, indicating a website created explicitly for the Web, exclusive of commercial interests. Nonprofit organizations often use the dot-org extension (.org).

Results of Chapter 6 Exercises

Figure 6.6 The files created by completing the Chapter 5 exercises are uploaded to a server using *Cyberduck, FireFTP*, and the Dreamweaver Files panel in the following exercises.

In the following exercises you will upload the HTML, CSS, and image files you created by completing the exercises in Chapter 5 (Figure 6.6). You will need a domain name and hosting (or server information) in order to complete these exercises.

Download Materials for Chapter 6 Exercises

There are no materials to download for the following exercises. I used my resulting files from Chapter 5 to demonstrate uploading. You may use any files, including those from previous chapters, available for download from the website. [http://viscommontheweb. wordpress.com/downloads/]

Exercise 1: Using an FTP Application

1. On my home computer, I use an application called Cyberduck to transfer files to my web server. PC users often transfer files with WS-FTP. In our Mac labs at school, Cyberduck, Transmit, and Fetch are installed. I will use Cyberduck to demonstrate the following steps, available as a free (or donation-based) download. Start by launching Cyberduck or any other FTP application (terminology and images of the interface may vary between applications, but the concept is the same).

> ### Reference
> Download Cyberduck for free. [www.cyberduck.ch]

2. Click the Quick Connection button and then enter your server information (the domain name of your website), user name, and password in the FTP dialog box (Figure 6.7). Click the Connect button.
3. The FTP dialog box now shows your server. You may be looking at your root directory. My host places my root directory inside a folder called "public_html." I have to double-click this folder to access my root directory.
4. Before uploading the Chapter 5 files to your server, you have to make a decision. Will you upload the exercises to your root directory or do you want to put them in a subdirectory? The implications of these choices are as follows: If you put the files in the root directory, the index page will be the first page to appear when a visitor types your web domain into their browser address bar. If you upload

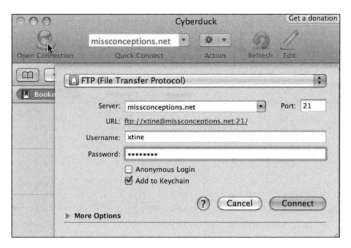

Figure 6.7 Open a new connection and add server information in *Cyberduck*.

the files to a subdirectory, viewers will only be able to see the files if they know where to look. If the files are transferred to a folder on your root directory—let's name it *test*—the path to the files will be www.yourdomain/test/. If you want to upload to your root directory, follow Step 5. If you want to make a subdirectory, skip ahead to Step 6.

5.   **Transferring files to the root directory:** Upload *all* of the Chapter 5 results files (the HTML, CSS, JPG, and PNG file) to the root directory of your server by choosing File > Upload (Shift+clicking will allow you to select all files) or by clicking and dragging all of the files from the *chapter05* folder on your hard drive to the root directory on your server (Figure 6.8). We have named our home page "index" throughout this book because the browser automatically opens the page named "index" when a user types a domain name into the browser's address bar. When you go to yourwebsite.com, you are actually seeing www.yourwebsite .com/index.html. (If you have finished uploading, skip ahead to Step 8).

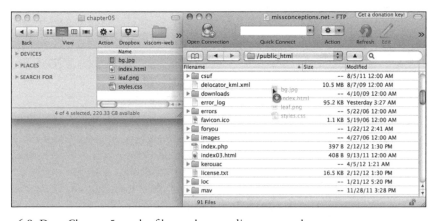

Figure 6.8 Drag Chapter 5 results files to the root directory on the server.

6.   **Creating and transferring files to a subdirectory:** Instead of transferring files to your root directory, you may want to store your files in a subdirectory, or a subfolder. Create a new folder: Choose File > New Folder or right-click inside the root directory to select New Folder (Figure 6.9).

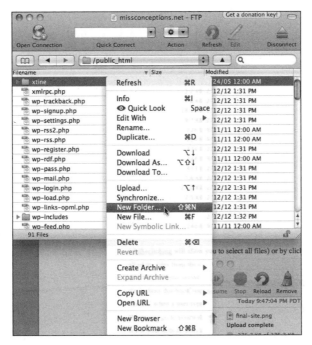

Figure 6.9 Right-click to create a new folder. Mac users can alternatively Control-click to access the contextual (or right-click) menu.

7. Double-click the name of the folder, and then drag your *chapter05* files into it (see Figure 6.8). For students who will upload several assignments to their websites, it makes sense to organize the root directory with a folder (or subdirectory) for each assignment.

> **Note**
>
> You can delete and rename files on your server using the contextual (right-click) menu. On a Mac, access the contextual menu by pressing Control and clicking the mouse in the server window.

8. Once your files are uploaded, access them in a browser. Remember, unless the file is named "index" you will have to type the name of the web page you want to see into the address bar.

Your Turn! If you didn't try it, upload your files to a subdirectory on your server. If you already created a subdirectory, try renaming your *index.html* file. Can you still find your file in the web browser? Remember, the file on your hard drive is not the version of the file that we will see on the Web. Delete everything you uploaded from your server. Since we are just practicing, you can't make a mistake by uploading or deleting these files. Continue these steps until you feel confident transferring files.

Exercise 2: FTP in a Browser

In some computer labs, FTP applications are either not installed or are inaccessible. If you do not have access to an FTP application such as Cyberduck, Transmit, or WS-FTP, you can transfer files through a web browser. One of the easiest browsers for this purpose is Firefox with an FTP extension such as FireFTP. If you have completed Exercise 1, you can skip this exercise.

1. Go to fireftp.mozdev.org to download FireFTP. Click the Install button in the pop-up dialog box (Figure 6.10).

Figure 6.10 Installing *FireFTP* in the *Firefox* web browser is simple.

2. Restart Firefox. Open Firefox and choose Tools > Web Developer > FireFTP from the top menu bar. In the dialog box, use the pull-down menu to choose QuickConnect (Figure 6.11).

Figure 6.11 Use the QuickConnect menu to connect to a server in *FireFTP*.

3. In the Account Manager dialog box enter your domain name in the Host field, your user name in the Login field, and your password. Click OK to save your settings (Figure 6.12).
4. You should see your domain name in the top-left corner of the dialog box. Click the Connect button to the right of your domain name to connect to your server (Figure 6.13).
5. Your server information loads on the right side of the screen.
6. You can create a new directory by right-clicking (or Control-clicking on a Mac mouse without a right-click) within your root directory. It may seem as though you have to select a file name or a directory before right-clicking (Figure 6.14).

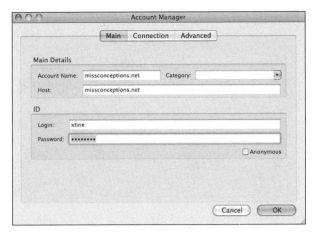

Figure 6.12 Add server information to the account manager before connecting to your server.

Figure 6.13 Connect to a server by pressing the Connect button.

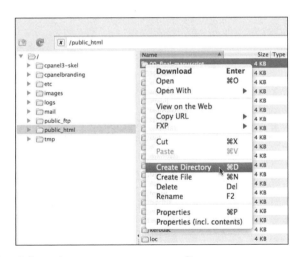

Figure 6.14 Right-click on the server to create a new directory.

7. Name the new directory in the untitled folder near the end of your file list.
8. Drag and drop files from your local computer (your hard drive) to the server in your root directory or in a subdirectory.
9. After you upload your files, take notice of the path to your HTML file, and then visit your files in the browser.

Exercise 3: FTP in Dreamweaver

1. Open Dreamweaver and choose Site > Manage Sites from the top menu bar.
2. Either set up a new site or double-click the name of the site you created when you began the Chapter 5 exercises (Figure 6.15).

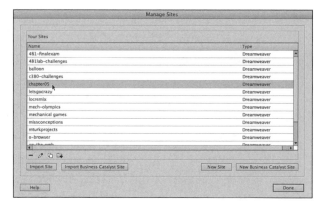

Figure 6.15 Edit site information in the Dreamweaver Site Definition/Manage Sites dialog box.

3. Choose Servers from the menu list on the top left of the Manage Sites dialog box, and then click the plus sign (+) to add your server to the list (Figure 6.16).

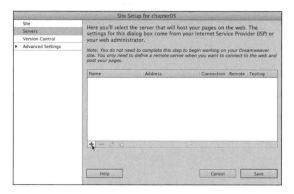

Figure 6.16 Add a new server connection in the Dreamweaver Site Setup dialog box.

4. Add the details for your server information. The server name can be any name you want to use in order to identify your server. The FTP address needs to be precise as it is the same as your domain name (Figure 6.17). Click the Test button to ensure that you have entered the correct user name and password. Then click the Save button to exit the dialog.

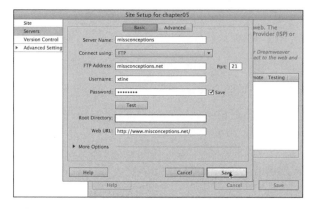

Figure 6.17 Set up the server account in Dreamweaver using your server name (or host, this is your domain name), user name and password. It's a good idea to test the server before exiting this box.

5. Click Save again to exit the Site Setup dialog. Click Allow to add your site user name and password to Dreamweaver's temporary memory. Then click the Done button to exit the Manage Sites dialog.

6. In the Files panel click the Expand button to view both the local files (on your hard drive) and the "remote site" (your server) (Figure 6.18).

Figure 6.18 Expand the Files panel view to display both the local and server windows.

7. In Dreamweaver versions prior to CS6 the File panel will automatically connect to the remote server when the Expand button is activated. CS6 users will need to click the Connect to Remote Server button (Figure 6.19) to view, add to, or delete from the list of files saved on your server. This button allows you to connect to or disconnect from your server.

Figure 6.19 Connect or disconnect with the server using the connection button.

8. Transfer files to your server by selecting them from the Local Files window (the right side) and dragging them to the Remote Server window (the left side) (Figure 6.20). You can create subdirectories on the server by right-clicking and choosing New Folder on the server side, just as you can create new folders using Cyberduck or FireFTP.

Close the connection to your server when you are finished by clicking the Connect to Remote Server button (Figure 6.19). Click the red button in the top-left corner of the window to collapse the layout of this panel into the original view of the Files panel (just the local view).

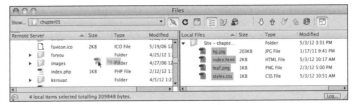

Figure 6.20 Drag files from the local files on the right side to the server on the left side of the panel.

The Art and Craft of Code

The Firefox add-on for FireFTP was created by Mime Čuvalo, a Croatian web developer who believes in open web standards (sharing, collaboration, and the noncommercialization of the Internet). FireFTP has been downloaded more than 4.5 million times, and it continues to be a free service, though donations are accepted. Čuvalo calls FireFTP his "charityware" project. Half of the donations support orphanages in Sarajevo and Vukovar.

Add-ons are created by thousands of developers—from amateurs and hobbyists to corporations. An ***add-on*** modifies the way a browser or application functions—often adding niche features or changing the display preferences. Browsing add-ons for Firefox is like browsing free samples in a paper warehouse. [https://addons.mozilla.org/en-US/firefox/]

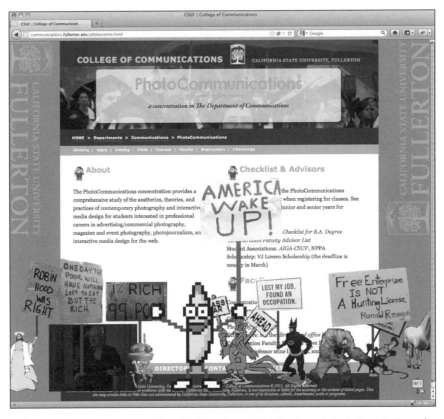

Figure 6.21 *Occupy Internet,* created by the Free Art and Technology Lab, is installed as a browser add-on in Firefox. This is a screen shot of the add-on at work when I open the California State University Fullerton Photocommunications web page.

Artists and experimenters create add-ons to challenge the way users think about using the Internet. In solidarity with the Occupy Movement, the Free Art and Technology Lab (F.A.T.) created an "Occupy Internet" add-on that displays an animated protestor in the bottom-right corner of your browser when it is installed (Figure 6.21). The code was developed for use with Chrome, Safari, and Firefox. If you have administrative rights to add extensions to the browsers in your office or lab, F.A.T. hopes you will secretly install the Occupy add-on there. [http://occupyinter.net/]

Create, Reflect, Critique

You will not learn the programming skills required for developing add-ons or extensions from this book. But in many cases those types of media are created by teams of developers. Suppose you were working with a team of programmers and anything would be possible. What add-on would you create? Summarize your idea in writing; then develop mock-up images to show the functionality of your add-on. Would you modify a browser, an application, or something else? Developing add-ons is like remodeling in the physical world. Can you think of an "add-on" that exists in the physical world? For real-world inspiration, see Instructables or Make. [http://www.Instructables.com] and [http://www.Makezine.com]

Glossary Words

browser add-ons, domain, FTP, hosting, taxonomy, web domain, web hosting

7   WEB TYPOGRAPHY

VIDEO
INTRODUCTION

Principles, History, Theory

Six Six Six

What is so special about the number six?

After all that talk about loving neighbors, helping strangers, and forgiving enemies found in most of the New Testament, the Bible ends with a curious tale of innumerable horrors, a result of a final battle between the forces of good and evil. Most likely written by John of Patmos (Turkey) in the first century, religious scholar Elaine Pagels in her book *Revelations: Visions, Prophecy, and Politics in the Book of Revelation* explains that the work is, in reality, an anti-Roman diatribe deftly hidden within a complex system of symbolism (Figure 7.1).

One of the most enduring symbols from the controversial book is that of the mark of the Devil. Chapter 13:18 of Revelation makes it clear: "Here is wisdom. Let him that hath understanding count the number of the beast: for it is the number of a man; and his

Figure 7.1 By all accounts, the 17th century Spanish painter and architect Alonzo Cano was not a particularly religious person. After a customer refused to pay his price for a statue of a saint, he risked his life when he smashed it to pieces—at the time a capital offense. When a priest tried to offer him the Sacrament on his deathbed and showed his crucifix, Cano refused the offer. Still, during his lifetime he had to make a living and became the chief architect for the Granada Cathedral and painted many religious-themed works including a portrait of John Patmos receiving inspiration from an angel for his *Book of Revelation. Courtesy of the Yorck Project.*

Note

Since Lincoln made the famous speech in 1863 and the country began in 1776, four score and seven years equals 87 years ago.

number is Six hundred threescore and six." If you have forgotten what a score is, recall President Lincoln's "Gettysburg Address" that started with "Four score and seven years ago our fathers brought forth on this continent a new nation...."

A score is 20. Therefore, Satan in the form of a man is named by the numbers $6 - 6 - 6$.

Why were three sixes chosen for the Devil? The answer comes from the power of numbers. As John Patmos was Jewish, he knew of Gematria, an ancient Greek method in which numbers were assigned to names or concepts. It was thought that things with the same numbers were somehow related. Gematria is still used in Jewish texts, such as the Kabbalah. Who hasn't played around with numerology? Using the numerical system, Patmos was slyly communicating to those in the know that $6 - 6 - 6$ stood for Emperor Nero, considered the worst of the worst Roman rulers and a contemporary of Patmos. He dared not say his name outright.

But that's enough of the doom and gloom of the end of the world, or at least one person's hope that the Roman Empire would end. There are plenty of positive references to the number six:

A Rubik's cube (and all others) has six sides.
A guitar usually has six strings.
Honeycomb cells are six-sided.
Insects have six legs.
The atomic number for carbon is six.
The number of points for a touchdown in American football is six.
The Star of David has six points.
LaBron James of the Miami Heat wears the number six.
All of the typefaces ever created can be divided into one of six families.

Johannes Gutenberg had an easy time selecting the typeface style for his Bible because there was only one—Textur. Since his time, at least 40,000 different typeface styles have been created, with more than 176,000 font variations. With so many choices, a method was devised to group all of the typefaces into families. The resulting six basic typeface families became blackletter, roman, script, miscellaneous, square serif, and sans serif. Think of each typeface family as separate colors or musical styles, each with their own mood and purpose. In fact, as letters are simply highly stylized line drawings, they are pictures with emotional meaning. Learning which typeface picture family and individual typeface work best for a graphic design is all about matching form and content for your audience (Figure 7.2).

Blackletter   Sometimes called gothic, old style, old English, renaissance, or medieval, the blackletter typeface family is highly ornate and decorative. Because it happened to be the style that scribes in monasteries used for their handwritten works, the family is associated with traditional, conservative, religious, or German content. A newspaper's name was often set in this typeface family to communicate to readers that the publication had traditional values and was long established.

Roman   The roman typeface family is the most commonly used of them all. Body copy in books, magazines, and newspapers use roman because it is familiar to readers and exceedingly legible. The gently curved serifs create lines that are easy to read. Development of the style of roman used today took approximately 300 years from the time it was introduced in 1465. During that period, three forms were introduced: *old style*, *transitional*, and *modern*.

Script This typeface family was designed to mimic the handwriting of ordinary people. Ironically, the script typeface family is now used almost exclusively for documents and publications that want to promote a high-quality, high-class appearance.

Miscellaneous Sometimes referred to as novelty or display type, the members of the miscellaneous typeface family, as the name suggests, cannot easily be sorted into the other families. Miscellaneous type first began appearing for advertising purposes during the Industrial Revolution. The miscellaneous family's unique feature is that its style purposely draws attention to itself.

Square serif In Chapter 11 the link between Napoleon's brief occupation of Egypt and a printer named Vincent Figgins is explained. Square serif is the least used of all six families because of its awkward, blocky appearance.

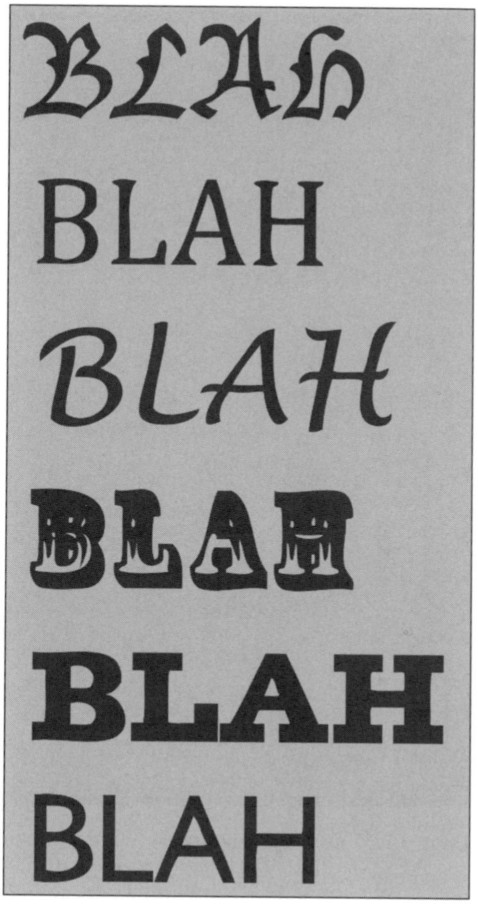

Figure 7.2 The same word can have different symbolic and emotional meanings depending on the choice of typeface. *Courtesy of Paul Martin Lester.*

Sans serif When this family was introduced, it was immediately controversial. William Caslon I simply took existing letters and trimmed off all their serifs. Typographical critics of the day immediately voiced their objections to the type family as being too simple and without style. Curiously, the creator of square serif, Vincent Figgins, came up with the name *sans serif*. Screen media presentations have demonstrated the importance of the sans serif style, as it is easy to read. Consequently, these typefaces are used most often in motion picture titles and credits; in captions for television news programs; and for computer, tablet, and smartphone screens.

Note

Sans serif font faces are easier to read on the screen because light is projected through the content to the viewer's eyes. In this environment a serif becomes a tiny contrasting graphic element that is more difficult to see than the sans serif letterforms.

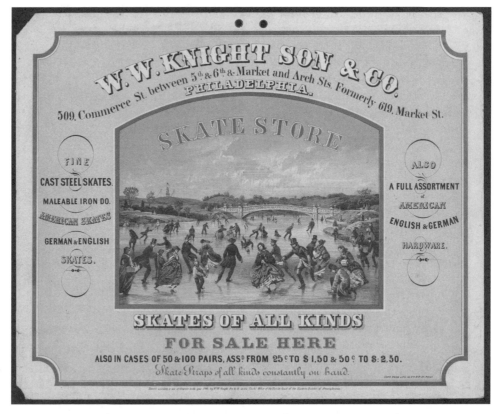

Figure 7.3 An 1860 advertising window display card for a Philadelphia ice skating store exhibits all six of the typeface families. Blackletter: AMERICAN SKATES; Roman: 509, Commerce St.; Script: Skate Straps of all kinds; Miscellaneous: W.W. KNIGHT SON & CO.; Square serif: PHILADELPHIA; and Sans serif: CAST STEEL SKATES. Was the printer a friend of the Devil? *Courtesy of the Library of Congress.*

Knowing the six typeface families and their different emotional qualities will aid you in creating designs that are best for your intended audience. Regardless, you should never use all six families for a single piece—you might be accused of being in league with the Devil (Figure 7.3).

Practice

Elastic Measurements

In CSS code, the most commonly used forms of measurement are pixels (px), percentages (%), and *elastic measurements* (em). Designers have to weigh the pros and cons of using these types of measurements. The advantage of pixels is your familiarity with the unit of measurement, and the precision and certainty of a pixel-based design. You know exactly how wide 25 pixels will be, regardless of user settings or browser choices. Percentages are a relative unit of measurement; as such you have to make sure that your CSS code knows what you mean when you declare something to be measured in percentages. We take for granted that declaring something as a percentage of something else implies the reference to the "something else." If you assign a CSS value of 50%, then the browser will look to a parent element in the code to determine 50% *of what*. Elastic measurements are the most user-friendly choice you can make because this relative format of measurement is based on user preferences. From the predigital days of typographic layout, 1em is equal to the value of the width of the capital letter "M" in a selected typeface. When measuring type using CSS code, the general rule is a simple calculation. But, 1em is still equivalent to the width of the capital letter "M" in the default font size.

This means that the default font and the default font size are both part of the equation. Since users can elect to modify their browser's default font and size, 1em does not hold a concrete value. However, most users do not bother to change their browser presets. Most browsers are set to the default type size, "medium." In many cases (but not all), this default size is 16 pixels. So, most designers will work under the following assumption:

1em = approximately 16px

Expanding Typeface Choices

By now you may have noticed that Dreamweaver offers a small selection of fonts when you select a typeface from a font pull-down menu. For instance, see Modify > Page Properties > Page Font. Only 13 font sets appear on the list (Figure 7.4).

Now that we are utilizing CSS code linked to our HTML document, we have greater flexibility in the design of the page, including in our typographic choices. The short list of fonts that appears as the default set of choices is true to HTML. When you are coding a web page for display in a browser, you have to consider what resources will be installed on the user's viewing device. Most computers and mobile devices have the fonts listed in Figure 7.4 installed at the time of manufacturing. These are the only typefaces you can rely on that your users will be able to see. So it is safest when just using HTML to choose one of these groups of typefaces (and if a user does not have, for instance, Verdana installed, then the typeface that will show up is the next one after the comma—Geneva).

A property new to CSS is called "at font face," that is, **@font-face**. This property allows the designer to upload a font to her server and use it in her design. For

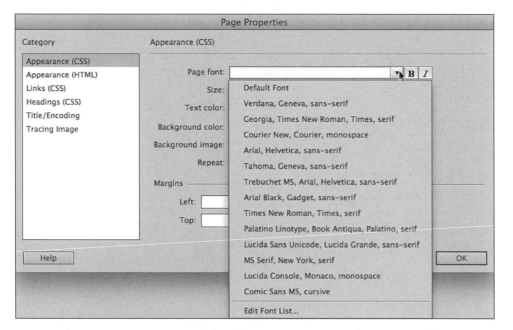

Figure 7.4 Notice the small choice of fonts from the Dreamweaver font pull-down list.

Reference

For more on using @font-face, see the Font Squirrel website [http://www.fontsquirrel.com/]. Also, see Jeffrey Way's screencast tutorial, which demonstrates using the Font Squirrel website [http://net.tutsplus.com/tutorials/design-tutorials/quick-tip-how-to-work-with-font-face/].

beginning students, **@font-face** can be a little overwhelming, so I will leave that for you to explore on your own when you are feeling confident with this material. I have found that students in my advanced interactive media design class have no problem integrating this property into their designs.

Instead of dealing with the property directly, we will use Google Web Fonts, which work similarly to the **@font-face** property but do not require as much coding and uploading because the font files are saved on Google's server [http://www.google.com/webfonts].

With the **link href** tag that we implemented in Chapter 5 (Exercise 2, Step 8) we connected our HTML document to an externally saved style sheet. This tag can also be used to connect to typefaces that have been uploaded to a server. This procedure will open our selection of "safe" fonts to a wide array of choices, not because the fonts are necessarily installed on a user's device, but because the fonts are accessible for download from a server. We will use this method of linking to a collection of fonts provided by Google in the following exercises.

Results of Chapter 7 Exercises

In the following exercises you will learn to use elastic measurements, make typographic choices for the web page using Google's Web Fonts, and add a **class** selector to the style sheet and the HTML document (Figure 7.5).

Figure 7.5 Chapter 7 results include new typefaces in the heading ("Anna Atkins"), first level headers, and body copy.

Download Materials for Chapter 7 Exercises

We will modify the resulting files from the Chapter 5 exercises to begin the exercises in Chapter 7. You can download the Chapter 5 results files from the website [http://viscom-montheweb.wordpress.com/downloads/].

Exercise 1: Measuring Type with Elastic Measurements

1. **Set up your workspace:** Copy and paste the final Chapter 5 exercise files to a new folder named *chapter07*. Open Dreamweaver and define or edit your site to point to the root directory, *chapter07*. Choose Window > Workspace Layout > Designer. Open *index.html* in Dreamweaver, modify the title tag (I titled my page "Chapter Seven"), and press Command+S or select File > Save.

2. View the CSS code linked to *index.html* by clicking the styles.css button just under the top-left tab. Modify the font size attributed to the **H1** tag selector to 1.5em, as follows:

Replacing px with em	

`h1 {`
`    font-family:`
`    Verdana, Geneva,`
`    sans-serif;`
`    font-size: 24px;`
`    color: #009;`
`}`
	The original code contains the font size in pixels

`h1 {`
`    font-family:`
`    Verdana, Geneva,`
`    sans-serif;`
`    font-size: `~~`24px;`~~
`    color: #009;`
`}`
	Delete the pixel measurement

`h1 {`
`    font-family:`
`    Verdana, Geneva,`
`    sans-serif;`
`    font-size: 1.5em;`
`    color: #009;`
`}`
	Replace the pixel measurement with elastic measurements

Note

If 16px is assumed to be the default pixel size of "medium" text, then 24px is approximately the same as 1.5em because 24px/16 = 1.5em.

3. Save your work and preview it in a browser (Figure 7.6). The typography of the heading most likely looks the same as it did before you converted its pixel dimensions to ems.

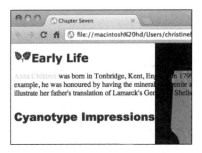

Figure 7.6 Pixel dimensions and ems may appear identical if your math is accurate and your default type size is "medium" or 16 pixels.

4. Find your browser preferences and change the default font size to make it much larger or smaller (Figure 7.7).

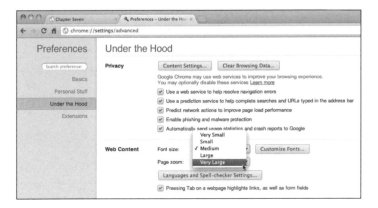

Figure 7.7 I used Chrome at this time of writing and pressed the tool bar icon in the top right corner of the browser window to change the preferences in the "Under the Hood" category.

5. Notice what happens to your typography! The heading appears much larger (if you selected "very large") and the paragraph text (surrounded by the p tag) is also bigger (Figure 7.8). Since we did not set a value for the **p** tag using CSS, the text on the page will default to the browser settings. For my code, that means the body copy appears larger and the heading, set to 1.5em, is much larger.

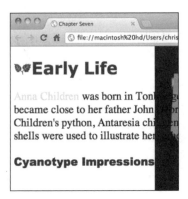

Figure 7.8 Notice the increase in size in the typography being measured with ems.

6. Did you notice that the text "Cyanotype Impressions" did not resize? Can you figure out why this text did not change? View the HTML code. This text is governed by an inline style in the HTML tag set to 24 pixels. This style will dominate over the browser preference due to the cascading nature of CSS code.

7. Set your browser preferences back to "medium" or the default font size settings to return to your normal viewing conditions.

Exercise 2: Using Google Web Fonts

1. Our next goal is to choose three Google Web Fonts for the display text (what we will name **header**), each of the page headings (the **h1** tags), and body copy (the **p** tags) on our page. Go to the Google Web Fonts page and click the Start Choosing Fonts button (Figure 7.9) [http://www.google.com/webfonts].

Figure 7.9 The *Google Web Fonts* home page displays three steps you should take: choose your fonts, review them, and use them in your own creations.

2. In Exercise 3 we will add Anna Atkins' name to the top of the page. Choose a display text for this header on our page. I filtered the selection of fonts by choosing Handwriting from the pull-down menu. Then I clicked the Add To Collection button next to the font named "Ruthie" (Figure 7.10). Add two more fonts to your collection for the **h1** tag and the **p** tag. I added "Ropa Sans" and "Ledger" to my collection.

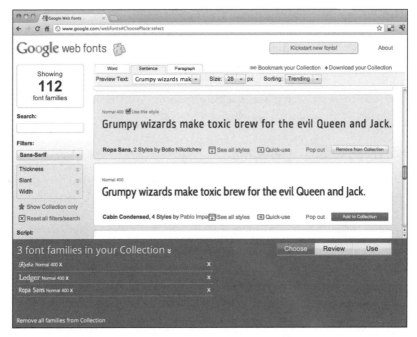

Figure 7.10 When you choose Google Web Fonts font-faces, Google adds them to your collection.

3. Click the Use button to verify your settings (Figure 7.11). The more fonts and font styles you select, the more you are asking your user to download (therefore, the longer it will take for your page to load).

Figure 7.11 On the top of the "Use" screen you will see a list of your fonts (you can check or uncheck styles you want to use) and the toll it will take, in terms of download time, on your audience.

4. Scroll, if you need to, and copy the code from Step 3 on the Google Use page (Figures 7.12 and 7.13). This **link href** tag will be inserted into the head area of your HTML page. It allows you to make a reference in your HTML code to the location on Google's server where these fonts are stored.

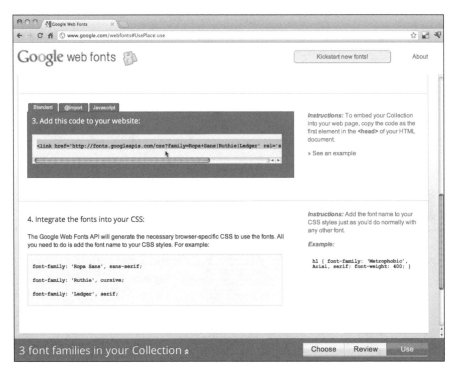

Figure 7.12 Copy the **link href** tag from Google to use it in your file.

```
1   <!DOCTYPE html PUBLIC "-//W3C//DTD XHTML 1.0 Transitional//EN"
    "http://www.w3.org/TR/xhtml1/DTD/xhtml1-transitional.dtd">
2   <html xmlns="http://www.w3.org/1999/xhtml">
3   <head>
4   <meta http-equiv="Content-Type" content="text/html; charset=UTF-8" />
5   <title>Chapter Seven</title>
6   <link href="styles.css" rel="stylesheet" type="text/css" />
7   <link href='http://fonts.googleapis.com/css?family=Ropa+Sans|Ruthie|Ledger' rel='stylesheet' type='text/css'>
8   </head>
9
```

Figure 7.13 Paste the **link href** code to the **head** section of *index.html*.

5. Now we will modify the CSS code saved in *styles.css* to add these fonts to our tag selectors. As a reminder, Step 4 on the Google Use page gives you the property and values for the three font choices you made. I will start with the h1 tag selector—copy the value **'Ropa Sans', sans-serif**; and paste it on top of the font-family property in the **h1** declaration block (Figure 7.14).

```
Source Code  styles.css*
@charset "UTF-8";
h1 {
    font-family: 'Ropa Sans', sans-serif;
    font-size: 1.5em;
    color: #009;
}
```

Figure 7.14 Add the Google Web Fonts **font-family** value to the externally linked style sheet, *styles.css.*

6. On a new line in *styles.css,* add a style for the **p** tag (Figure 7.15).

Code view in Dreamweaver	Adding a declaration block for the **p** tag
| ```
body,td,th {
    color: #000;
    background-image: url(bg.jpg);
    background-repeat: no-repeat;
    background-position: center top;
}
p {
    font-family: 'Ledger', Georgia, serif;
}
``` | ```
p {
    font-family: 'Ledger',
    Georgia, serif;
}
``` |

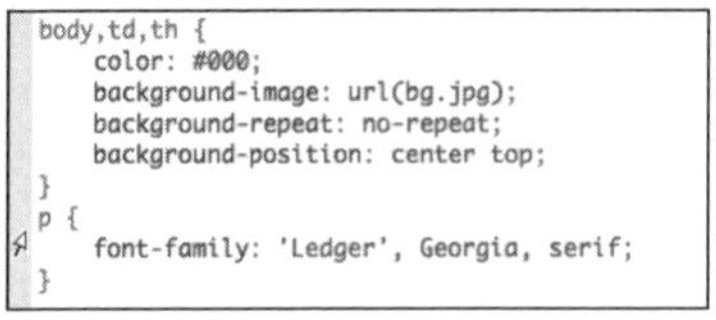

Figure 7.15 Create a new style for the **p** tag.

7. **Your Turn!** Now add more content to the HTML document (in Dreamweaver, this will be the "source code" document). Try working just in code view. Remove the inline style on the "Cyanotype Impressions" text, and then add some copy for the separate headings Cyanotype, Photography, and Later Life and Work. I copied a small amount of text from the Anna Atkins Wikipedia page [http://en.wikipedia.org/wiki/Anna_Atkins]. Your copy should mimic the page views in Figures 7.16 and 7.17. You might notice that you will have to add a list of content to the page. The unordered list tag **<ul>** tells the browser that the enclosed list uses bullet points (or other decorative symbols) rather than numbers to create a list where the order of items is insignificant. The li tag **<li>** is used to separate each listed item. Both tags, **<ul>** and **<li>**, need to be closed at the end of the entire list **</ul>** and at the end of each listed item **</li>**. You will need to add **<p>** and **</p>** around paragraphs, **<h1>** and **</h1>** around headings, and **<ul>** and **</ul>** around the list of items where **<li>** and **</li>** is used to list each item. When you are finished, save your work and preview it in a browser.

8. Notice that the listed items (the text following the bullet points) is not set in the font that is used throughout the body copy. Since this text is encoded with the list tag **<li>**, it uses the default page font. We have not set a default font for the page, so this will simply be the default browser font. Copy the font property and value from the CSS declaration block you created for the **p** tag and paste it on a new line following the last set of properties and values in the **body, td, th** tag selector (Figure 7.18). Save your work and preview it in a browser.

> **Note**
>
> Place **<ul>** and **</ul>** around the entire list and use **<li>** and **</li>** around each listed item (each bullet point).

> **Watch out**
>
> When you remove your inline style, be sure to look in the head area of the HTML document. You should not need a **<style>** or **</style>** tag if you are not using inline or internal styles. Delete these tags if you see them.

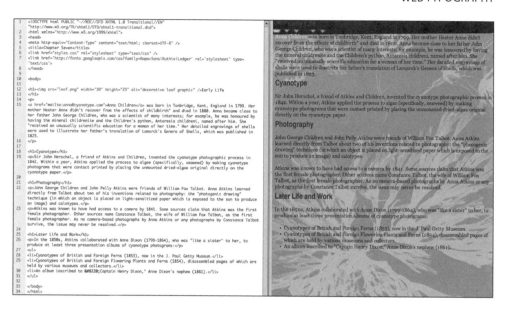

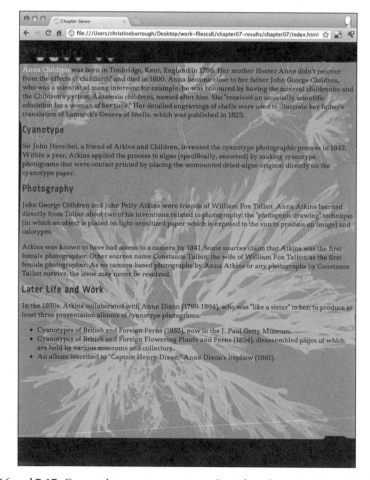

Figures 7.16 and 7.17 Copy and paste new content to the code and preview the results in a browser.

```
body,td,th {
    color: #000;
    background-image: url(bg.jpg);
    background-repeat: no-repeat;
    background-position: center top;
    font-family: 'Ledger', Georgia, serif;
}
p {
    font-family: 'Ledger', Georgia, serif;
}
```

Figure 7.18 Add the Google Web Fonts **font-family** value (**'Ledger'**) to the **body** tag selector.

VIDEO
WALKTHROUGH

Exercise 3: Creating a Class Selector

1. Finally, let's add Anna Atkins' name to the top of the page. In code view, place the cursor just beneath the body tag. Type "Anna Atkins." In design view it may be hard to see this new text, as it appears in black on a dark blue background.

2. We will apply a CSS style to this text. This time we will use a class rather than a tag selector. First we will create the style; then we will apply it in the HTML document. Click the New CSS Rule button in the bottom of the CSS Styles panel (Figure 7.19). In the New CSS Rule dialog box, select Class from the Selector Type pull-down menu, name it **.header**, and save it in the *styles.css* external styles sheet (Figure 7.20).

Note

You will learn more about the different types of CSS selectors in Chapter 8.

Figure 7.19 Click on the New CSS Rule button in the CSS Styles panel.

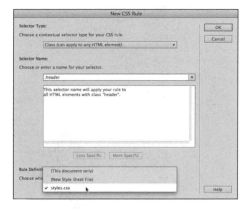

Figure 7.20 Save a new class selector named **.header** in the externally saved style sheet, *styles.css.*

3. Did you notice that the Google Web Fonts are not listed in the Font-family pull-down menu in the Type category of the CSS Rule Definition dialog box for **.header**? These fonts are available for you to use because you are linking to them on Google's web server. However, Dreamweaver does not know that you are using these linked files, so it only presents the fonts that it "thinks" you can rely on having installed on both your computer and the viewer's device. We will outsmart Dreamweaver. Select Verdana, Geneva, Sans-serif from the pull-down menu (Figure 7.21).

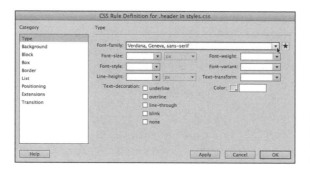

Figure 7.21 Select "back up" type families for the browser to display if the first family listed is unavailable.

4. Switch views to the *styles.css* style sheet. The declaration block for **.header** will appear as the last item on the page. Modify the values that are associated with the **font-family** property by copying/pasting the name of the font you selected to use on the Google Web Fonts page. I selected **'Ruthie', cursive,** so I added these two typefaces to the beginning of my list of values (Figure 7.22). If for some reason the Google page does not load on my viewer's device, the viewer will see my type set in whatever default font is used to display "cursive" text, or it will display using Verdana, then (if that is not installed), Geneva, then, finally, whatever font is used to display as "sans serif."

```
.header {
    font-family: 'Ruthie', cursive, Verdana, Geneva, sans-serif;
}
```

Figure 7.22 Add additional primary and secondary **font-face** values to the CSS code.

5. Click back to the source code view to see your HTML document. We have not yet applied our CSS style to the text "Anna Atkins." Highlight this text in code view, as it is easier to see right now in code view than in design view. In the Properties panel at the bottom of the screen, click the HTML button to add an HTML property, and then use the Class pull-down menu to assign the "header" class to this text (Figure 7.23). As a result, the code will be modified to include the span tag, **<span>**, around the text "Anna Atkins." The span tag is used to add style to a selection of content in the HTML document. We just applied the header class to the text "Anna Atkins." Save your work and preview it in a browser.

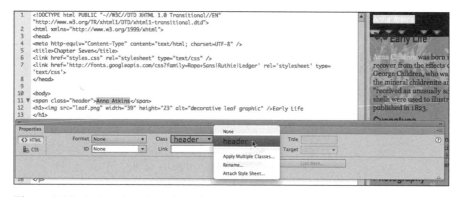

Figure 7.23 Assign the **.header** class to the HTML **span** tag in the source code.

6. I am happy with the fonts that are in use on my page, but I want the header "Anna Atkins" to appear much larger so that it is a focal point on the page. Contrast through size is one method for creating hierarchy in a layout. I will modify the **.header** class to increase the size of the typography. Expand the styles.css menu in the CSS Styles panel, and you will see a list of all of the properties we have created CSS rules for in our style sheet. Double-click **.header** to open the Rule Definition dialog box for this CSS *class selector*. Remember that 1em is approximately 16 pixels. Assign a value of 3em to the **font-size** property (Figure 7.24). This is 48 pixels (assuming the default font is 16 pixels).

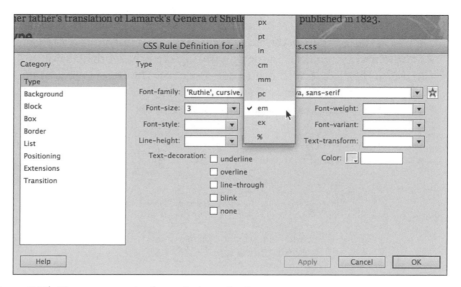

Figure 7.24 Change a type size from pixels to elastic measurements.

Note

Did you notice that in Dreamweaver you will not see a preview of the font face that is being saved on and accessed from Google's server? You will only be able to preview this font face when you are connected to the Internet and capable of accessing Google's server. There is a Live View button in Dreamweaver that will display the page more accurately, but my policy is to always preview work in a browser.

7. In the font that I selected, 3em does not seem too terribly large. I will make just a couple of minor adjustments to the header typography by modifying the properties and values directly on the style sheet. Click to view *styles.css*. Change the font size value from 3em to 6em. Make sure that you do not accidentally remove the semicolon at the end of the line of code—the syntax is vital. Extra spaces, typos, a forgotten dash, colon, or semicolon could throw off your whole page.

8. Finally, change the color of the type using the color property. I copied and pasted the color property from the **a:link** declaration to the **.header** declaration, assigning to it a bright shade of yellow, **#FF3** (Figure 7.25).

```
.header {
    font-family: 'Ruthie', cursive, Verdana, Geneva, sans-serif;
    font-size: 6em;
    color: #FF3;
}
```

Figure 7.25 Change the type size (**font-size**) directly in the CSS code.

The Art and Craft of Code

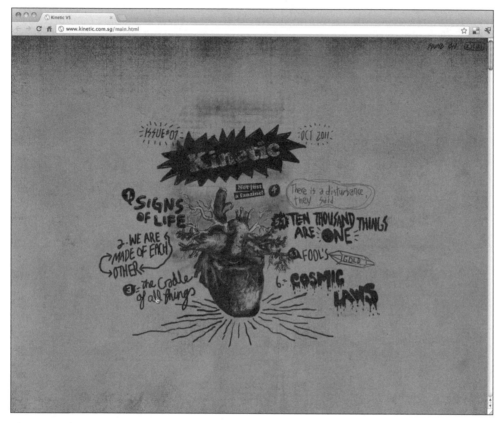

Figure 7.26 The 2012 Kinetic home page displays a hand-drawn navigation that functions as a free form illustration. © *Kinetic*.

Kinetic is a web design agency located in Singapore. The inaugural issue of "Not just a fanzine!" online zine is a unified freeform collage of hand-drawn typography and illustrations with accompanying science fiction audio effects [http://www.kinetic.com.sg/main .html].

Create, Reflect, Critique

Create a version of your résumé using HTML and CSS. If you have a résumé that you designed in another application, see if you can match the formatting that you have already created. Use Google Web Fonts and explore CSS properties and values that we did not use in this chapter. For instance, you can apply small caps and adjust line height using the Text-transform and Line-height properties in CSS (these are also available in the

Dreamweaver CSS Rule Definition dialog box). How will you create hierarchy on your page? Were you able to keep the basic principles of design and typography in mind while applying CSS styles? Were you tempted to use as many variations as you could learn how to code? Remember the all-important rule: Create repetition and then break it to create contrast.

Reference

See Jason Santa Maria's "On Web Typography" article on *A List Apart* for an in-depth discussion of typography online [http://www.alistapart.com/articles/on-web-typography/].

Glossary Words

Blackletter, class selector, elastic measurement, miscellaneous typeface, roman typeface, sans serif, script typeface, square serif

8 NAVIGATION TOOLS

VIDEO
INTRODUCTION

Principles, History, Theory

Navigation: Learning from Failures

Does your life depend upon knowing where you're going?

Usually, when someone makes a serious navigational mistake, bad things happen. Take Columbus, La Salle, and Riegels.

To celebrate the end of his apprenticeship at the weaving shop of Guglielmo di Brabante of Genoa, Italy, 21-year-old Domenico Colombo married Suzanna Fontanarossa. About 13 years later, a son was born to the hard-working couple. Despite his modest birth, Christopher Columbus, as he eventually became known, would sail across the Atlantic Ocean four times wrongly thinking he was on his way to India. His navigational error resulted in the start of the conquest of the Americas and the admiral's downfall. When he died in 1506, he was buried with only a handful in attendance in a small monastery in Valladolid, Spain. His body wore the habit of the third order of Saint Francis and, according to his wishes, was wrapped in the chains he wore upon his arrest after his third voyage in which he again failed to find a good tandoori chicken recipe. Only three lines of text marked his obituary in the official record. No paintings were ever made of the seaman during his lifetime because no one knew of the significance of his discoveries (Figure 8.1).

The French explorer René-Robert Cavelier, known as La Salle, was the first to travel the entire length of the Mississippi River from Canada. He reached the end in 1682 and named the land *Louisiana*, in honor of his king, Louis XIV (Figure 8.2). But five years later he and his men were in desperate shape. Running out of supplies and with their simple fort near Houston, Texas, surrounded by hostile natives, La Salle set out with 17 others in an attempt to find the Mississippi River and sail north to the protection of the French missions in the Great Lakes region. But a navigational error sent him west when he should have traveled east. The doomed expedition made it as far as the present-day town of Navasota, about 300 miles west of the Mississippi. His frustrated and angry crew murdered La Salle and "left his body for the animals to eat" (Lester, 2009). *Ouch.*

One of the most memorable college football plays in the history of the game was caused by a navigational error. On New Year's Day of 1929, the University of California played Georgia Tech in Pasadena's Rose Bowl. During the second quarter, the center for California, Roy Riegels, scooped up a fumble and ran 65 yards toward the goal line on his way to what he thought would be hero status. Trouble was, he ran the wrong way. A teammate stopped him three yards from the Georgia goal to avoid a safety, but on the next play a punt was blocked and two points were awarded to the Yellow Jackets, who went on to win the game. Although some praised Riegels for overcoming his emotions and playing hard during the second half, he blamed himself for the loss. For the rest of his life he was known as "Wrong Way" Riegels (Figure 8.3).

Figure 8.1 A statue of Christopher Columbus overlooks the main reading room of the Library of Congress. His confused expression is probably due to the fact that he is in Washington, DC and not India. *Courtesy of the Library of Congress.*

Navigation, whether in life or on web pages, is vital to a successful experience (Figure 8.4).

In 1974 Vincent Flanders graduated from Wabash College, a small, private school in western Indiana. His degree specialized in ancient Greek culture from which he learned three important principles for living and web design: moderation, proportion, and beauty. After college, he was an associate editor of a computer magazine in Austin, Texas, a webmaster for an Internet company, and taught HTML to business site designers. In 1996 he launched a website that would make him famous: "Web Pages That Suck." The praise about the site resulted in two published books, one of the same title with fellow designer Michael Willis and the other, *Son of Web Pages That Suck*. His lists of the ugliest and worst websites are valuable and entertaining lessons in what to avoid on your pages.

In his list of the 16 biggest mistakes of web design, Number 7 features navigational failure. Flanders writes, "All web navigation must answer these questions: Where am I? Where have I been? Where can I go next? Where's the Home Page?" He makes the observation, probably learned from Aristotle, that "navigation must be simple and consistent." He adds, "Common mistakes include different types of navigation on the same site, a link to the current page on the current page (home page link on the home page), poorly worded links so the visitor doesn't know where he'll go if he clicks, no links back to the home page, and confusing links to the home page."

Eye-tracking studies, in which volunteers wear headsets and hunt for navigational buttons while a computer records where and how long their eyes gaze, have also concluded that buttons and links should be placed in the same location on different pages, combined with text when possible, in a logical order, be large enough for elderly users to click, never blink or be overly cute, and should be accessed without the need for scrolling.

Writing for *Smashing* magazine, Matt Cronin names "50 Beautiful and User-Friendly Navigational Menus." For Cronin, "Usable navigation is something every

Figure 8.2 As the translation of the illustration is, "The unhappy adventures of the Sieur de la Salle," at least during the moment engraved by Jan Van Vianen in 1698 all is well. La Salle, priests, and others can be seen on shore while supplies are unloaded from a ship. *Courtesy of the Library of Congress.*

website needs. Without usable navigation, content becomes all but useless. Menus need to be simple enough for the user to understand, but also contain the elements necessary to guide the user through the website—with some creativity and good design thrown in." The main concept that connects the 50 website menu pages on his site is brand specificity. Regardless if the website is a personal blog or a large corporation's display, the choices of typography, color, illustrations, placement on the page, and so on reflect the unique personality of the person or culture of the creators and

Figure 8.3 Photographer Sam Sansone, who later became the chief photographer for the *Los Angeles Examiner*, took this picture of Roy Riegels running the wrong direction during the Rose Bowl game of 1929. *Courtesy of the* Los Angeles Examiner.

Figure 8.4 California resident Mike Rowe, an Eagle Scout, high school chorus singer, and performer for the Baltimore Opera Company, was lured away from the stage to pitch products for the QVC channel. He eventually became famous as the creator and amiable host of the Discovery Channel's "Dirty Jobs," and was willing to take on tasks few would want. His website reflects the unique actor's eclectic tastes as a user discovers when rolling a mouse over the objects in the room. *Courtesy of mikeroweWORKS.com.*

the potential audience. Cookie-cutter and template-driven designs may save time and money, but they will never compete with unique Web pages that a visitor finds useful and beautiful (Figure 8.5).

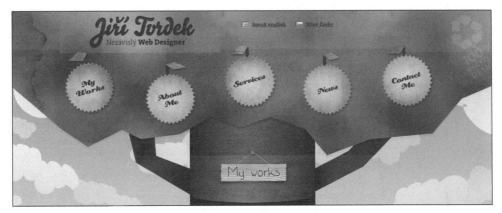

Figure 8.5 Czech web designer *Jiří* Tvrdek gets inspiration from trees. He writes that his work "just like the trees, is simply never the same." Matt Cronin calls his CSS-based navigation menu as leaves on a tree, "Creative, unusual and memorable." *Courtesy of* Jiří *Tvrdek at www.tvrdek.cz/en.*

Hopefully, if the navigational controls on your website contain errors and your visitors get lost, you won't be put in chains, left to die in the woods, or ridiculed until your death, but your site will lose credibility and eyeballs if your users cannot successfully navigate through your work, enjoy the journey, and return home.

Practice

Using Lists for Navigation Toolbars

When you begin to think about designing a web page, there are two necessary questions to ask yourself: How will users link from one page to the next? How will content on the page be organized? In fact, these two questions are often under-considered because we have developed a standard set of answers: Users should link from one page to another using the navigational tool (usually on the top, side, and/or bottom of the page) in addition to links embedded in the copy. In addition, as with a newspaper, book, or magazine, the page should be organized in columns. To translate this idea into code, you will have to modify the styles associated with an unordered list so that it assumes the properties you want to see in a navigational bar. To create a top bar, the unordered list should be presented on one horizontal baseline (that is, set the **display** property to **inline**), and you will probably want to hide the default bullet points that are the visual indicators of a list (set the **list-style-type** property in CSS to **none**).

Creating Boxes with the Division Tag

Creating a column of text, or more than one column, requires an HTML tag named **<div>**. The **div** tag applies an invisible box around content that is used for positioning elements

The DIV Rules Out TABLES!

If you ever created HTML tables using **<table>** in order to position content on you page, you should know that this practice is dead. You can still use tables to organize information (as you would in a spreadsheet—something we won't need for the web page we are assembling). However, for designing columns on a page or positioning assorted page content, you should be using the division tag.

on the page. We will use the **div** tag to divide areas of content into a navigation area, a heading, and two columns to create order and hierarchy on the page. The most commonly used **div** tags are called "container," "header," "nav," "sidebar," and "footer." We will focus on the container div in the next chapter, and on the footer in Chapter 10. In the following exercises we will create a navigation tool and a set of divs for "nav," "header," and "column." While exploring the division tag, we will also continue to use two of the three CSS selector types: **class** and *ID*. We have already explored the third selector type, **tag**, in Chapters 5 and 7.

Results of Chapter 8 Exercises

In the following exercises you will learn to separate sections of the web page using the division tag, **<div>**. You will also make a navigational tool from an unordered list and define divisions as half columns with CSS code (Figure 8.6).

Figure 8.6 In the following exercises you will create a web page that includes a navigation tool derived from an unordered list and several **div** tags that reference class and *ID selectors*.

Download Materials for Chapter 8 Exercises

We will modify the resulting files from Chapter 7 to begin the exercises in Chapter 8. You can download the results files from Chapter 7 exercises on the website. {http://viscommontheweb.wordpress.com/downloads/}

Exercise 1: Adding Divisions in HTML

1. Set up your workspace: Copy and paste the final Chapter 7 exercise files to a new folder named *chapter08*. Open Dreamweaver and define or edit your site to point to the root directory, *chapter08*. Choose Window > Workspace Layout > Designer. Open *index.html* in Dreamweaver, modify the title tag (I titled my page "Chapter Eight"), and save your work.
2. Select the header text "Anna Atkins" in design view. Add a division at the top of the page to separate "Anna Atkins" from the rest of the page by choosing Insert > Layout Objects > Div Tag. Since page content is selected, Dreamweaver will ask you to select how you want to add the **div** tag to the code. Choose the first option in the pull-down menu: Wrap Around Selection (Figure 8.7).

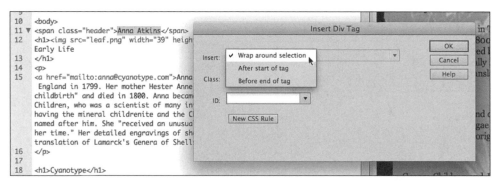

Figure 8.7 Select media in Dreamweaver design view then create a new **div** tag using the Insert menu.

3. View your code (Figure 8.8).

```
10    <body>
11    <div><span class="header">Anna Atkins</span></div>
12    <h1><img src="leaf.png" width="39" height="23" alt="decorative leaf graphic" />
      Early Life
13    </h1>
```

Figure 8.8 The HTML code created to span (or wrap) the header class around the text "Anna Atkins."

Notice the **div** tag is applied around the **span** tag, which is applied around the header text "Anna Atkins." The **span** tag, **<span>**, was used in order to attach a class called "header" to the content that the tag surrounds. Now that we are using the **div** tag, we can eliminate the **span** tag and apply the class to the division. Edit your code to make it more efficient.

Remove excess tags in the HTML code	
`<div><span class="header">` `Anna Atkins</span></div>`	The original code includes the **div** and **span** tags.
`<div class="header">` ~~`<span class="header">`~~ `Anna Atkins`~~`</span>`~~`</div>`	Remove the **span** tag and assign the class to the **div** tag.
`<div class="header">` `Anna Atkins</div>`	The modified code is simpler, more efficient, and results in a smaller file size.

4. Save and preview your files in a browser. So far, it will seem as though nothing has changed.

5. Add two more divisions to break the content of the page into two columns. Select just the first paragraph of text and create a **div** tag around the **<h1>** and paragraph content. Then select the remaining heading and paragraph content, and apply a **div** tag around it (Figure 8.9).

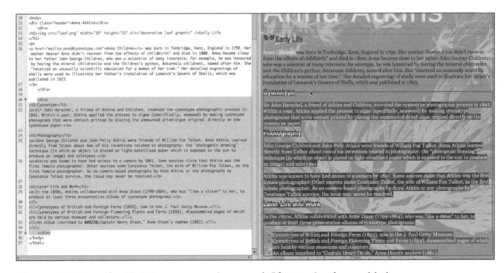

Figure 8.9 View the HTML page once the second **div** tag has been added.

6. To add the final division for a navigation tool on the top of the page, place your cursor just beneath the **body** tag in code view. Choose Insert > Layout Objects > Div Tag and select At Insertion Point from the pull-down menu (Figure 8.10). Dreamweaver will insert the placeholder text, "Content for New Div Tag Goes Here." We will modify that text in the next exercise.

Exercise 2: Creating a Navigation Tool from an Unordered List, Part A—HTML

1. Select the placeholder text surrounded by the first set of **div** tags in code view and then press the Delete key. You might notice that it is difficult to see where

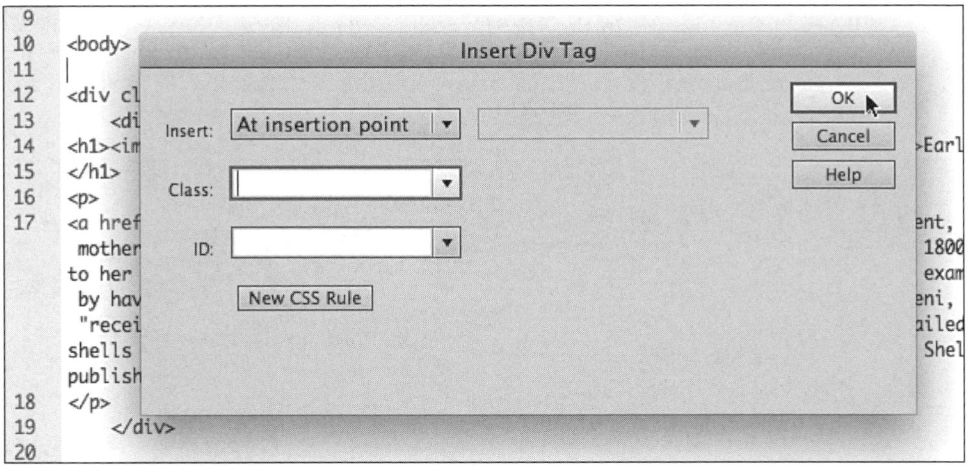

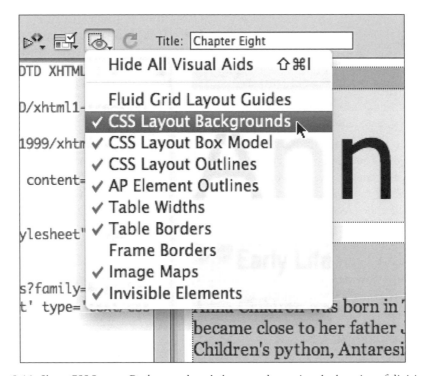

Figure 8.10 Insert a **div** at the "insertion point" or at the location of the cursor in design view.

the new content should be inserted, as the **div** happens to overlap a dark portion of the background image. Select CSS Layout Backgrounds from the Visual Aids pull-down menu (Figure 8.11). Dreamweaver will convert your design view to a series of rectangles, with bright background colors housing the content surrounded by each **div** tag.

Figure 8.11 Show CSS Layout Backgrounds to help see and perceive the location of division tags using the Visual Aids Menu.

2. In the first (empty) div create an unordered list by using the Properties panel or working in code view with **<ul>** and **<li>**. Our list elements will be the navigation buttons for the Anna Atkins website: "Biography," "Timeline," and "Algae and Ferns" (Figure 8.12).

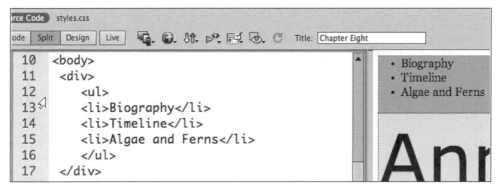

```
10    <body>
11      <div>
12          <ul>
13              <li>Biography</li>
14              <li>Timeline</li>
15              <li>Algae and Ferns</li>
16          </ul>
17      </div>
```

• Biography
• Timeline
• Algae and Ferns

Figure 8.12 Create an unordered list **<ul>** of listed items **<li>** near the top of the page to use as a navigational tool.

Note

If you are using the Properties panel, be sure to select HTML properties (not CSS properties) and then click the Unordered List button.

Exercise 3: Creating a Navigation Tool from an Unordered List, Part B—CSS

Reminder

You created an unordered list in Chapter 7, Exercise 2, Step 7.

Reference

Listamatic is a website that provides the HTML and CSS code you can use or modify in your own projects to generate different types of navigation tools. [http://css.maxdesign.com.au/listamatic/]

1. The CSS required to transform our bulleted list into a horizontal set of links with no bullet points requires a simple declaration block for the listed items in the navigation tool. At this point, you might be comfortable working directly in the CSS code, or you may want to continue to work with the Dreamweaver panels. What follows is a series of screen shots from the CSS Rule Definition panel and the code created by those panel settings. We want to apply these settings to our navigational list, so we'll set up a new rule definition for the *tag selector*, **li**, in the externally linked style sheet, *styles.css*.

Creating a new rule using the Dreamweaver CSS Style and Rule Definition panels	The result of working with the Dreamweaver panels is a New CSS declaration block for **li**
See Figures 8.13, 8.14, 8.15, 8.16, and 8.17	```li { display: inline; padding-right: 20px; list-style-type: none; }```

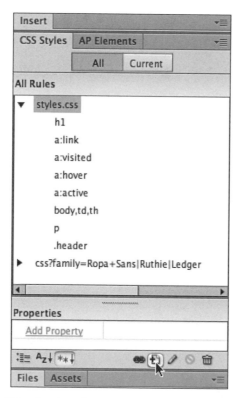

Figure 8.13 Add a new CSS rule using the Dream-weaver CSS Styles panel.

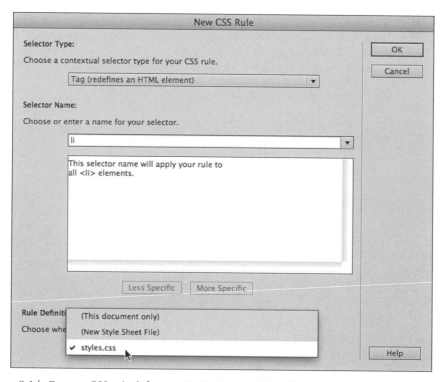

Figure 8.14 Create a CSS rule definition (or declaration block) for the **li** tag selector in the external style sheet named *styles.css*.

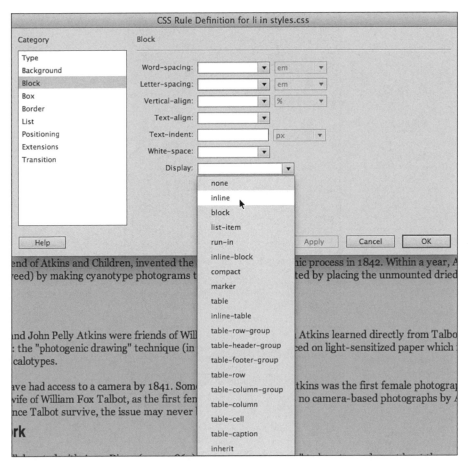

Figure 8.15 **Display**: While there are many display values, the two most commonly used are inline and **block**. If the inline value is applied to a line of text, no paragraph breaks are forced and the text only takes up as much space as it needs. The block value creates a column of text with a paragraph break before and after the block. A block will span the entire width of space that is available.

Figure 8.16 **Padding-right:** This property is used to add space between the elements contained within the selector and its right edge.

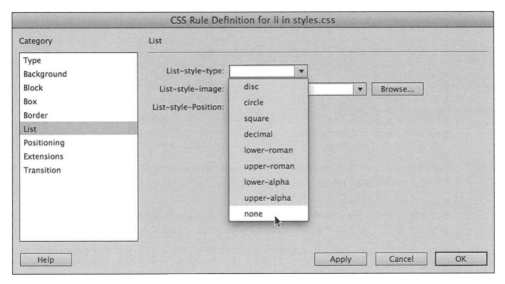

Figure 8.17 **List-style-type:** This property is used to define how the marker will appear in front of each listed item. In this case, we wanted to hide any bullet points (or circles or squares, for instance) so we used the value: **none**.

2. Save your files and preview the page in a browser. You may not have noticed it yet, but we've created a bit of a monster with this code. What happened to the bullet points in the list under the "Later Life and Work" headline? Since we told the HTML code to treat all listed items (anything that is displayed using the **li** tag) with the CSS styles defined with the **li** selector, a bulleted list of content that should have remained as such is now displaying as if it were a navigational tool. *Yikes!* We will make a minor modification to our code as a brief introduction to parents and children, a topic that is addressed in greater detail in Chapter 9, Exercise 5.

3. Since the navigation tool for our page only appears once (in our case, at the top of the page), it makes sense to create a CSS selector with the ID named "nav." View *styles.css* and locate the declaration block for the **li** selector. Place your cursor at the beginning of this selector and type "#nav" (press the spacebar once after the letter v). Your code will be the same, with the addition of the ID **#nav** acting as a parent element to the tag **li**:

```
#nav li {
    display: inline;
    padding-right: 20px;
    list-style-type: none;
}
```

4. Let's review what we just did. Instead of using the tag selector named **li** (which modifies all listed items in the HTML document), we added a "parent" ID named "nav" to the selector (narrowing the power of the selector). Now, if you save and preview your work (you may need to refresh your browser), you will notice that you are back to seeing bullet points everywhere, including the listed items in the navigation area. We need to add "nav" to our source code for the magic to happen.

5. Return to your source code. Add the "nav" ID to your navigation **div**:

```
<div id="nav">
```

6. Save your files and preview the page in a browser. *Voila!* You have a top naviga-tion bar that is horizontal and does not display bullet points, and you have listed items in the last paragraph block on the page that ignore the styles in the navi-gation bar. Our CSS code indicates that every **<li>** in the section of the HTML document governed by the ID named "nav" should be styled with the display, padding, and list-style-type values we selected. Another way to say this is that all **<li>** who are children of **#nav** will be styled with the properties and values defined in our declaration block.

7. Finally, add **<a href>** to the three items in order to define them as links (Figure 8.18). I will simply add the code **<a href = "#">** to indicate that I intend to create a link. The pound sign (#) is a placeholder for a link reference. Don't forget to close the tag **</a>** around all three navigational links.

Exercise 4: Creating a Half-page Column Using CSS

VIDEO WALKTHROUGH The **<div>** tag by itself simply puts a box around an area in the design window, as we have seen in the first exercise. Nothing will change on your web page if you preview it in the browser—that is why we turned on our visual aids to show the CSS layout back-grounds. The **<div>** tag is most commonly used with a CSS selector—it either assumes properties declared in an ID or a class. In your HTML file, you will always write the code as in one of the following two examples, where "name" represents the name of the ID or class specified in the CSS file:

```
<div id="name">
<div class="name">
```

Before we can assign an ID or class to a **<div>** we need to create one in the style sheet. For this exercise we will create a new class selector. A class can be used repeatedly within an HTML file.

1. Click the New CSS Rule button in the bottom of the CSS Styles panel. Select Class from the Selector Type pull-down menu, name the class **.halfcol**, and make sure that the *styles.css* page you created is selected in the Rule Definition pull-down menu.

Note

CSS naming conventions hold that the period (.) always precedes the name of a class, while the pound sign (#) precedes the name of an ID. Think about this from the browser's point of view—there has to be some indication in the declaration block that you intend to create a class or an ID. So a name is more than a name—it is also the place where you assign the value of class or ID to the CSS declaration block.

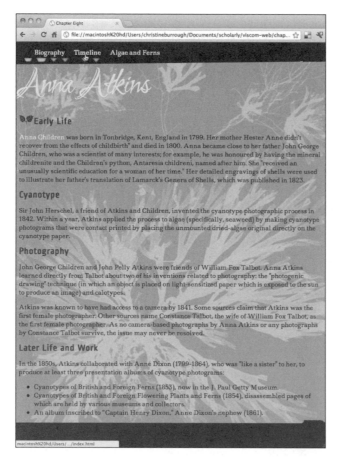

Figure 8.18 View the web page with its new navigational links. As a result of completing these exercises, the final HTML code in the navigation area looks like this:

```
<div id="nav">
    <ul>
       <li><a href="#">Biography</a></li>
       <li><a href="#">Timeline</a></li>
       <li><a href="#">Algae and Ferns</a></li>
    </ul>
</div>
```

The final CSS declaration block for the listed items in the navigation area looks like this:

```
#nav li {
    display: inline;
    padding-right: 20px;
    list-style-type: none;
}
```

2. In the Rule Definition dialog box, choose the Block category and select Left from the Text-align pull-down menu. The **Text-align** property is used to align contents of the **<div>**. You will most often align contents with left-alignment, but sometimes you will want to center or even right-align elements. Next, click the Box category and add 15 pixels of padding to the top, right, bottom, and left sides. Padding is used to create space between the edges of the inside of the **<div>** container and the content held within it. Click OK to exit the dialog. The resulting CSS code in *styles.css* should look like this:

```
.halfcol {
  text-align: left;
  padding: 15px;
}
```

Note

In CSS, padding and margin values are listed in the order of the face of a clock: top, right, bottom, left. When a property that can contain four values (one for each edge of the box) is set to just one value, that value is applied to all four sides of the box. That is, **padding: 15px;** is the same as **padding: 15px 15px 15px 15px;**

The CSS Box Model

The CSS box model demonstrates the overall size (most importantly, the width) of the rectangular boxes that result from employing the **div** tag. The main reason for understanding the **div** tag as a box model is to gain insight into the formula for arriving at the width and height of a box created with a CSS rule. You can create and modify box elements in the CSS Rules Definition dialog box by selecting the Box category. Using CSS, you may add width, margin, border, and padding properties to a selector. These four properties are combined together when measuring the width of a box. For instance, a box with a width of 200 pixels, a margin of 10 pixels, a border of 5 pixels, and 15 pixels of padding would take up the sum space of the left border + left margin + left padding + box width + right padding + right margin + right border, or 10 + 5 + 15 + 200 + 15 + 5 + 10 = 260 pixels (Figure 8.19). You can read more about the box model on the W3 site [http://www.w3.org/TR/CSS21/box.html], but it might be even more fun to interact with the box model on Tstme. [http://www.redmelon.net/tstme/box_model/]

3. None of the divisions in the HTML document are styled with the properties established in **.halfcol**. Styles must be applied to the HTML document, and when the selector is a class or an ID, this means you have to purposefully apply the style in the HTML code. Apply the "halfcol" ID to the HTML file by selecting the two **<div>** tags in the design window (one at a time) and choosing Halfcol from the Class pull-down list in the Properties panel (Figure 8.20). Alternatively, edit each of the two **<div>** tags in your HTML document so they read **<div class="halfcol">**.

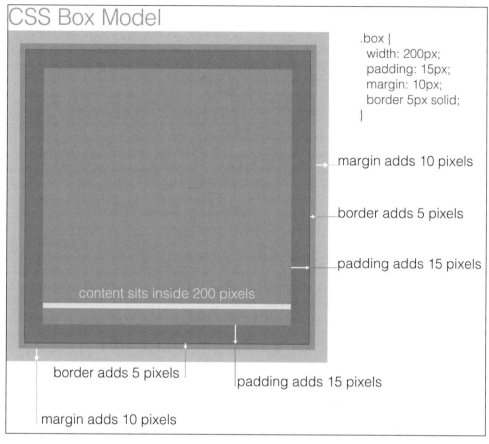

Figure 8.19 The CSS box model illustrates that the ultimate width of a "box" created with CSS width, margin, padding, and border values is the sum of those values on the left and right sides. *Illustration courtesy of xtine.*

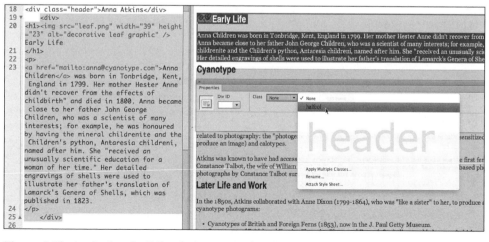

Figure 8.20 Apply the **.halfcol** class to the first division using the Dreamweaver Properties panel.

VIDEO
WALKTHROUGH

> **Note**
>
> Dreamweaver will support you with code hints that help you choose your selector when you type class or ID followed by the equal sign (=) in code view.

4. Save your files and then preview your page in a browser. You will notice only minimal changes (if any). Next we will modify **.halfcol** in a way that will result in visible changes to the layout of the page.

5. Columns of text are easiest to read when the line length is not too terribly long. Right now, the lengths of the lines of text in our divisions are as long as the browser is stretched open. To create better legibility, we will control the width of the columns, which will force the lengths of each line of text to become shorter. Double-click **.halfcol** from the list of selectors in the CSS Styles panel. Edit the Rule Definition dialog box by selecting the Box category and changing the width and the float properties. By assigning the **<div>** tag a width, you can control how large the div container will be before content wraps to the next line. Set the **width** value to 400 pixels. Change the **float** value to **Left**. **Float** is a property used to position a **<div>** with respect to other elements on the page. In this layout, the float property (with the left value) on the first division is responsible for the left alignment of the second division along the same baseline. Click OK. View *styles.css* where **.haflcol** should look like this:

```
.halfcol {
  text-align: left;
  padding: 15px;
  float: left;
  width: 400px;
}
```

> **Note**
>
> You can add a width value to a selector using pixels, percentages, or ems (elastic measurements).

6. Save your files and preview the page in a browser.

 ### The Art and Craft of Code

In 2007, Young-Hae Chang Heavy Industries created a spoof of their résumé using Flash that does (eventually) list some of their accomplishments, embedded in a layered audio/visual typographic experience (Figures 8.21, 8.22, and 8.23). It is debatable now whether Adobe Flash will be a dominant tool for developing animated web content (or strictly gaming content) in the future, but the design of Young-Hae Chang Heavy Industries' "Résumé I?" web page is a timeless work of graphic, networked art. [http://www.yhchang.com/RESUMAY_I.html]

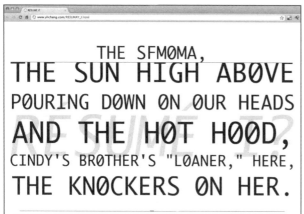

Figure 8.21

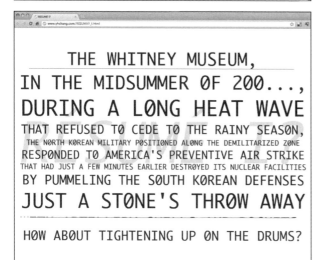

Figure 8.22

Figures 8.21, 8.22, and 8.23 In *Resumé I?* Young-Hae Chang Heavy Industries showcase their accomplishments after an audio/ textual narrative that could take place in a swanky lounge club. *Courtesy of Young-Hae Chang Heavy Industries.*

Create, Reflect, Critique

View the two-column layouts listed on Mashable's article, "80+ Free 2-Column Website Templates." [http://mashable.com/2007/09/29/2-column-website-templates/] Can you draw a sketch (using primitive tools such as paper and pencil) of where the **div** tags would be placed on several of those layouts?

For a more challenging activity, revisit the résumé you created in Chapter 7. Add a second column and separate the sections of the document using **div** tags. Remember: The optimal line length for legibility on a printed document is about three to four inches in length (or about 50 to 75 characters).

Reference

See Christian Holt's "Readability: The Optimal Line Length" as an additional resource for this chapter. [http://baymard.com/blog/line-length-readability]

Glossary Words

Class selector, ID selector, tag selector, **<div>**, **<li>**, **<ul>**

9 PAGE CONTAINERS

VIDEO
INTRODUCTION

Principles, History, Theory

Wertheimer, Gestalt, and Unity

Isn't it appropriate that the word *unity* needs "u" and "i"?

After the Vikings outgrew their surroundings in the Normandy region of northern France during the 12th century, they looked for other lands to conquer. Since these Normans, as they came to be called, had lived in the country for about 150 years, put away their pagan ways, adopted the Christian religion, incorporated the French language into their own, and intermarried as much and as often as they could, they held no animosity toward their French hosts. Consequently, William, the Duke of Normandy (also known as William II and William the Bastard, but ended up with the more exciting name of William the Conqueror), chose not to send his troops south, but looked north and decided England was ripe for the picking. After several encounters between the opposing forces, the British Saxons were defeated at the Battle of Hastings on October 14, 1066, in which Harold II, the last Anglo-Saxon King of England, was killed. A detailed visual description of the confrontation was depicted in a 75-yard-long, handmade embroidered work named the Bayeux Tapestry. It is considered one of the first examples of narrative storytelling in a cartoon-like format produced by Western civilization (Figure 9.1).

Figure 9.1 The fierce fighting is evident in this panel from the Bayeux Tapestry that shows spears and swords used to slay soldiers and their steeds. *Courtesy of Serge Lachinov.*

Equally important, Garrison Keillor in "The Writer's Almanac" notes that the Norman victory "had a larger and more pronounced effect on the development of the English language than any other event in history. Within the course of a few centuries, English went from being a strictly Germanic language to one infused with a large Latinate vocabulary, which came via French."

As positions of power, from landowners to government officials, were handed out to French-speaking compatriots over many years, Old English was gradually transformed into Middle English, the basis for the modern version of the language today. Nevertheless, because

French was the official language of the Court in England until the 15th century, Keillor observes that such English words as *allegiance, coroner, governor, regal, royalties, sovereign,* and *subject* are a result of the merger of the two cultures. Another common Anglo-French word invented during the occupation of England was *unity*.

Along with contrast (discussed in Chapter 2), balance, rhythm, and unity form the basis for what might be considered "good" design. However, such a designation is fraught with caveats because, like beauty, "good" is often a highly subjective determination. Good design changes over time and varies among cultures. Styles, as do fads, capture immediate interests but become outdated just as quickly. One method for determining good design is to be aware of the needs of your audience.

Unity in visual communication on the Web is a presentational concept in which separate elements are seen as a consistent whole. Colors, lines, typography, illustrations, navigational buttons, and so on all combine to achieve a coherent visual style (Figure 9.2).

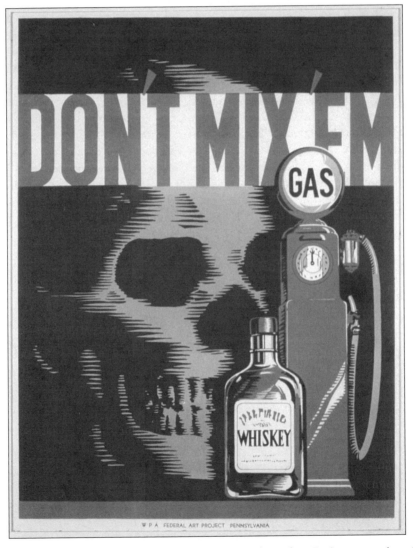

Figure 9.2 In this 1937 WPA Federal Art Project poster by Robert Lachenmann, the color red unifies the stark graphics of the visual messages. *Courtesy of the Library of Congress.*

Important to the concept of unity is the ***gestalt theory of visual perception*** with its famous phrase:

The whole is different from the sum of its parts.

Every designer works with a palette of hundreds of possible elements or variations to include in a piece. After much experience, experimentation, and inspiration, individual components mesh into a unified, synchronized, and organized work in which no one part is more noticeable or important than any other.

German psychologist Max Wertheimer received his inspiration for the gestalt theory of visual perception during a train trip in the summer of 1910. As he looked out the windows of the moving train, he realized that he could see the outside scene even though the opaque wall of the train and the window frame partially blocked his view.

He left the train in Frankfurt, went to a toy store, and bought a popular children's toy of the day—a stroboscope, similar to a flipbook. The flipbook is a simple form of cartoon animation. On the first page of the book, a drawing—say, of a cartoon character in a running position—is displayed on the right side of the page. On each subsequent piece of paper, the drawing of the figure is slightly different, depending on the actions intended by the artist. To see the effect of the moving character, a viewer uses a thumb to rapidly flip the pages (Figure 9.3). A modern example of this animation technique can be seen in a music video from the Dutch pop group Kraak & Smaak for their 2007 hit, "Squeeze Me."

Figure 9.3 Dogs cannot do this. A flipbook becomes animated when its pages are flipped by a viewer's thumb. *Photo courtesy of Paul Martin Lester.*

Wertheimer's observations during the train trip and play time with the flipbook led to more research at the University of Frankfurt. He concluded that the eye merely takes in all the visual stimuli, whereas the brain arranges the sensations into an image. It is the cohesiveness of an entire presentation that creates the concept of unity.

Visual communicators create unity when they use similar elements placed close together that are repeated with frequency to create rhythm. Sections of a web page that are meant to be separate are often divided by white space or a fine rule, but the overall graphic look of the presentation is unified through a consistent choice of similar visual elements (Figure 9.4).

The use of unity helps create a graphic style that joins the visual elements within an individual web page and all the other pieces that are a part of your website. It gives your work a sense of stylistic consistency so that a visitor will not feel lost after she clicks a button. Just as you don't want a reader of *The New Yorker* magazine to turn a page and suddenly find herself confronted with design elements better suited for *Wired*, your web users should appreciate when the visual language you start with has not suddenly been transformed by marauding Vikings.

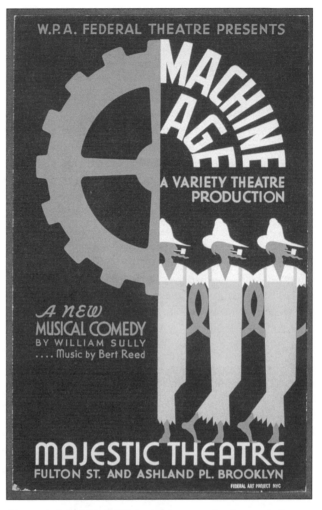

Figure 9.4 In Martin Weitzman's poster for the musical comedy "Machine Age," unity is expressed through the similarly shaped and dressed corncob smoking and dancing hillbillies. *Courtesy of the Library of Congress*

Practice

Containing the Page to Create Unity in the Viewport

We have already been using similar styles in marked-up areas on our page in order to see the kind of continuity of form required for achieving unity. In the following exercises we will continue to modify our body copy and headings so that there is repeated visual treatment to similar elements on the page. However, all visual elements relate not only to each other but also to the confines of the "page" itself. In the case of designing for the browser (with its inescapably unknown, user-defined size), the most commonly practiced method of establishing a unified area for the page content is to create what I will refer to as a *"container div."* This division will define the edges of the space that holds all of the page content and can then be related to the remaining space between itself and the browser.

In the last chapter we implemented **div** tags to organize the web page layout. We used the **Float** property with the value **Left** to keep two columns side by side. By default, content flows from the top left of the browser page to the bottom-right corner. So far, all of our page content hugs the left margin of the browser.

The next logical question is: How can I center web page content in the space of the browser?

In short, the answer is to use another **<div>**. In fact, this is such a standard procedure that most coders and designers use a **<div>** with an ID called "container," "wrapper," or "content." This tag will be set to a width that is "safe" for the majority of online viewers (see the "How Big Is the Web?" area in the Practice section of Chapter 2). At the time of this writing, 960 pixels is considered to be a safe width for containing the content of a page. In addition to establishing a width, we will tell the browser to divide any remaining margin space outside the container division in half in order to center the container on the page.

Let's view the code of a few websites to see the container **div** in action. In Chrome, I selected View > Developer > View Source from the top menu bar. In other browsers, you will find an equivalent to "View Source," most likely in the View menu. We will see the HTML code and any other programming languages used in it or linked to it (such as CSS and JavaScript).

What you might notice is that while the container divisions identified in Figures 9.5, 9.6, and 9.7 all assume different names (*container, wrap,* and *shell*), they do share similar properties and values in the CSS code. Namely, a container division is utilized to center

---

Fixed, Fluid, or Elastic Layouts?

Containers can be set to a specific number of pixels, as we will see in the following exercises. This style of treating the relationship of the content in the container to the space on the page is called a *fixed-width layout*. Instead of using pixels, you can set the container to a width in ems or a percentage of the page for a *fluid-width* layout. However, in the case of a fluid layout you run the risk of long lines of typography, which can result in decreased legibility.

An *elastic layout* is entirely based on ems, rather than pixels or percentages.

We will use a fixed-width layout for the container division, and we will also use ems to measure other areas of the page.

Reference

See Kayla Knight's "Fixed vs. Fluid vs. Elastic Layout: What's the Right One for You?" article on the Smashing website for more information on these different approaches to setting up the container. [http://coding .smashingmagazine.com/2009/06/02/ fixed-vs-fluid-vs-elastic-layout-whats-the-right-one-for-you/]

Note

Other commonly used names for the "container" of the page are "wrapper" and "content." I often use "content" to name some of the material that is placed inside the container.

---

content in the web browser that has two key features: the margins are set to the value "auto" on the left and right sides, and the width property is established (in these screen shots you can see that the widths take on different values, from 960 pixels wide to 980 pixels to 1000 pixels).

Figure 9.5 The content for the *Salon.com* home page is blurred to avoid copyright infringement. Notice that the CSS code seen in the bottom right panel reveals the code for two container classes assigned to the div id, "contentContainer."

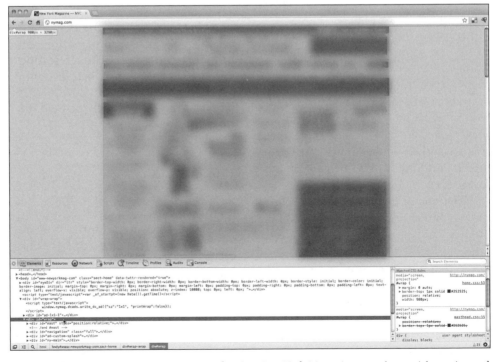

Figure 9.6 *NYmag.com* is the home page for the *New York Magazine*, seen here with stories and images blurred. Using developer tools in Chrome, you can see that the programmers labeled the container "wrap." The **div** id, "wrap," keeps all of the content centered in the web browser.

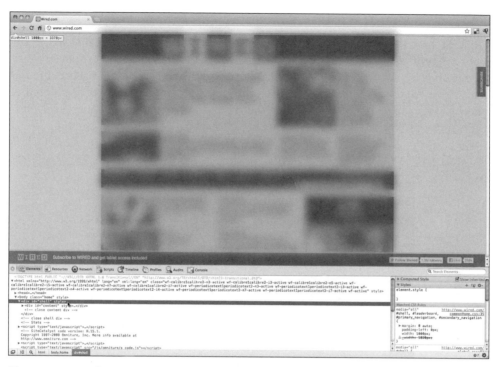

Figure 9.7 *Wired.com* is the home page for *Wired Magazine*, seen here with stories and images blurred. The programmers at *Wired* named the container **div**, "shell."

Containing Floating Elements

A container **div** is used to keep all of the content items on the page organized within a bounding box. But you will soon find that there is one challenge when it comes to using a container **div**: any divisions that are placed inside the container that are assigned the **float** property will not be vertically recognized by the container. There are a couple of ways to overcome this annoyance: use an **overflow** property on the container or use a **clear** property on an HTML element that appears after the floating divisions. In this chapter we will use the **overflow** property on the container to remedy our problem. In Chapter 10 you will learn about the **clear** property.

Comments

If you are viewing the code on other websites, you may notice that *comments* are often added to create clarity for onlookers or teammates. This area of the code is essentially "skipped" by the web browser. There is a syntax for writing comments in the HTML and CSS code, as follows:

In HTML you can use the syntax "open angle bracket-exclamation point-dash-dash" before comments, and "dash-dash close angle bracket" to close the comments, as follows:

```
<!-- HTML comments should be inserted here -->
```

In CSS code, surround comments with slash asterisk (**/***) before the comments and an asterisk slash (***/**) after them:

```
/*CSS comments should be inserted here*/
```

Results of Chapter 9 Exercises

While the main focus of this chapter is to learn how to add a container division to the page, you will also modify the design of the web page after analyzing visual issues of spacing and alignment. Adjustments will be made to the body copy and the background image. You will use parent and children selectors to adjust the alignment of a set of bullet points (Figure 9.8). Finally, after completing the last exercise you will have added comments to your CSS and HTML documents.

Figure 9.8 In the following exercises you will create a container **div** in order to center the page content within a web browser. You will also add comments to your code.

Download Materials for Chapter 9 Exercises

We will modify the resulting files from the Chapter 8 exercises to begin the exercises in this chapter. Create a copy of these files on your hard drive, or download them from the website. [http://viscommontheweb.wordpress.com/downloads/]

Exercise 1: Adding the Container

VIDEO
WALKTHROUGH

1. **Set up your workspace**: Copy and paste the final Chapter 8 exercise files to a new folder named *chapter09*. Open Dreamweaver and define or edit your site to point to the root directory, *chapter09*. Choose Window > Workspace Layout > Designer. Open index.html in Dreamweaver, modify the title tag (I titled my page "Chapter Nine"), and save your work.

2. In the HTML code, add a **<div>** at the top of the page, just beneath **<body>** (Figure 9.9). Don't forget to close the tag, **</div>**, at the end of the page, just before the close body tag, **</body>**. The new **<div>** is used to contain (or wrap around) all of the content on the page. For this reason, this particular **<div>** often utilizes a CSS ID named "container."

```
10   <body>
11   <div>
12 ⌐    <div id="nav">
13       <ul>
```

Figure 9.9 Place an additional division tag directly beneath **<body>** to begin what will become the container **div**.

3. Since the container is used only one time on the page, we will create a new ID selector in the external style sheet to define this rule. Click the New CSS Style Rule button to create the ID named "container" in the external style sheet (Figure 9.10).

Note

Remember, the name of a CSS ID should always start with the pound sign (#).

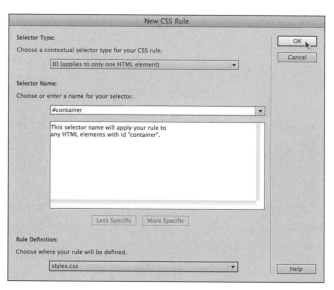

Figure 9.10 Define the container ID selector (saved to the external style sheet, *styles.css*) in the Dreamweaver Rule Definition Dialog box.

4. In the CSS Rule Definition dialog box, select the category Box and set the width to 960 pixels and the margins to 0, auto, 0, auto—for the top, right, bottom, and left sides of the element (Figure 9.11). This action is the most important part of creating the container. Before you exit the dialog box, also be sure to set the text-align property to Center (this will center elements inside the container div tag). Use the Block Category to select Center from the text-align pull-down menu.

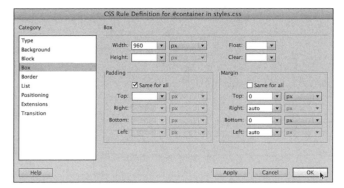

Figure 9.11 Set the width and margin properties in the Box category of the Rule Definition Dialog Box.

You must define a box width. Since many users view web pages with screen resolutions of approximately 1024 pixels wide, choosing a value that is less than 1000 pixels is essentially making a safe bet that most people will be able to see all of the content on the page without having to scroll left or right. The margin values are also significant. The top and bottom margin values are negotiable; however, the right and left margins must be set to Auto in order to center the container **<div>** in the browser. Applying the Auto value translates to "make the remaining browser spacing even on the left and right sides, given that the box is 960 pixels wide."

Consolidating CSS Code

Margin and padding values are always written in CSS in the order top-right-bottom-left (clockwise). In the CSS code you might see something like this, where the margins are set to 5 pixels of space on the top and bottom and 10 pixels on the right and left sides:

> **Margin: 5px 10px 5px 10px;**

However, this code could also be simplified to:

> **Margin: 5px 10px;**

In this case, the first number (5px) is applied to the top and bottom of the selected content and the second number (10px) is the value applied to the right and left sides of the content.

---

5. So far we inserted an unnamed **<div>** tag in the HTML file and we have created a CSS ID named "container" with the properties that will create a centered box in the web browser. Save and preview your work in a browser. You will notice that it seems nothing has happened. Nothing will happen until you assign the CSS style to your HTML content (in this case, the first div on the page). In the HTML code, type a space next to the word "div" before the closing bracket (Figure 9.12), and then type "id" (Figure 9.13). You may notice the code help in Dreamweaver assists you with menu items such as id and class. Select id and press the Return key. Select Container from the list and press the Return key again. If you do not see the code help menus, simply type the code **<div id="container">** into your HTML document (Figure 9.14).

Figures 9.12, 9.13, and 9.14 Use Dreamweaver code hints to add the container ID to the division tag in code view.

Note

If you modify the code in Dreamweaver's code view, you will not see changes occur in the design view until you click any part of the design view in the application.

6. Save your HTML and CSS files and preview your page in a browser (Figure 9.15).

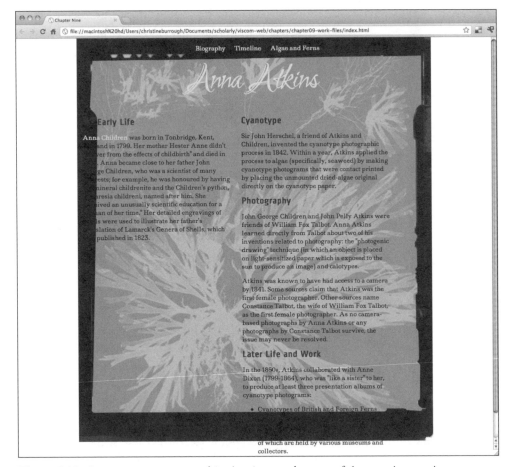

Figure 9.15 Content appears centered in the viewport because of the container settings.

7. Right now it looks as if our page layout is behaving our commands. However, turn on the Visual Aids in Dreamweaver to see CSS Layout Backgrounds. There is something fishy about the layout—it doesn't appear that a background for the container **div** stretches all the way to the end of the page. In other words, if you gave the container a border (nothing we want to do in this design, but just for the sake of argument, let's see it), it would not surround all of the content on the page. Double-click **#container** from the CSS Styles panel in Dreamweaver. Select the Border category and apply a solid, thick, yellow (#FF0) line to all sides of the **div** (Figure 9.16). Save your files and preview the page in a browser (Figure 9.17).

Figures 9.16 and 9.17 Add a border to the container rule definition and see that it does not appear to extend to the bottom of the page.

8. *Doh!* The bright yellow border only surrounds the heading area on the page. It ignores all of the content in the two columns. What do those two columns have in common? The text in those columns is placed inside a division that has been

assigned the CSS **float** property. A container **div** will ignore nested divisions that utilize the **float** property. This omission can be annoying, as it is highly common to use a container **div** in conjunction with nested divisions that are assigned the **float** property. To correct it, add one more property and value to the **#container** declaration block in the CSS style sheet as follows. Then save *styles.css* and preview the page in a browser (Figure 9.18).

```
#container {
  text-align: center;
  width: 960px;
  margin-top: 0px;
  margin-right: auto;
  margin-bottom: 0px;
  margin-left: auto;
  border: thick solid #FF0;
  overflow:hidden;
}
```

Note

The **overflow** property in CSS tells the selected element (usually a division) what to do with content that extends beyond its borders.

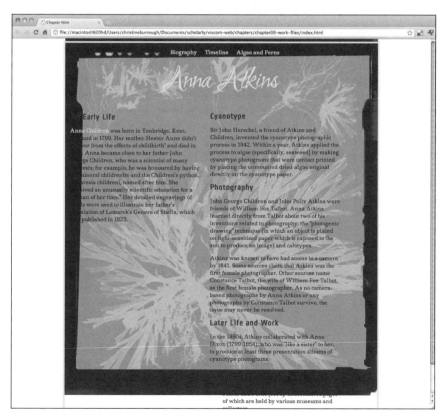

Figure 9.18 Due to the **overflow** property, the container extends to the bottom of the page. We can now delete the border properties.

9. The border extends all the way to the edge of the content. Our content does surpass the bottom edge of our background image (something we'll address next and remedy in the following chapters), but at least there is a border at the bottom of the page. Return to Dreamweaver and see that your design view (with CSS Layout Backgrounds enabled) shows a background color in a rectangle surrounding all page elements (Figure 9.19).

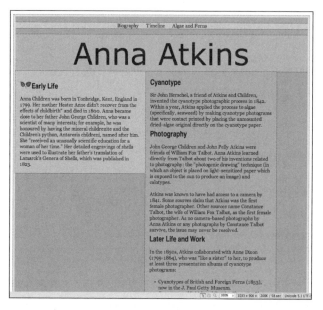

Figure 9.19 Notice that the visual aids help us to know if the container surrounds all page elements.

10. Make a final adjustment to the CSS code for the container **div**. View *styles.css* and modify the container selector to consolidate all of the margin declarations on one line and remove the border declaration:

```
#container {
  text-align: center;
  width: 960px;
  overflow: hidden;
  margin: 0px auto;
  border: thick solid #FF0;
  margin-top: 0px;
  margin-right: auto;
  margin-bottom: 0px;
  margin-left: auto;
}
```

Note

When you assign the value zero you do not need to add a unit of measurement. Zero pixels is the same as zero ems, which is the same as zero percent: zero is zero. You can use 0px or you can simply code with 0.

11. Save your files and preview the page in a browser.

Exercise 2: Spacing and Alignment

1. Eliminating strange spaces will probably take a lot of your time when you are first starting to learn how to code with HTML and CSS. In our current document, there is unwanted margin space at the top of the browser, just before the navigation tool. The following CSS code provides a quick, simple way to eliminate that extra spacing using a universal selector:

```
*  {
  margin: 0px;
  padding: 0px;
}
```

The asterisk (*) is a **universal selector**—it applies a style to all elements. This is a common way to reset various browser default behaviors. We will use it to set the margins and padding to zero. Type this CSS declaration block into the top of your style sheet. Save the CSS file and preview your work in a browser.

2. Overall, the design elements in the positive space of the page are in need of some negative space (or you might say "breathing room"). We will add that space now with the **padding** property. Let's start with the navigation tool. Add 1em, or approximately 16 pixels of padding, to the navigation tool by adding the following code to your style sheet:

```
#nav {
  padding: 1em;
}
```

In the style sheet the **nav** id is referenced only in the declaration for "children" of **#nav** using the **<li>** tag. We will investigate *parents* and *children* in Exercise 5. For now, we simply declared that everything within a division that takes the styles for **#nav** should have 1em of padding on the top, right, bottom, and left sides (approximately 16 pixels of padding if the user does not change her default typography settings).

> **Note**
>
> You could have created **#nav** using the Dreamweaver Rule Definition dialog box. However, when you become familiar with typing the CSS code into the style sheet, you will find that it is more efficient to type the code.

3. Modify the padding that is already established in the **halfcol** declaration block. Either modify your CSS code in *styles.css* or use the Rule Definition dialog box in Dreamweaver. This time we will add padding only to the top and left sides of the selector (Figure 9.20):

```
.halfcol {
  text-align: left;
  padding: 1em 0 0 3.75em;
  float: left;
  width: 400px;
}
```

4. Save your files and preview your page in a browser.

```
.halfcol {
    text-align: left;
    padding: 1em 0 0 3.75em;
    float: left;
    width: 400px;
}
```

Figure 9.20 If you used the CSS Rule Definition dialog box, click to your style sheet to see the modified code.

5. **Your turn!** Add 1em (about 16 pixels) of padding to the top of the **h1** selector and 0.5em (about 8 pixels) to the bottom of the **h1** selector. Save your files and preview the page in a browser.

Exercise 3: Adjusting the Body Copy

Since we wrapped the paragraph tag, **<p>**, around all of the body copy in the HTML document, we can modify the CSS styles applied to that tag by adjusting the **p** selector in *styles.css*.

1. View your work in a browser and notice that the background interferes with your ability to read the body copy (what should be clearly understood as a foreground design element). We will adjust the **line-height** property, which is the CSS property that most closely resonates with the typographic concept of leading (the space between lines of text). View your source code in Dreamweaver, and double-click the **p** selector in the Dreamweaver CSS Styles panel. Enter 1.2em in the Line-height field (Figure 9.21). Notice that the space between the lines of text in the body copy decreases and the paragraphs become slightly darker in value for greater contrast with the background graphic.

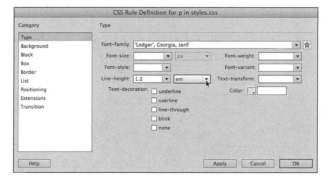

Figure 9.21 Modify the **line-height** property in the Type category of the Rule Definition dialog box.

2. View *styles.css* and add the text-indent property to the declaration block for the **p** selector with the same value, as follows:

```
p {
  font-family: 'Ledger', Georgia, serif;
  line-height: 1.2em;
  text-indent: 1.2em;
}
```

Now the body copy is easier to read and new paragraphs are indented.

Exercise 4: Positioning an Image as the Background of a CSS Selector

The first heading on the page has a decorative leaf image file positioned to the left of its text. View the HTML code and notice that this image is embedded in the source document (Figure 9.22).

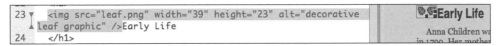

Figure 9.22 Select the **`<img src>`** tag for *leaf.png* from the HTML code where it is inserted or embedded on the page. We will delete the image from the HTML code and insert it into the CSS code using the **background** property of the **h1** selector.

Suppose we want to see this leaf image appear to the left of every heading on the page—can you imagine how we would modify the CSS code to facilitate this idea?

1. In the HTML source code, remove the image tag that appears near the first heading, **<h1>**, or click the image of the leaf in the design view window and press the Delete key.
2. Double-click the **h1** selector from the CSS Styles panel in Dreamweaver and select the Background category. Modify your settings so they match those in Figure 9.23: the background is set to *leaf.png*. It will not tile, or repeat on the page (no-repeat), and it appears in the top-left corner of the selector area.

Figure 9.23 Add *leaf.png* to the **background** property (in the Background category) via the Rule Definition dialog box for **h1**.

3. If you have CSS Layout Backgrounds turned on (or checked) in the Visual Aids menu, you will not see background CSS images in design view. Turn them off using the Visual Aids pull-down menu to see that the image is added to the **h1** selector wherever it appears on the page.

Note

Dreamweaver does not always preview your web layout accurately. Always view your work in a browser for an accurate view of your design.

4. The leaf appears near all of the level-one headings on the page, but they are not positioned correctly (Figure 9.24).

Figure 9.24 View where the background image appears on the web page due to the **h1** selector.

5. First we will take care of the vertical placement of the leaf image; then we will correct the horizontal relationship between the image and the type. Replace the value "top" in the **background-position** property of *styles.css* using elastic measurements. "Top" positions the background image at the top of where the **<h1>** content might appear. This does not relate well to the actual typography displayed on the page. Push the leaf down, away from the top, by using a positive value. I set mine to 0.9em because I did not like seeing the leaf dip below the baseline of the typography at 1em (Figure 9.25). Keep in mind that all browsers will display your settings a little differently, so although you are modifying based on what you see in Chrome, Firefox, or Safari, for instance, you cannot assume that the precision of your eye for design will be upheld in all online viewing situations. (Don't despair—we will test our work in multiple browsers in Chapter 14).

Using Numeric Values to Position a Background Image in CSS	
| ```
h1 {
    font-family: 'Ropa Sans', sans-serif;
    font-size: 1.5em;
    color: #009;
    background-image: url(leaf.png);
    background-repeat: no-repeat;
    background-position: left top;
}
``` | The original **h1** declaration block positions the leaf to the top left of the heading area |
| ```
h1 {
    font-family: 'Ropa Sans', sans-serif;
    font-size: 1.5em;
    color: #009;
    background-image: url(leaf.png);
    background-repeat: no-repeat;
    background-position: left .9em;
}
``` | Replace the value "top" with a numeric value to nudge it away from the border area |

Figure 9.25 The background image is positioned in accordance with the numeric measurement in the **background** CSS property, as you will discover in Step 7.

6. If you try to set the leaf away from the type horizontally, you might run into a little trouble. Try replacing "left" in the background position property with a negative value (such as −1em), and you will soon see that the leaf image appears cut off because there is not enough space. Instead of realigning the leaf image, we will adjust the typography using the padding property as follows:

```
h1 {
    font-family: 'Ropa Sans', sans-serif;
    font-size: 1.5em;
    color: #009;
    padding: 1em 0 0 1.8em;
    background-image: url(leaf.png);
    background-repeat: no-repeat;
    background-position: left .9em;
}
```

7. Finally, consolidate the background properties in the CSS code to make it easier to read. The order is important: you set the image first, then the horizontal position, then the vertical position, and then if or how the background image repeats. Save your work and preview it in a browser (Figure 9.26). The final **h1** declaration block is as follows:

```
h1 {
    font-family: 'Ropa Sans', sans-serif;
    font-size: 1.5em;
    color: #009;
    padding: 1em 0 0 1.8em;
    background: url(leaf.png) left .9em no-repeat;
}
```

Link

See the W3 specification for the complete order of background properties. [http://www.w3.org/wiki/CSS/Properties/background]

Figure 9.26 When the background leaf image is properly placed in the **h1** tag selector, it should display to the left of each first-level headline, on or near the baseline of the typography.

Exercise 5: Parent and Children Selectors

In the last paragraph on the page, notice that the text next to the bullet points appears in alignment with the body copy. However, the bullet points are in the gutter (the mostly negative space between the two columns on the page). We do not want to disrupt this important column of negative space. Instead, the bullets should be indented beneath the paragraph, while the listed items of text should be indented even farther. To modify the design, we will declare padding specifically for this content. Look in the source code and you will find that the list items are surrounded by the **<ul>** tag. Also, **<ul>** is nested inside a **div** that is defined by **.halfcol**. In other words, to target the list items, we will create a declaration block for the child tag **ul** of the parent selector **.halfcol**. All unordered list items inside the half column will have the properties and values ascribed to the rule set **.halfcol ul**. Add the following declaration to your style sheet to add top and left padding to the unordered list and then save and preview your page in a browser (Figure 9.27).

```
.halfcol ul {
    padding: .25em 0 0 1.5em;
}
```

Figure 9.27 Listed items in the second column, adorned with bullet points, are nudged to the right so the line of continuation at the left edge of the list is tucked under the preceding paragraph.

Exercise 6: Adding Comments

Finally, add comments to the HTML and CSS code as a reminder (or hint) about what you had intended to achieve. Use **<!--insert code hints here -->** to add comments to your HTML document and **/* insert code hints here */** to add comments to your CSS document (Figures 9.28 and 9.29). You may want to reposition declaration blocks in order to group similar treatments together. Be careful! When you copy and paste you risk losing or adding a curly bracket, semicolon, or other important element. This could result in some frustration when it's time to validate and debug your code (we will tackle this in Chapters 13 and 14).

```
<!DOCTYPE html PUBLIC "-//W3C//DTD XHTML 1.0 Transitional//EN"
"http://www.w3.org/TR/xhtml1/DTD/xhtml1-transitional.dtd">
<html xmlns="http://www.w3.org/1999/xhtml">
<head>
<meta http-equiv="Content-Type" content="text/html; charset=UTF-8"
/>
<title>Chapter Nine</title>
<!--LINK HREF TO THE EXTERNAL STYLE SHEET AND GOOGLE FONTS -->
<link href="styles.css" rel="stylesheet" type="text/css" />
<link href=
'http://fonts.googleapis.com/css?family=Ropa+Sans|Ruthie|Ledger'
rel='stylesheet' type='text/css'>
</head>

<body>
<div id="container"> <!--CONTAINER DIV-->
<div id="nav"> <!-- NAV TOOL -->
  <ul>
    <li><a href="#">Biography</a></li>
    <li><a href="#">Timeline</a></li>
    <li><a href="#">Algae and Ferns</a></li>
  </ul>
</div><!-- CLOSE THE NAV TOOL-->
<div class="header">Anna Atkins</div> <!--HEADER DIV-->
<div class="halfcol"> <!--1ST HALF COLUMN DIV-->
  <h1>Early Life</h1>
  <p>
    <a href="mailto:anna@cyanotype.com">Anna Children</a> was born
  in Tonbridge, Kent, England in 1799. Her mother Hester Anne
  didn't recover from the effects of childbirth" and died in 1800.
  Anna became close to her father John George Children, who was a
  scientist of many interests; for example, he was honoured by
  having the mineral childrenite and the Children's python,
  Antaresia childreni, named after him. She "received an unusually
  scientific education for a woman of her time." Her detailed
  engravings of shells were used to illustrate her father's
  translation of Lamarck's Genera of Shells, which was published in
  1823.</p>
    </div><!--CLOSE THE 1ST HALF COLUMN DIV-->
<div class="halfcol"><!--OPEN THE SECOND HALF COLUMN DIV -->
  <h1>Cyanotype</h1>
  <p>Sir John Herschel, a friend of Atkins and Children, invented
  the cyanotype photographic process in 1842. Within a year, Atkins
  applied the process to algae (specifically, seaweed) by making
  cyanotype photograms that were contact printed by placing the
  unmounted dried-algae original directly on the cyanotype paper.</p
  >

  <h1>Photography</h1>
  <p>John George Children and John Pelly Atkins were friends of
  William Fox Talbot. Anna Atkins learned directly from Talbot about
  two of his inventions related to photography: the "photogenic
  drawing" technique (in which an object is placed on
  light-sensitized paper which is exposed to the sun to produce an
  image) and calotypes.</p>
    <p>Atkins was known to have had access to a camera by 1841. Some
  sources claim that Atkins was the first female photographer.
  Other sources name Constance Talbot, the wife of William Fox
  Talbot, as the first female photographer. As no camera-based
```

```
@charset "UTF-8";
* { /* a universal selector is used here to reset margins and
padding to zero */
    margin: 0;
    padding: 0;
}
/* LINKS */
a:link {
    color: #FF3;
    text-decoration: none;
}
a:visited {
    text-decoration: none;
    color: #FF3;
}
a:hover {
    text-decoration: none;
    color: #FFF;
}
a:active {
    text-decoration: none;
    color: #FFF;
}
/* PAGE SELECTORS */
body,td,th {
    color: #000;
    background-image: url(bg.jpg);
    background-repeat: no-repeat;
    background-position: center top;
    font-family: 'Ledger', Georgia, serif;
}
/* CONTAINER INFO */
#container {
    width: 960px;
    margin: 0px auto;
    overflow:hidden;
}
/* NAV TOOL */
#nav {
    padding: 1em;
}
#nav li {
    display: inline;
    padding-right: 20px;
    list-style-type: none;
}
/* HEADER */
.header {
    font-family: 'Ruthie', cursive, Verdana, Geneva, sans-serif;
    font-size: 6em;
    color: #FF3;
}
/* HEADING TAGS */
h1 {
    font-family: 'Ropa Sans', sans-serif;
    font-size: 1.5em;
    color: #009;
    padding: 1em 0 0 1.8em;
    background: url(leaf.png) left .9em no-repeat;
```

Figures 9.28 and 9.29 Comments in the HTML and CSS documents are helpful as you learn new tags and properties.

The Art and Craft of Code

Traveass Smalley is a 2010 graduate of The Cooper Union in New York. His background in painting and digital printmaking converges into a perfectly unified web presence for his online exhibit Vector Drawings (Figure 9.30). [http://www.travesssmalley.com/vector_drawings/] On his web page, the background image is the repeated checkerboard of gray and white squares that all digital natives recognize as the indication of a transparency in Adobe programs. The vector drawings couldn't be better placed than they are—

Figure 9.30 *Vector Drawings* by Travess Smalley include a Compact Disc on a checkerboard background. *Courtesy of Travess Smalley.*

right in the center of the browser among that grid of "transparent" checkers. Though a simple container should have been used here to center the vector images on the page, this is an excellent display of design (the checkered background image) supporting its content (the vector drawings).

Create, Reflect, Critique

Create a two-column layout for an article of your choice from an e-mag such as *Salon.com, Nymag.com,* or *Wired.com.* Designing a mock-up layout for a website as developed by these three publications is similar to writing a single episode for a long-standing television show. Use the logo or masthead of the original site, but create a new page layout. Can you create a variation on the design of the web page layout that adheres to the original site's visual properties? Too much similarity will result in pure mimicry, while too much difference will result in a lack of consistency between the design of your article and the original site. Pay attention to the unity of design elements on the page. Don't use too many font faces. Do create variations in style, size, and color of the typography to develop contrast and hierarchy on the page. Don't use too many colors in the background, images, or typography. Do create a color palette that relates different types of content to one another on the page. How does your experience with creating unity include the back and forth play of allowing enough contrast to achieve a focal point and hierarchy while retaining visual similarities?

Glossary Words

comments, container **div**, elastic layout, fixed layout, float, fluid layout, gestalt theory of visual perception, parents and children, unity, universal selector

10 ADDING A FOOTER WITH HTML5 AND CSS3 ELEMENTS

VIDEO
INTRODUCTION

Principles, History, Theory

Last But Not Least

How do you know when your footer needs a massage?

Since the beginning of human congregation, cultures throughout the world have devised games in which balls are kicked toward a goal. The ancient Greeks played one of the oldest foot games in history from about the third century BCE that was later adapted and made popular by the Romans (Figure 10.1). Called *harpustum*, roughly translated as "carried away," players used a ball about the size and weight of a modern softball with rules that were thought to be similar to what later became known as rugby. Although the game was praised by one of the most revered figures in Greek history, the physician and philosopher Galen, because of the extent of its required vigorous exercise, it was also criticized for being too violent, with players and spectators sometimes severely hurt. Brutality on and off the field would be a common criticism of various foot games by government officials, religious leaders, social critics, and the athletes themselves throughout the centuries up until the present time.

Figure 10.1 One of the first football games was called *Episkyros* and invented by the Greeks in about 2000 BCE. Depicted on marble is an adult showing a boy how to balance a ball on his leg. Although predominantly a man's sport, women also sometimes participated. Regardless, contestants played the game in the nude and no doubt were careful where they kicked. *Courtesy of the National Museum of Archeology, Athens.*

During the first century BCE, the Chinese military played *cuju*, or "kick ball," while the Japanese about 600 years later played a popular game called *kemari* (Figure 10.2). Similar to kicking a hackie sack, kemari players formed a circle and tried to keep the ball off the ground with their feet.

Figure 10.2 A woodcut from an anonymous engraver created during Chinese's Ming Dynasty (1368 – 1644) shows servants playing an early football game called *cuju*. *Courtesy of Outlaws of the Marsh.*

Known as soccer in the United States, early versions of football were played in England and Ireland, but in these iterations, hands were as important as feet in moving the ball along. It wasn't until the 15th century that the first description of the game included a rule that except for the goalie, a player must be true to the game's name and avoid using hands. With such emphasis on the feet, those who play non-American-style football, the most popular game in the world, are sometimes called *footers*.

A *footer* is also the name for a horizontal strip of information and links at the bottom of a web page that is often overlooked by users and designers. Sven Lennartz, a co-founder of *Smashing Magazine*, writes that "most footers are rather boring and uninspiring" because they are often the last element placed on a page by Web designers. Many think that footers at the bottom of a page are simply the place that informs a visitor that no more scrolling is possible. Footers can also inform a user

> **DDR**
>
> Whether dancing for fun, exercise, or as a student at the California Institute of Technology and the University of Kansas for class credit, one of the most popular video games in the world, whether in its arcade or PlayStation 2, Xbox, or Wii versions, is "Dance Dance Revolution" (DDR). Produced by the Japanese company Konami in 1998, players earn points when they step on a complicated sequence of synchronized colored arrows and other symbols that flash to trendy tunes. Users advance through the game by successfully completing a dance routine to receive a passing score. The five main levels of performance—beginner, basic, difficult, expert, and challenge—are divided into additional levels called *footers*. For example, a DDR song "Can't Stop Fallin' in Love" performed by Cut N Edge is rated a 9-footer.

about the website, provide contact details, present copyright and legal information, and include other miscellaneous links. Dull, right? But the space can also be another area where your style can shine through the clutter.

Paulo Taneda, based in São Paulo, Brazil, is an interactive designer with more than ten years of experience as an illustrator and web creator. His work is both playful and professional. For an educational website, Taneda's footer uses a picture of green grass in a horizontal orientation that connotes a yard filled with growing possibilities. For the marketing company Comunika, his footer blends seamlessly with a drafting table background picture that communicates a casual, but effective work environment (Figure 10.3). For a high-end kitchen product company, the footer is composed of text-based links set in a classic sans serif typeface that doesn't distract from the main messages of the site.

As Lennartz suggests, footers with thoughtful combinations of colors, illustrations, advanced features, and new ways to express traditional components, especially if they respect your audience, will be noticed and appreciated.

Practice

Progressive Enhancement

The bottom of the web page is perhaps less viewed than the top, but it is still an important part of a design. In this chapter, we will create a footer area with accompanying styles, and we will explore HTML5 and CSS3 elements on our page.

HTML and CSS are programming languages that are always in the process of being developed. When HTML is revised, some tags become *deprecated*, or extinct. For instance, you may have been familiar with the HTML center tag, **<center>**, which was widely

Figure 10.3 Brazilian illustrator and web designer Paulo Taneda creates pages for corporate clients in which the footers integrate seamlessly, usually through typography alone, into the style of the product or service being depicted. *Courtesy of Paulo Taneda at paulotaneda.com.br.*

used before HTML4. The tag became obsolete in HTML4 when the CSS `text-align` property was introduced as the favored method of centering HTML content. (And yes, the center tag remains obsolete according to HTML5 standards).

But, as tags become deprecated over time, new features are introduced (sometimes it seems they arrive almost one browser at a time). Since these programming languages are developed by many and owned by none, a new "version" of the code isn't exactly like a new version of an Adobe software application—you don't have the luxury of simply installing it on your system.

Instead, you must learn new code and appreciate where some of the new features will work. You also need to know what to look out for when the new features you experiment with don't appear in your favorite (or least favorite) browser.

HTML5 is the fifth major revision of the primary language used to code web pages, Hypertext Markup Language (HTML). The fifth revision is still a work in progress (see "Is HTML5 Ready Yet" for a sort of concrete date of completion, and be sure to read the source code). [http://ishtml5readyyet.com/] While all browsers do not support all of the newest tags or developments, *most* browsers are ready for the new code.

You will see in the following exercises that some browsers are still working on integrating new properties to the third version of CSS, so we will have to add lines of code repeating the CSS3 rule to target specific browsers.

At least with CSS, the good news is that we can always insert a rule for older browsers before a rule that displays the latest features. Steven Champeon, a steering committee member of the Web Standards Project, introduced the design concept of "*progressive enhancement*" with the idea of "graceful degradation." Remember, if there are two conflicting CSS rules in a document, the browser will always display whichever CSS rule is nearer to the end of the file. This cascading feature allows us to "degrade gracefully." We can add the older code first and then insert a rule using newer features. Browsers that display the newest feature will display the page with the newer code, while older or less updated browsers will simply show the older, more trustworthy CSS rule. With the idea of progressive enhancement in mind, pages are designed for the future while retaining stability in older browsers. Don't rely on new features to deliver important items of content. Instead, use them in decorative places where you know that the old rules will suffice for a viewer who does not have an up-to-date viewing platform.

Results of Chapter 10 Exercises

In the following exercises you will learn to use the **clear** property, some CSS positioning, CSS3 properties and HTML5 code (Figure 10.4). Although the resulting file is not as beautiful as the results of Chapter 14, the exercises in this chapter contribute steadily towards progress on the final web page design.

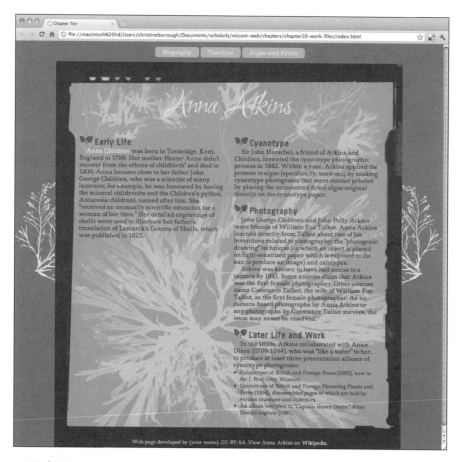

Figure 10.4 Chapter 10 results include a footer element that uses a **clear** property then **fixed** positioning (later discussed in Chapter 11). You will also create a design treatment for the top navigational tool that achieves greater hierarchy due to its isolation from the background graphic and the contrast between a rounded form and a sharp line.

Download Materials for Chapter 10 Exercises

In addition to the results files from Chapter 9, you will need the files *bg-left.png* and *bg-right.png* to complete the exercises in this chapter. Download them from the website. [http://viscommontheweb.wordpress.com/downloads/]

Exercise 1: Surpassing Floating Divisions

1. **Set up your workspace:** Copy and paste the final Chapter 9 exercise files to a new folder named *chapter10*. Open Dreamweaver and define or edit your site to point to the root directory, *chapter10*. Choose Window > Workspace Layout > Designer. Open *index.html* in Dreamweaver, modify the title tag (I titled my page "Chapter Ten"), and save your work.

2. Create a new set of division tags between the closing **</div>** tag for the right column and the final closing **</div>** tag on the page as you want the footer to display within the boundaries of **#container**. Add the following text, inserting your name as the page developer (Figure 10.5).

Add This Text to Your Footer	HTML Code View
Web page developed by (your name). CC-BY-SA. View Anna Atkins on Wikipedia.	**</div><!--CLOSE THE 2ND HALF COLUMN DIV-->** **<div><!--footer area-->** **Web page developed by (your name). CC-BY-SA. View Anna Atkins on** **<a href="http://en.wikipedia.org/wiki/Anna_Atkins">Wikipedia</a>.** **</div><!--close the footer area-->** **</div><!--CLOSE THE CONTAINER DIV-->**

Save the HTML file and preview your work in a browser.

```
41      </ul>
42      </div><!--CLOSE THE 2ND HALF COLUMN DIV-->
43       <div><!--footer area-->
44        Web page developed by (your name). CC-BY-SA. View Anna
         Atkins on <a href="http://en.wikipedia.org/wiki/Anna_Atkins">
         Wikipedia</a>.
45        </div><!--close the footer area-->
46      </div><!--CLOSE THE CONTAINER DIV-->
47   </body>
48   </html>
```

Figure 10.5 Add a footer area in the HTML source code.

3. Did you expect the footer text to appear at the bottom of the page? Instead it simply follows the normal flow of the page. Within the container **div**, you

have an unordered list followed by two **div** tags that are set to **float: left**. After all of this, the footer area is defined by a new **div** tag. The footer content appears after everything else on the page—which is not the same as being near the bottom of the browser window. In this case, the footer is left aligned next to the second column because **.halfcol** is floating left. While Dreamweaver's design window does not always provide an accurate representation of the browser view, in this case, you can get a pretty good visual reading of the flow of **div** tags by looking at your work with the CSS Layout Backgrounds selected from the Visual Aids pull-down menu (Figure 10.6).

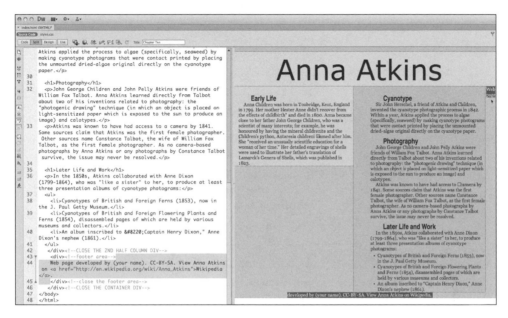

Figure 10.6 Notice that the start of the sentence, "Web page" appears in the top right corner, just following the right column on the page.

4. Create a declaration block for the footer **div** tag in order to control its positioning. You may continue using the Dreamweaver Rule Definition dialog box, but it would be more efficient (and better practice for learning code) to write the code without the hassle of the dialog box. Most of the following code in the declaration statement for the ID selector named "footer" will be familiar. However, we do have to deal with positioning the footer beneath the two floating divisions. The **clear** property is often used in this situation. It basically tells the browser to skip past any floating items and move to the next line. Add a footer declaration to your style sheet as in Figure 10.7.

```#footer { clear: left; color: #CCC; padding: .5em; font-size: small; }```	**CLEAR:** The clear property can be set to left, right, or both. It simply tells the browser to clear anything before it that was floating left or right (or all floating objects). Since I knew that our prior **divs** were floating left, I simply cleared all "left" floating elements.

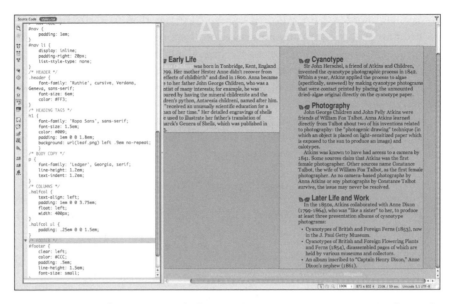

Figure 10.7 Since the footer clears left floating divisions, the content in the footer division appears in a new box beneath the two columns.

Be sure to go back to your HTML code and insert "id=footer" into the footer **div** tag so it reads **<div id="footer">**.

Reference

Chris Coyier's "All About Floats" article from 2009 provides a set of helpful illustrations for learning to use the **float** and **clear** properties. [http://css-tricks.com/all-about-floats/]

Exercise 2: Fixed Positioning

VIDEO
WALKTHROUGH   In many web page designs, the **clear** property would be the perfect solution for our footer. We would see the footer at the end of the content by clearing floating divisions, and the page would come to a succinct end. There would be no fuss about integrating the design of the page layout with the background image. However, that is not true for our page. For us, the background image dictates the positioning of the footer.

Notice that the text in the right column extends just a little bit past where the content of the page should seem to end—the cyan area of the frame at the bottom of the page (Figure 10.8). We will modify our content and then deal with an unfortunate surprise.

1. Adjust the text for the bullet points by using the **small** property. Add the following line to your code for **.halfcol ul**:

```
.halfcol ul {
    padding: .25em 0 0 1.5em;
    font-size: small;
}
```

Save your style sheet and view your page in a browser (Figure 10.9).

Figure 10.8 The footer text is overlapped by overflowing text in the right column.

Figure 10.9 Now that the page content fits inside the background graphic, the footer has snuck up into the light gray area.

2. *Oh no!* The bulleted items are smaller and the page content ends in a decent loca-
    tion, but the footer has snuck up into the content area. This is a losing situation.
    Our only solution is to use another method that will keep the footer stuck to
    the bottom of the page in precisely the location where the cyan border (in the
    background image) appears. For this we need to use a positioning property. There
    are four **position** properties (static, fixed, absolute, and relative) that are the
    focus of Chapter 11. In this exercise, we will see a preview of fixed positioning to
    define the footer. The *fixed position* value places the **div** tag on the page accord-
    ing to the top, right, bottom, or left values assigned *as these values relate to the
    browser window*. In other words, when **position: fixed;** and **bottom: 0px;**
    is declared for a **div** tag, it is placed at the bottom of the browser window. The
    fixed position placement remains true regardless of scrolling. Adjust the footer ID
    declaration in your style sheet to remove the **clear** property and add positioning
    and bottom properties. View your work in a large browser, then reduce the size of
    the web page. Notice where the footer lands (Figures 10.10 and 10.11).

```
#footer {

clear: left;

    position: fixed;
    bottom: 0;
    color: #CCC;
    color: #CCC;
    padding: .5em;
    font-size: small;
}
```

Figure 10.10 The results of sticking the footer to the bottom of the browser (*oops*—we will need
to center the content in the division).

Figure 10.11 *Yikes!* The footer moves when the browser moves. Fixed positioning is strictly in relation to the edges of the browser window.

> **Note**
>
> Positioning with CSS is a two-part process, as you will have to assign a type of positioning (static, fixed, absolute, or relative) and top, right, bottom, or left values (for which you will need to understand the reference point each uses in order to predict the visual results of those values). Positioning is the focus of Chapter 11.

3. Add a **width** property and the **text-align** property to the footer ID to center the contents of the division in 960 pixels (the same width as the container).

```
#footer {
    position: fixed;
    bottom: 0;
    text-align: center;
    width: 960px;
    color: #CCC;
    padding: .5em;
    font-size: small;
}
```

While the footer is not yet behaving perfectly on our page, the content is in place and you have learned something new about positioning elements in CSS using the **clear** property and the **fixed** positioning value. If our web page design did not include a background graphic that appears light in value throughout the main area of the page and dark cyan near the bottom of the page (requiring a precise placement of light-valued footer text), we would be finished. Since it is a little more complicated than most page layouts, we will complete the footer in the next chapter.

Exercise 3: CSS3 Properties

As of this writing, there are CSS3 properties supported in many, but not all, browsers. Some of these properties allow us to create design elements with CSS code instead of having to rely on uploaded images. This procedure results in a faster load time, which is especially helpful for viewers on mobile devices or with slow connections to the Internet.

This timing issue is a constant battle for visual communicators using the Web as a primary platform for creative output. While we want to use the most up-to-date code, we also usually want our work to be accessible and viewable in most or all browsing situations. Programmers and developers make contributions to the growing list of CSS properties. The W3C is responsible for creating standards, as they proclaim, "The World Wide Web Consortium (W3C) is an international community where member organizations, a full-time staff, and the public work together to develop Web standards. Led by Web inventor Tim Berners-Lee and CEO Jeffrey Jaffe, W3C's mission is to lead the Web to its full potential" (http://www.w3.org/Consortium/).

Note

You should always validate HTML documents before publishing them on the Web by using the W3C Markup Validation Service (or search the Web for "W3C validator" if the link has moved). Validation is one of the main topics in Chapter 13. [http://validator.w3.org/]

Which Browsers Are Safe?

As of this writing, **border-radius** is supported in Chrome 3+, Firefox 1+, Internet Explorer 9 beta, Opera 10.5+, and Safari 3+.

rgba is supported in Chrome 3+, Firefox 3+, Internet Explorer 9 beta, Opera 10+, and Safari 3.2+.

Multiple background images are supported in Chrome 2+, Firefox 3.6+, Internet Explorer 9 beta, Opera 10.5+, and Safari 1.3+.

For a list of CSS3 features and the browsers where they are supported, see the Preview page on CSS3.info [http://www.css3.info/preview/].

Although the following CSS3 properties are not fully supported in all browsers, we can use them for browsers that do read and display them properly and include back-up code for older browsers (i.e., graceful degradation).

1. Instead of using hex values to define color, with CSS3 you can define a color with RGB values *and* an additional opacity value using the *RGBa* (where "a" stands for "alpha," referring to transparency) color model. We will explore this with the background property in the **#navlist li** selector. Add this line of code to your style sheet and then save and preview your work:

```
#nav li {
    display: inline;
    padding-right: 20px;
    list-style-type: none;
    background: rgba(255, 255, 255, .5);
}
```

The background for each listed item (or navigation link) takes a red, green, and blue value of 255. Since RGB colors are defined on a scale of 0 (white) to 255 (black), the RGB translation of the set (255, 255, 255) is the color black. In addition, the decimal value, .5, tells the browser to display the RGB color as 50% transparent. The background color for each link item is 50% black—but

Figure 10.12 The RGBa color model is used to define the background color of the listed items.

that percentage is not the same as middle gray. Black registered at 50% opacity will appear as a mid-value gray, but it will also seem to blend with the background image or color due to its transparency (Figure 10.12).

2. If a browser does not support the **background** RGBa declaration, you simply would not see a background color on the navigation tool. We will add a **background-color** declaration to ensure that a color will appear in all browsers. However, be sure to add this line of code before the **rgba** background declaration. The browser applies styles based on their order in the declaration block—if there are conflicting declarations, the last declaration is the one that is displayed. By putting the **rgba** declaration at the end, it will rule over the **background-color** property when it can be displayed. Here we are programming for graceful degradation with the progressive enhancement of the RGBa value.

```
#nav li {
    display: inline;
    padding-right: 20px;
    list-style-type: none;
    background-color: #69F;
    background: rgba(255, 255, 255, .5);
}
```

3. Next, we will apply the **border-radius** property, which is also only functional in some browsers at the time of this writing. Add the following to your **#navlist li** declaration block:

```
#nav li {
    display: inline;
    padding-right: 20px;
    list-style-type: none;
    background-color: #69F;
    background: rgba(255, 255, 255, .5);
    -webkit-border-radius: 7px;
    -moz-border-radius: 7px;
    -o-border-radius: 7px;
    border-radius: 7px;
}
```

Safari, Firefox, and Opera are currently developing support for the **border-radius** property. For now, you have to include code that speaks just to each of these browsers, as we do with the dash webkit, dash moz, and dash o (-webkit, -moz, -o) statements. We are basically saying, "Turn on border radius with a value of 7 pixels" in a language specific to the Safari browser, then the

Figure 10.13 The **border-radius** property is used to create rounded edges for the listed items.

Firefox browser, then the Opera browser. For all browsers that currently support **border-radius**, and for browsers that will support this property in the future, the last property declared is simply **border-radius**. Save and preview your page in a browser (Figure 10.13).

Reference

Jacob Bijani is a product engineer at Tumblr. [http://jacobbijani.com/about] In his spare time, he creates useful, elegant Internet "offerings," such as the border-radius website. You'll never have to remember all of the browser-specific code for the **border-radius** property, because border-radius.com is so simple to use. [http://border-radius.com]

4. If you delete the padding declaration from **#nav li** you will see that the text for each link is centered just inside the background color. Let's modify the padding property now so the text is centered with negative space surrounding all sides. Replace your padding property with the following line of code, which applies 3 pixels of padding to the top and bottom of the rounded button and 20 pixels of padding to the right and left sides. Remember, the value is read by the browser clockwise from the top.

```
#nav li {
    display: inline;
    padding: 3px 20px 3px 20px;
    list-style-type: none;
    background-color: #69F;
    background: rgba(255, 255, 255, .5);
    -webkit-border-radius: 7px;
    -moz-border-radius: 7px;
    -o-border-radius: 7px;
    border-radius: 7px;
}
```

Note

The padding rule could be made simpler by consolidating the values:
`padding: 3px 20px;`

5. In the final site design, the navigation tool appears above the background image. In order to move the image down the page and make space at the top for the navigation, we need to create another container. This time, we will call it "content," as it will be the division that holds all of the content on the page between the navigation tool and the footer. Insert the tag **<div id="content">** beneath

the **</div>** where the navigation ends. Close the tag, **</div>** at the end of the page, just before the footer **div** is opened. Then, be sure to create the **#content** class in the style sheet as follows:

```
#content {
    width: 960px;
    text-align: center;
    height: 1062px;
    background:#CCC url(bg.jpg) no-repeat;
}
```

Save your files and preview the page in a browser (Figure 10.14).

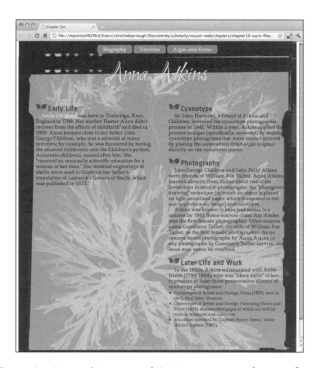

Figure 10.14 The navigation tool is centered in its own space, but we forgot to remove the background image from the **body** selector.

6. *Whoops!* We forgot to remove the background image from the **body** selector. Delete the **background-image**, **-repeat**, and **-position** properties from the selectors **body, td,** and **th**. Modify the selector so it only declares rules for **body** (not **td** or **th**, selectors for table data and table header, which we will not use in this design). Then add the following code to the **body** selector:

```
body {
    color: #000;
    font-family: 'Ledger', Georgia, serif;
    background: url(bg-left.png) no-repeat center
left,url(bg-right.png) no-repeat center right;
    background-color: #669;
}
```

In the browser, notice we are using two background images, one for the left side and one for the right (Figure 10.15). Both images share the values **no-repeat** (meaning only display the image one time on the page) and **center** (position the background image vertically in the center of the page). The **left** and **right** values position the images in reference to the browser horizontally. The ability to assign multiple background images is new to CSS3. The property is **background**, the two URL values are separated by a comma, and the declaration is ended with a semicolon, as usual. We are also assigning a medium-value periwinkle color (#669) to the background of the page, which will be viewable outside of the container.

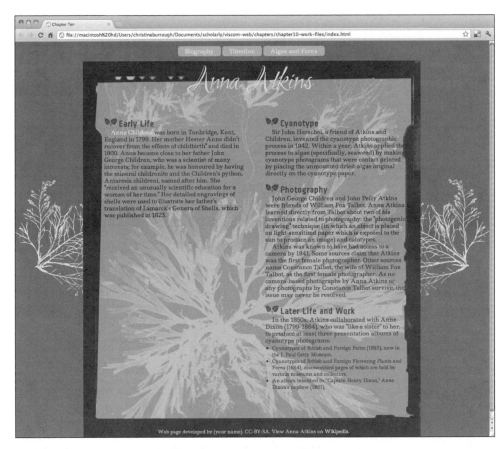

Figure 10.15 Now that the navigation area has been separated from the rest of the content, the top spacing is incorrect for the header and columns.

7. By moving the background image down into the content area of the page, the navigation tool is now isolated with more negative space, so it takes greater hierarchy on the page. Of course, now that we've moved the background image to a lower position, the spacing around the columns and header text is off. Add 60 pixels of top padding to the header. We will use pixels, as we are concerned with the distance between the header and the top of the graphic. The graphic is measured in pixels.

```
.header {
   font-family: 'Ruthie', cursive, Verdana, Geneva,
sans-serif;
   font-size: 6em;
   color: #FF3;
   padding: 60px 0 0 0;
}
```

The Grid Revisited

This design treatment alludes to a slight break in the grid that is established by the evenly sized boxes (created by the division tags) inside the container. However, the organic background images are not necessary to reading the content on the page. They provide a visual layer of information that acts as a textural component for the design. Though the multiple background images may not appear in certain browsers (ahem, old versions of Internet Explorer), the browsers that do display the graphics (both in terms of reading this newer code and having a wide enough viewport) provide a visual "bonus" (Figure 10.16). It is a good idea to experiment with new code (CSS3, HTML5, or whatever comes next) in a way that does not inhibit the user's ability to read all of the content on the page.

Figure 10.16 The two background images appear in all of the browser windows seen here (on a Mac): Chrome (version 18), Firefox (version 11), and Safari (version 5.1.4).

8. The two columns of text also seem tight in terms of the space (or lack of space) near the margins. Meanwhile, the gutter (the space between the two columns) is too wide. If you try to fix this by adjust the padding in **.halfcol** you will find that by assigning separate values to the left and right sides of the box (the division), you will never be able to achieve a repetition of negative space (inherently, different values are different, meaning you would lose the design property of repetition). To fix all of this, we will assign each column separate classes in order to control the amount of space on the left and right sides. Replace **.halfcol** with the following two classes, where again, we'll use pixel dimensions, as we are concerned with the width of the cyan edges on the background graphic. We'll remove all padding from the top, since this has been achieved by separating our navigation from the content on the page:

Copy and rename the half-column class to create two new classes: **.leftcol** and **.rightcol**	Adjust the padding of **.leftcol** and **.rightcol**

~~**.halfcol**~~ {
    text-align: left;
    float: left;
    width: 400px;
    padding: ~~**1em 0 0 3.75em;**~~
}
	.leftcol {
	    text-align: left;
	    float: left;
	    width: 400px;
	    padding: 0 15px 0 65px;
	}
	
	.rightcol {
	    text-align: left;
	    float: left;
	    width: 400px;
	    padding: 0 65px 0 15px;
	}

Note

Notice that the padding is set to zero on the top and bottom of the divisions that are ruled by these two classes. The left column (**.leftcol**) has 15 pixels of padding on the right side (toward the gutter) and 65 pixels of padding at the left margin (to clear the edge of the cyanotype background graphic). The right column uses the same numeric values of padding in reverse: 65 pixels at the right margin (to clear the background image) and 15 pixels in the gutter (on the left side).

Go to the HTML source code and replace the first **class="halfcol"** with **class="leftcol"**. Replace the second **class="halfcol"** with **class="rightcol"**. Save your files and preview the page in a browser (Figures 10.17 and 10.18).

9. The list items in the content area of the page are once again misaligned. Look in your style sheet. The **ul** that is being modified is a child of **.halfcol**. Since

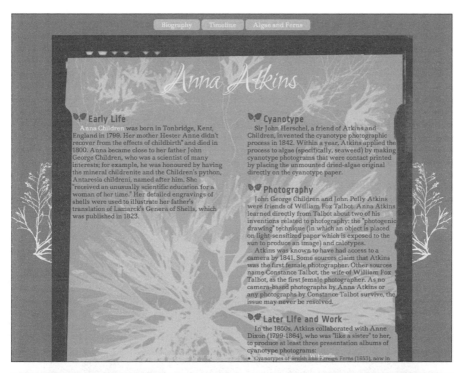

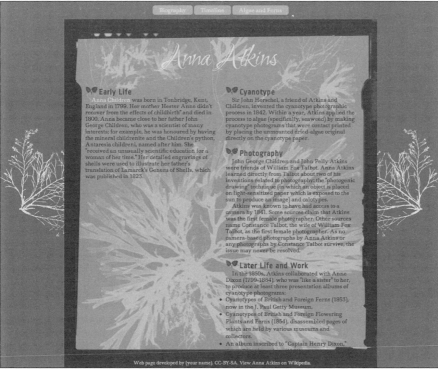

Figures 10.17 and 10.18 Can you see the differences in these two images between the negative space at the left and right margins and in the gutter between the two columns? Figure 10.17 displays both columns as they would appear with the same **.halfcol** class. Figure 10.18 displays the two columns when they are styled by **.leftcol** and **.rightcol**.

we are no longer using **.halfcol** this declaration will not have an effect on the page you see in the browser. Modify your code so that you declare padding properties for the child (**ul**) of the right column (**.rightcol**). Save and view your work in a browser (Figure 10.19).

The child of **.halfcol** targeting the bulleted items is now the child of **.rightcol**. Delete the selector then rename it.	Name the selector **.rightcol ul**

~~.halfcol ul {~~
        padding: .25em 0 0 1.5em;
        font-size: small;
}
	.rightcol ul {
	        padding: .25em 0 0 1.5em;
	        font-size: small;
	}

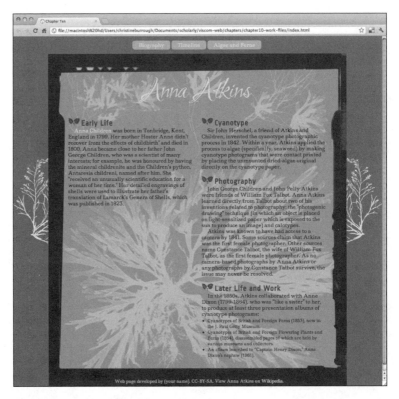

Figure 10.19 The list in the right column is now the child of **.rightcol** (not **.halfcol**). Here is what the web page looks like when **.halfcol ul** has been renamed **.rightcol ul** in the CSS code.

Exercise 4: HTML5 Elements

The main purpose of retooling HTML for the fifth version was to create a language that better supports the way designers and developers create web content and the way users have become familiar with interacting with media displayed in a browser. You may have heard the terms, "the semantic Web," or "Web 3.0." Both of these terms allude to the idea that the code used to format web content (HTML as well as other programming languages) should be structurally sound. The names of tags or elements in the languages should refer to what it is that the tag (or element) does. As such, some of the HTML5 tags make so much sense that we're almost already using them—you will see we have named division classes or IDs with the names that can be used now as tags. In the following exercises we will update some of our HTML source code to conform to HTML5 protocols.

> **Note**
>
> See the W3 website for thorough documentation regarding the differences between HTML4 and HTML5. [http://www.w3.org/TR/html5-diff/]

1. Update the **doctype**. We should start at the very beginning—the document type. As per the W3 website, "The doctype declaration is **<!DOCTYPE html>** and is case-insensitive in the HTML syntax." Replace the first line of the code that Dreamweaver wrote for you with the simple doctype declaration, as follows.

Delete the long **doctype** tag from the original HTML code

```
<!DOCTYPE html PUBLIC "-//W3C//DTD XHTML 1.0
Transitional//EN"
"http://www.w3.org/TR/xhtml1/DTD/xhtml1-
transitional.dtd">
```

Add the HTML5 **doctype** tag

```
<!DOCTYPE html>
```

> **Note**
>
> Throughout this exercise you will be typing in your source code. Be careful! One typo could lead to a miserable experience debugging your code. Every space and letter is important.

2. Update the navigation area. The new tag, **<nav>**, should be used for major navigational elements on the page. In our exercise, the main navigation tool is set inside a division tag with an ID named "nav."

Delete the navigation **div** from the original HTML code

```
<div id="nav">
```

Add the HTML5 **nav** tag in its place

```
<nav>
```

> **Note**
>
> While you can use the **nav** tag more than once, Bruce Lawson and Remy Sharp (2011) wrote in *Introducing HTML5* that it should not be used for a page of search results or a group of sponsored links, for instance, as these are not major navigational elements on a page.

Be sure to close the nav tag, **</nav>**, in lieu of closing the division tag, **</div>**. This does mean that we will have to update our CSS document.

Rename the two CSS tag selectors for the navigation tool

~~#nav~~

and

~~#nav li~~

By deleting the pound signs, the new selectors refer to tags instead of IDs

nav {padding: 1em;}

and

```
nav li {
    display: inline;
    padding: 3px 20px 3px 20px;
    list-style-type: none;
    background-color: #69F;
    background: rgba(255, 255, 255, .5);
    -webkit-border-radius: 7px;
    -moz-border-radius: 7px;
    -o-border-radius: 7px;
    border-radius: 7px;
}
```

Note

When writing CSS code, you can list the declaration inside the curly brackets on a single line (as in the **nav** rule set) or open the curly bracket and then list each declaration on a new line (as in the **nav li** rule set). For beginners, it can be easier to see the properties and values when they are listed on separate lines. As you become more familiar with writing code, you may begin to save space in your documents by placing the declaration on the same line as the selector.

Note

If you create a page with more than one **nav** tag, you can always assign a CSS ID or class to the tag, just as you would have treated a division tag.

---

3. Update the header area. The W3C states that the **header** tag "represents a group of introductory or navigation aids." We have separated our navigation from the header, so for us it will simply be Anna's name, which is currently nested inside a **div** tag assigned a class named, of course, "header."

Delete the header **div** from the original HTML source code

~~<div class="header">Anna Atkins</div>~~
~~<!--HEADER DIV-->~~

Replace it with the **header** tag

<header>Anna Atkins</header>

Note

Notice that when the new tag, **<header>**, is used, the need for a comment tag specifying that the generic "div" was acting as a header is no longer necessary.

Again, we will have to modify our style sheet to reflect our changes.

Delete the period, indicating the header as a CSS class selector

~~.header~~

Instead, **header** becomes a CSS tag selector

```
header {
        font-family: 'Ruthie', cursive, Verdana, Geneva,
        sans-serif;
        font-size: 6em;
        color: #FF3;
        padding: 60px 0 0 0;
}
```

---

4. Update the footer area. The **footer** tag should be used in place of a division with an ID or class named "footer." We will modify the source code to simplify the tag, close the tag properly, and then modify the style sheet to update the selector format to a tag selector rather than an ID.

Replace the **div** in the footer area of the HTML source code

~~<div id="footer"><!--footer area-->~~

Use the footer HTML5 tag

```
<footer>
```

* Don't forget to rewrite the close division tag so that you close the footer tag:

```
</footer>
```
.

Replace the footer CSS class selector

~~#footer~~

Use the footer CSS tag selector

```
footer {
        position: fixed;
        bottom: 0px;
        text-align: center;
        width: 960px;
        color: #CCC;
        padding: .5em;
        font-size: small;
}
```

Save your work (Figure 10.20) and preview it in any browser but Internet Explorer (IE). We'll deal with IE in Chapter 14.

```
<!DOCTYPE html>                                              nav {
<html xmlns="http://www.w3.org/1999/xhtml">                      padding: 1em;
<head>                                                       }
<meta http-equiv="Content-Type" content="text/html; charset=UTF-8" />   nav li {
<title>Chapter Ten</title>                                       display: inline;
<!--LINK HREF TO THE EXTERNAL STYLE SHEET AND GOOGLE FONTS -->    padding:3px 20px 3px 20px;
<link href="styles.css" rel="stylesheet" type="text/css" />      list-style-type: none;
<link href='http://fonts.googleapis.com/css?family=Ropa+Sans|Ruthie|Ledger' rel='styl   background-color: #69F;
</head>                                                          background: rgba(255, 255, 255, .5);
                                                                 -webkit-border-radius: 7px;
<body>                                                           -moz-border-radius: 7px;
<div id="container"> <!--CONTAINER DIV-->                        -o-border-radius: 7px;
<nav> <!-- NAV TOOL -->                                          border-radius: 7px;
  <ul>                                                       }
    <li><a href="/">Biography</a></li>                      /* HEADER */
    <li><a href="/">Timeline</a></li>                       header {
    <li><a href="/">Algae and Ferns</a></li>                    font-family: 'Ruthie', cursive, Verdana, Geneva,
  </ul>                                                          font-size: 6em;
</nav><!-- CLOSE THE NAV TOOL-->                                  color: #FF3;
<div id="content">                                               padding: 60px 0 0 0;
<header>Anna Atkins</header>                                 }
<div class="leftcol"> <!--1ST HALF COLUMN DIV-->             /* HEADING TAGS */
  <h1>Early Life</h1>                                        h1 {
  <p>                                                            font-family: 'Ropa Sans', sans-serif;
    <a href="mailto:anna@cyanotype.com">Anna Children</a> was born in Tonbridge, Kent    font-size: 1.5em;
  childbirth" and died in 1800. Anna became close to her father John George Children,    color: #009;
  having the mineral childrenite and the Children's python, Antaresia childreni, named    padding: 1em 0 0 1.8em;
  her time." Her detailed engravings of shells were used to illustrate her father's tre   background: url(leaf.png) left .9em no-repeat;
    </div><!--CLOSE THE 1ST HALF COLUMN DIV-->                  }
<div class="rightcol"><!--OPEN THE SECOND HALF COLUMN DIV -->   /* BODY COPY */
  <h1>Cyanotype</h1>                                         p {
  <p>Sir John Herschel, a friend of Atkins and Children, invented the cyanotype photo      font-family: 'Ledger', Georgia, serif;
  (specifically, seaweed) by making cyanotype photograms that were contact printed by      line-height: 1.2em;
  p>                                                             text-indent: 1.2em;
                                                             }
    <h1>Photography</h1>                                     /* COLUMNS */
    <p>John George Children and John Pelly Atkins were friends of William Fox Talbot. A   .leftcol {
  to photography: the "photogenic drawing" technique (in which an object is placed on       text-align: left;
  calotypes.</p>                                                 float: left;
    <p>Atkins was known to have had access to a camera by 1841. Some sources claim that    width: 400px;
  Talbot, the wife of William Fox Talbot, as the first female photographer. As no camer    padding: 0 15px 0 65px;
  survive, the issue may never be resolved.</p>              }

    <h1>Later Life and Work</h1>                             .rightcol {
    <p>In the 1850s, Atkins collaborated with Anne Dixon (1799-1864), who was "like a s     text-align: left;
  photograms:</p>                                               float: left;
    <ul>                                                        width: 400px;
      <li>Cyanotypes of British and Foreign Ferns (1853), now in the J. Paul Getty Muse    padding: 0 65px 0 15px;
      <li>Cyanotypes of British and Foreign Flowering Plants and Ferns (1854), disassen  }
      <li>An album inscribed to &#8220;Captain Henry Dixon," Anne Dixon's nephew (1861)   .rightcol ul {
    </ul>                                                        padding: .25em 0 0 1.5em;
  </div><!--CLOSE THE 2ND HALF COLUMN DIV-->                     font-size: small;
  </div><!--CLOSE THE CONTENT DIV-->                         }
<footer>                                                     /* FOOTER */
Web page developed by (your name). CC-BY-SA. View Anna Atkins on   footer {
<a href="http://en.wikipedia.org/wiki/Anna_Atkins">Wikipedia</a>.   position: fixed;
</footer><!--close the footer area-->                           bottom: 0;
</div><!--CLOSE THE CONTAINER DIV-->                            text-align: center;
                                                                width: 960px;
```

Figure 10.20 When new HTML5 tags are used in the source code, their supporting CSS selectors may need to be modified.

The Art and Craft of Code

Jacob Broms-Engblom's *Playing in the Surf* (2009) and *It's All About the Lighting* (2011) are two projects where the concept of the "footer" directly relates to the way the user interacts with the web page. In *Playing in the Surf*, the user is instructed to "scroll downwards to play in the surf." The page appears almost entirely devoid of content, save the background color (surf blue) and a small (238 by 183 pixels) JPG image of a dolphin positioned near the bottom of the page (Figure 10.21). As you scroll down, the dolphin and scrollbar both seem to hop back up. The web page is a trickster with the joke on the user. The dolphin image and the scrollbar can never come to an end. Instead they demand endless "play" from the user. [http://www.likeneveralways.com/playinginthesurf] [http://www.likeneveralways.com/itsallaboutthelighting/]

Usability Note

Playing in the Surf seemed to work perfectly in any browser I used prior to January 2012. Visual experiments created for the Web often "break" over time. Be sure to resize your browser window so there is some place to scroll before playing in the surf.

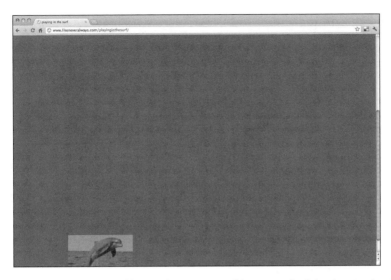

Figure 10.21 *Playing in the Surf* by Jacob Broms-Engblom is a playful spin on what happens in the area of the page traditionally used as the footer. *Courtesy of Jacob Broms-Engblom.*

Broms-Engblom's *It's All About the Lighting* is an interactive page that seems to dim or brighten depending on where the user positions or drags her cursor (Figure 10.22). Vector graphics simulating an abstract sun rising over a grassy hill on a blue sky lighten when the mouse is dragged from the bottom of the browser window to the top. Drag from the top to the bottom, and the virtual sun fades below the grass while the "lighting" dims. Here, the grass, positioned at the bottom of the browser window, could be abstractly understood as the "footer" of the page.

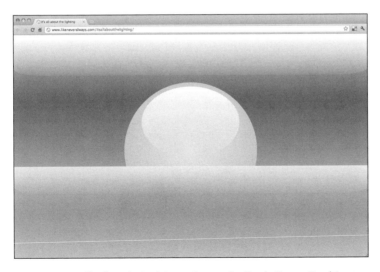

Figure 10.22 On the *It's All About the Lighting* web page by Jacob Broms-Engblom, you can set the sun and watch the page dim by dragging the yellow, circular vector shape into the footer area, where it hides behind a green abstraction for grass green, abstract "grass" area. *Courtesy of Jacob Broms-Engblom.*

Create, Reflect, Critique

The footer does not have to be a banal part of the web page layout. After finding inspiration in Jacob Broms-Engblom's works, can you create a footer that plays with the concept of the finality of the page? What does your footer represent? Is it a conceptual page ending or a visual stamp of something that terminates?

Glossary Words

deprecated tag, fixed positioning, HTML5, footer, progressive enhancement, RGBa

---

11   ALIGNMENT WITH CSS POSITIONING

VIDEO
INTRODUCTION

Principles, History, Theory

Columns and Modular Design

What in this world can be iconic, ironic, and ionic?

One of the most famous portraits of the Emperor Napoleon Bonaparte is the iconic painting by fellow Frenchman Jacques-Louis David. Completed in 1812 at the height of David's career but near the end of Napoleon's, the troubled conqueror stands in his study at the Tuileries Palace looking confidently at the viewer (Figure 11.1). With its late night, writing-desk setting with rolled papers that represent his legacy, the Napoleonic Code for civil law, subdued lighting with a nearly exhausted candle, and a clock that revealed the early morning time of 4:13, the painting is meant to convey the hard work required to move away from military conquest toward a more peaceful domestic reign. But after the disastrous loss trying to invade Russia the same year eloquently explained by Charles Minard's informational graphic, Bonaparte would be exiled three years after the completion of the painting.

Napoleon's stance is considered iconic because he rests his right hand comfortably within his unbuttoned tunic, a conventional pose that has been mimicked and satirized in such motion pictures as *Time Bandits* (1981) and *Night at the Museum: Battle of the Smithsonian* (2009).

Perhaps the hand-between-the-buttons pose was an affectation of the day requested by the artist or, less likely, an indication of an itch he couldn't quite scratch. Bonaparte died nine years later of stomach cancer.

Regardless, there is no doubt that Bonaparte had a more serious itch—to be emperor of Europe. Toward that end, in 1798 his army invaded Egypt to prevent England's trade route to India, but he was defeated by naval forces led by Vice Admiral Horatio Nelson. Ironically, one of the most striking sights within central London is the 50-meter-high Corinthian-style column, a monument to Nelson at Trafalgar Square (Figure 11.2). The statue is ironic because it was Napoleon's invasion of Egypt that started a world-wide craze for all things Egyptian—interior design, furniture, hieroglyphics with the discovery of the Rosetta Stone, and most importantly for this discussion, columns.

Four thousand years before Napoleon was born, the Egyptians invented columns. They were initially tall, narrow structures with carvings that looked like the reeds seen growing along the Nile River. Later, the Persians, Greeks, and Romans adopted their variations of the architectural staple with animal figures, tapered or fluted tops, and flat and curved arches within five divisions, or orders—Composite, Doric, Tuscan, Ionic, and Corinthian.

Egyptian columns also inspired two important innovations in graphic design—a typeface family to join the other five of blackletter, roman, script, sans serif, and miscellaneous—and a layout standard that became one of the most common ways to present words on any substrate.

Figure 11.1 "Napoleon Bonaparte in his Study at the Tuileries," 1812, Jacques-Louis David. The iconic pose of the Emperor, imitated many times throughout history, comes from this famous painting. Three years after the portrait, his forces were defeated at the Battle of Waterloo. For David, a mishap while fencing left a scar on his face so severe that he had trouble eating and speaking. In addition, a non-cancerous growth from the injury resulted in his nickname, "David of the Tumor." *Courtesy of the National Gallery of Art.*

Figure 11.2 British architect William Railton designed the 169-foot high Corinthian column honoring Admiral Horatio Nelson, killed during the Battle of Trafalgar in 1805. Completed in 1843, it cost £47,000 (adjusted for inflation, the price would be $1.7 million), and can be admired with a zoom lens in Trafalgar Square in central London. Ironically, despite the history of the square serif, there is no historical record that the Corinthian order of columns ever made it to Egypt. *Courtesy of David Castor.*

If you wanted a job as a trade worker in 18th-century England, you had to first be hired as an apprentice to learn a craft. At the time, William Caslon was the most famous typeface designer in the world (the first version of America's *Declaration of Independence* was printed in a Caslon typeface). One of his apprentices was Joseph Jackson, who later started his own workshop and hired 16-year-old Vincent Figgins, who learned the art of typeface making so well that he later began his own company in London. When the Egyptian cultural tsunami hit England, Figgins was inspired to invent a new typeface family that resembled Egypt's columns. Named slab serif, square serif, Antique, or Egyptian, the style made Figgins and his sons, who followed in his business, rich (Figure 11.3). In 1955 Howard Kettler designed the square serif typeface Courier to resemble the look produced with a typewriter. Today, the blocky column look is out of fashion but still used for Hollywood westerns on posters and for initials of universities curiously printed on sweatshirts and baseball caps.

Figure 11.3 In 1815 British printer Vincent Figgins designed the first square serif typeface (also called slab serif or Egyptian) and named it Antique. Ironically, the memorial's message for him and his wife, located at Nunhead Cemetery in London, was not set in his typeface style. However, the Tuscan columns are the least ornate of all the orders with bases that are most like square serif type families. *Courtesy of James Stevens.*

Although the moveable-type printing press inventor Johannes Gutenberg did not originate the idea of dividing lines of words on a page in discrete columns in 1455—his assistant Peter Schöffer most likely was the graphic designer for the famous and irreplaceable bibles—the success of the printing press popularized the column style. With each page containing two blocks of text, this grid approach would dominate newspaper and magazine printing for the rest of its history. For example, the *Haarlems Dagblad* from the Netherlands first published in 1655, the *Oxford Gazette* from 1665, *The New England Courant* published by Benjamin Franklin's older brother James in 1721, and today's version of your local online news website present their words and images in easily readable column formats (Figure 11.4).

Today the grid approach is exemplified by the De Stijl and **Bauhaus** styles (see Chapter 5). In the summer of 1917 several Dutch painters, including Piet Mondrian and Theo van Doesburg, perceived the use of a grid as a way to search for universal harmony in the wake of World War I. Mondrian and van Doesburg composed abstract paintings of thick

Figure 11.4 The two-column style of early newspapers mimicked the graphic design choice that Johannes Gutenberg's graphic designer, Peter Schöffer made in 1455. Abraham Casteleyn's *Weekly European News* first printed one hundred years later is no exception. *Courtesy of Haarlems Dagblad.*

black lines that divided canvases into basic shapes filled with primary colors. Their artwork inspired graphic designers to use the same system with text and images. From jewelry to apartment buildings, many products mimic this iconic, systematic design (Figure 11.5).

The architect and designer Le Corbusier, a pseudonym for the Swiss-born Charles-Édouard Jeanneret, made an important contribution to the use of the grid in architecture with his 1948 book *Modulor*. By the 1960s *modular design*, named after Le Corbusier's book, became the dominant force in modernizing the front pages of newspapers around

Figure 11.5 A single family house in Long Beach, California employs a grid design for its façade. *Courtesy of Paul Martin Lester.*

the world. In modular design, text and images for a story are placed within rectangular shapes called modules.

The other art movement that inspired the use of the grid approach was Bauhaus. In 1919, architect Walter Gropius headed a design workshop in Weimar, Germany, called the *Das Staatliches Bauhaus*. Bauhaus comes from the German words *bauen*, "to build," and *haus,* "house." Bauhaus was originally intended as an architectural school, but included classes in typography, advertising, and textiles. Like De Stijl, Bauhaus is characterized by its emphasis on useful, simple, and clearly defined forms. Abstract painter Paul Klee; designer and photographer Laszlo Moholy-Nagy; and designer, author, and educator Gyorgy Kepes were advocates of the Bauhaus style.

The popularity of columns, whether in architecture, typography, or graphic design, is easily understood. Because we humans can be split down the middle symmetrically, most of us prefer order. With an organized grid approach, balance and alignment are keys in producing layouts for print and screen media that are both highly legible and aesthetically soothing.

Practice

Static, Fixed, Absolute, and Relative Positioning

The web page we are building is organized into two columns. So far we have used the **float: left** CSS rule to organize the columns. Alternatively, we could have used positioning to establish the first column with *relative positioning* and the second with *absolute positioning*, but this would overcomplicate the code.

The Two-column Layout with Positioning

Again, this would overcomplicate the CSS code, but if you want to see absolute and relative positioning in another block of code, here is how the two-column layout could be interpreted *without the float property:*

First, **#content** would need to declare absolute positioning in order to act as the point of reference containing both columns:

```
#content {
  width: 960px;
  text-align: center;
  height: 1062px;
  background:#CCC url(bg.
    jpg) no-repeat;
  position: absolute;
}
```

Now you can declare absolute positioning on the left column (at the left edge of the content **div**) and relative positioning on the right column (480 pixels from the left—400 pixels to clear the width of the left box and 80 pixels to clear the sum of the padding on the left box):

```
.leftcol {
  text-align: left;
  position: absolute;
  left: 0;
  width: 400px;
  padding: 0 15px 0 65px;
}
.rightcol {
  text-align: left;
  position: relative;
  left: 480px;
  width: 400px;
  padding: 0 65px 0 15px;
}
```

A centered web experience is typical for blogs and personal sites, but some websites (currently Gmail and Amazon) keep their navigation tools fixed, either on the top or the left side of the browser while the rest of the page is free to stretch as large as the user opens a window. You can control how elements display on the page using four types of CSS positioning values, as follows:

Static positioning is the default. If no position is declared, in essence, you are using static positioning.

Fixed positioning displays an element according to values measured from the top, right, bottom, or left edge of the browser window. When fixed positioning is declared, the fixed item remains in place, regardless of the size of the browser or scrolling. When an element is declared with fixed positioning, it is no longer considered as being a part of the HTML page flow. We modified the **footer** tag selector in Chapter 10 using fixed positioning to keep it in place at the bottom of the page. However, when the browser window isn't in exactly the right position, the footer content overlaps the wrong areas of the page layout. For our page design, fixed positioning is not the best solution for keeping the footer in place on the page.

Absolute positioning is used to remove an element from the normal flow of the page and position it according to an offset value (top, right, bottom, or left) from the edges of its first (relative or fixed) positioned ancestor element. If a relative position is not declared in a parent element, the absolute positioned element will be in relation to the entire page.

Relative positioning is used to offset an element by values from the top, right, bottom, or left sides from where it would have been according to the normal page flow.

Absolute and relative positioning can (and often) work in tandem. Relative positioning is often declared as a point of reference for another selector that declares absolute positioning. You can add the code **position: relative;** to any selector.

Once a selector is defined as "relative" you can assign another selector **position: absolute;** and define top, right, bottom, and left values in order to declare a position in relation to a "relative" item on the page. If you declare absolute positioning without declaring relative positioning, then the selector is likely positioned in relationship to the **<html>** tag.

If no selector is defined as **position: relative;** the following code would basically set the footer to 0 pixels from the bottom of the page upon loading in the browser:

```
footer {
position: absolute;
bottom: 0px;
}
```

However, if you add a selector such as

```
#content {
position: relative;
}
```

to the code, the footer would be placed 0 pixels from the bottom of the content element.

> **Note**
>
> It makes sense to assign relative positioning to a selector before declaring absolute positioning. Remember: the absolute positioning values are measured from the first selector that declares **position: relative;**.
>
> You can overlap elements on the page by using fixed, relative, or absolute positioning in your CSS code. The stacking order of overlapping elements is controlled by the **z-index** property, as you will see in the following exercises.

Results of Chapter 11 Exercises

In the following exercises you will expand your growing knowledge of CSS positioning (Figure 11.6).

Download Materials for Chapter 11 Exercises

We will modify the results files from Chapter 10 to begin the exercises in this chapter. You can download the results files from the website. [http://viscommontheweb .wordpress.com/downloads/]

Exercise 1: Absolute Positioning without a Reference

1. **Set up your workspace:** Copy and paste the final Chapter 10 exercise files to a new folder named *chapter11*. Open Dreamweaver and define or edit your site to point to the root directory, *chapter11*. Choose Window > Workspace Layout > Designer. Open *index.html* in Dreamweaver, modify the title tag (I titled my page "Chapter Eleven"), and save your work.

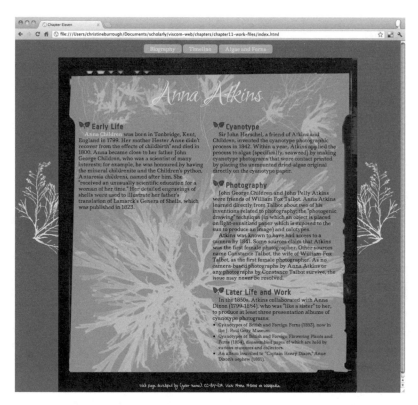

Figure 11.6 In the Chapter 11 exercises you will explore positioning with the footer division and make stylistic changes to the typography in the footer area.

2. We already created a footer defined with fixed positioning in Chapter 10. Change the property to **absolute** and preview your work in a browser—you can use the CSS Rule Definition for Footer dialog box in Dreamweaver (Figure 11.7), or you can simply replace the code in your style sheet.

Figure 11.7 The Positioning category in the CSS Rule Definition Dialog Box can be used to add the **position** property to the CSS code.

3. It may appear as though nothing has happened when you first view your page, but resize your browser window, scroll, and you will see that the footer remains positioned in the location that was "the bottom" of the browser when the page loaded (Figure 11.8). So **bottom: 0px;** in conjunction with absolute positioning is not the best declaration in this situation.

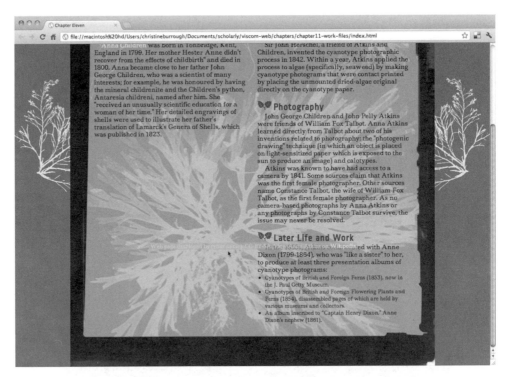

Figure 11.8 The footer content stayed in place at the "bottom" of the page when I first loaded it. When the browser is expanded, you can scroll to see that the footer content stays in its original "bottom" position, rather than sticking to the bottom of the window (as it would with fixed positioning). If you haven't noticed, this is still not a solution to our footer positioning problem.

4. You can make the footer stay at the bottom of the photograph by deleting **bottom: 0px;** and adding **top: 1062px;** This will make the footer stay 1062 pixels away from the top of the page (the **html** tag), since no other selector is defined with relative positioning.

``
footer {
    position: absolute;
    bottom: 0;
    top: 1062px;
    text-align: center;
    width: 960px;
    color: #CCC;
    padding: .5em;
    font-size: small;
}
``
	Since the bottom of the page varies according to how the user stretches the browser window, measuring positioning from the top of the document is more secure.

For our purposes, this procedure produces the results we want to see. But I'd feel better about defining the footer position in relation to something specific on the page, namely the content **div**.

Exercise 2: Absolute Positioning with Relative Positioning

VIDEO WALKTHROUGH

1. Now we will set the footer on the page using **absolute** positioning to offset the footer specifically from the top of the content division. We will do this by declaring **relative** position in another area of the page. It would make sense to think of the footer either as a fixed distance from the top of the browser, or an absolute distance relative to the content on the page. The content **div** is a parent to the footer **div**, so it would make sense to relate the positioning of the footer to it. In the style sheet, add relative positioning to the **#content** declaration.

| ```
#content {
    width: 960px;
    text-align: center;
    height: 1062px;
    background:#CCC url(bg.jpg) no-repeat;
    position: relative;
}
``` | Add relative positioning to the content division so we can relate the absolute positioning of the footer to it. |

By setting the position to relative, this class is now a point of reference for the footer, which has a position value of **absolute**.

2. Elements that declare an absolute position are removed from the normal flow of the page. In other words, as far as the rest of the document is concerned, this element doesn't exist (in terms of the flow of the page). Right now the footer appears to be sitting on a new line at the bottom of the page. However, we should consider what would happen if the columns didn't exactly fill the width of the container. We could end up with a **div** that ends halfway across the page and a footer that begins in the middle of the page instead of at the left margin of **#content**. Use the **Clear** property to bypass the floating divisions (see Chapter 10). The values that can be assigned to **clear** are **left**, **right**, and **both**. Although it does not seem (visually) necessary, add a left **clear** to the **footer** declaration block.

| ```
footer {
    position: absolute;
    top: 1062px;
    text-align: center;
    width: 960px;
    color: #CCC;
    padding: .5em;
    font-size: small;
    clear: left;
}
``` | "Clear" the left floating divisions to ensure the footer sits beneath the floating divisions applied to the left and right columns. |

Note

If you want to see this in action, add `clear: left;` to the `.rightcol` declaration block. Save your files and preview it in a browser—you will see the second column aligned beneath the first at the left margin (Figure 11.9). Return to your style sheet and use Command+Z to undo your last step(s) (or delete the `clear` property), as we don't actually want to clear the floating division before `.rightcol`.

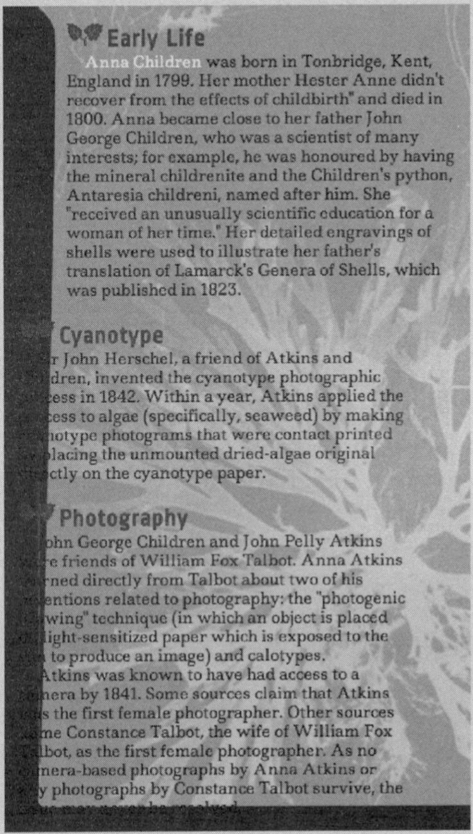

Early Life

Anna Children was born in Tonbridge, Kent, England in 1799. Her mother Hester Anne didn't recover from the effects of childbirth" and died in 1800. Anna became close to her father John George Children, who was a scientist of many interests; for example, he was honoured by having the mineral childrenite and the Children's python, Antaresia childreni, named after him. She "received an unusually scientific education for a woman of her time." Her detailed engravings of shells were used to illustrate her father's translation of Lamarck's Genera of Shells, which was published in 1823.

Cyanotype

r John Herschel, a friend of Atkins and dren, invented the cyanotype photographic ess in 1842. Within a year, Atkins applied the ess to algae (specifically, seaweed) by making otype photograms that were contact printed lacing the unmounted dried-algae original ctly on the cyanotype paper.

Photography

ohn George Children and John Pelly Atkins e friends of William Fox Talbot. Anna Atkins rned directly from Talbot about two of his entions related to photography: the "photogenic wing" technique (in which an object is placed light-sensitized paper which is exposed to the to produce an image) and calotypes. tkins was known to have had access to a era by 1841. Some sources claim that Atkins s the first female photographer. Other sources me Constance Talbot, the wife of William Fox lbot, as the first female photographer. As no era-based photographs by Anna Atkins or y photographs by Constance Talbot survive, the

Figure 11.9 If the right column cleared all left floating divisions, the second column would appear under the first.

Exercise 3: Using Z-index to Control Overlapping Items

1. You may have noticed that your footer content displays on top of the main content area of the page (it may have slipped your mind, but consider this a happy accident). **z-index** is a property used to set the stacking order of overlapping **div** tags. You can assign a positive or negative integer to the value. For instance, with a negative **z-index** value, your footer content will disappear. See this by modifying your code.

```
footer {
    position: absolute;
    top: 1062px;
    text-align: center;
    width: 960px;
    color: #CCC;
    padding: .5em;
    font-size: small;
    clear: left;
    z-index:-1;
}
```

A **z-index** with a negative integer will fall behind overlapping divisions with positively assigned indexes (or none at all).

With a negative **z-index** value, we are telling the browser to display the footer behind overlapping divisions on the page. This is not particularly advisable for our page, but it demonstrates how indexing works. Save your files and preview the page (Figure 11.10).

2. Set the **z-index** value to 1 (a positive integer) and save and preview your work to see the footer restored to its original stacking order (Figure 11.11).

Figures 11.10 and 11.11 The **z-index** property controls the stacking order of overlapping elements. In Figure 11.10 the footer element is indexed with a negative one (−1), so the footer falls behind other divisions. In Figure 11.11 the footer is indexed with a positive one (1) and no other elements are indexed. Therefore the footer displays on top of everything else on the page.

``css
footer {
    position: absolute;
    top: 1062px;
    text-align: center;
    width: 960px;
    color: #CCC;
    padding: .5em;
    font-size: small;
    clear: left;
    z-index:1;
}
``
	Set the **z-index** value in the footer declaration to 1 (or any positive integer, as we do not assign an index value anywhere else on the page).

Reference

Our footer is different from most because it has to land in the bottom margin of the cyanotype background print. Most page layouts for the Web are less strict about the height of a page, allowing more flexibility for the length of articles or other page content. In those cases, a "sticky footer" is a great solution. See http://ryanfait.com/sticky-footer or http://www.cssstickyfooter .com for code you can use in your own work. [http://ryanfait.com/sticky-footer/] [http://www.cssstickyfooter.com/]

Exercise 4: Adding a New Typeface to Footer Content

As we reviewed in Chapter 10, the footer area should not be overlooked. Since our footer content sits on top of the edges of a background graphic representing a cyanotype print, we should reconsider the typographic treatment so that the type is consistent with the format of the design.

This web page highlights information about and photographs made by Anna Atkins, who is well known for her collection of cyanotype prints of British algae. To create a cyanotype print, the photographer applies the sensitizer to the paper (or printing area) with a brush. When the formula dries, the negative is contact-printed (it lies directly on top of the sensitized paper) in the sunlight for the duration of the exposure. In its simplest format, the print is then washed in water and dried. Since the process involves contact printing, any notes written at the edges of the large-format negatives are possible to see in the resulting print. We'll assign a typeface to the footer area that mimics a handwritten note.

1. Search Google.com/webfonts for a hand-drawn font to use in the footer area (see Chapter 7, Exercise 2 for more on using Google Web Fonts). [http://www .google.com/webfonts] I narrowed my selection to four font-faces before deciding on Zeyada. Place the link to the new web font in the HTML source code and assign the font-family in the style sheet. I had to modify the size of my font from small to medium because hand-drawn fonts tend to have a smaller x-height, making them difficult to read when they are too small.

Add the reference link to the **head** area of the HTML source code

```
<!--LINK HREF TO THE EXTERNAL STYLE SHEET AND GOOGLE
FONTS -->
<link href="styles.css" rel="stylesheet" type="text/css"
/>
<link
href='http://fonts.googleapis.com/css?family=Ropa+Sans|R
uthie|Ledger' rel='stylesheet' type='text/css'>
<link
href='http://fonts.googleapis.com/css?family=Zeyada'
rel='stylesheet' type='text/css'>
</head>
```

Add the **font-family** names and a new **font-size** to the CSS style sheet

```
footer {
      position: absolute;
      top: 1062px;
      text-align: center;
      width: 960px;
      color: #CCC;
      padding: .5em;
      clear: left;
      z-index:1;
      font-size: medium;
      font-family: 'Zeyada', cursive;
}
```

2. Notice the redundancy in the HTML source code. We can consolidate the two links to the Google Web Fonts by adding a vertical line, or pipe (|), followed by the family selected for the footer to the string of code in the first **link href**.

Simplify the HTML code by consolidating two **link href** tags into one

```
<!--LINK HREF TO THE EXTERNAL STYLE SHEET AND GOOGLE
FONTS -->
<link href="styles.css" rel="stylesheet" type="text/css"
/>
<link
href='http://fonts.googleapis.com/css?family=Ropa+Sans|R
uthie|Ledger|Zeyada' rel='stylesheet' type='text/css'>

<link
href='http://fonts.googleapis.com/css?family=Zeyada'
rel='stylesheet' type='text/css'>

</head>
```

The Art and Craft of Code

ON THE WEB is xtine's translation of Jack Kerouac's 1957 scroll manuscript, *On The Road,* crafted for the experience of scrolling on the Web (Figure 11.12). This project tests how applicable Kerouac's road commentary is written in the contemporary virtual landscape of a web browser. Scrolling and browsing today is as popular as hitchhiking and road trips were in 1950s' American culture. In many cases, the work still speaks to wanderers—whether hitchhiking the open road or browsing the information superhighway. Every appearance of the word "road" was crossed out and replaced with the word "web" in a paperback edition of the book (there are, by the way, more than 150 instances of the word "road" in the original manuscript). Once each page was inked, it was scanned and uploaded into a design reflecting the original manuscript scroll, enabling the user/reader to scroll through the complete text on a single page. Click the last occurrence of the word "web" on any page where it is found to skim the book from the first "road/web" phrase to the next, to the last. {http://www.missconceptions.net/on-the-web/index-otw-original .html}

Figure 11.12 View the source code of the original version of xtine's *On the Web* to see all forms of positioning in play. *Courtesy of the artist.*

At http://www.missconceptions.net/on-the-web users can click to the original version of the project, see the "5K" and "Half-K" editions, and learn how absolute and relative positioning were used in tandem to create the illusion of paper taped together on a virtual scroll (Figure 11.13). View the source code and you will see fixed, absolute, and relative positioning all at play in this web page design. {http://www.missconceptions.net/ on-the-web}

Figure 11.13 The *On the Web* home page links to the Half-K edition and teaching tools. *Courtesy of the artist.*

Create, Reflect, Critique

Now that you can position a division any place on a page, use your new skills to create a design that does not adhere to the grid. How difficult is it to think in terms of collage and juxtaposition after you have spent chapters working in boxes that flow on top of, to the left, or to the right of one another? What types of design issues are challenging when you are creating a focal point and legibility in a dynamic, freeform composition?

Glossary Words

absolute positioning, Bauhaus style, fixed positioning, modular design, relative positioning, static positioning, z-index

12 INCORPORATING OTHER CODE

VIDEO
INTRODUCTION

Principles, History, Theory

Appropriation and Sampling

What do André the Giant, John Carpenter, and Barack Obama have in common?

André René Roussimoff was a renowned French wrestler and actor. He was best known as Fezzik in *The Princess Bride* and nicknamed "The Eighth Wonder of the World" because of his enormous size—he stood seven feet tall and weighed more than 500 pounds. Carpenter became noticed as an important Hollywood director with his 1978 indie slasher classic *Halloween*. The film made Jamie Lee Curtis a household scream queen, grossed more than $45 million, and spawned nine sequels and remakes. Obama, a social worker and community activist in Chicago, became a senator from Illinois, was elected the first African American president of the United States in 2008, and won the Nobel Peace Prize the next year.

You might take a wild guess and say that the link between them is that they are all men, successful in their respective fields, and put their pants on one leg at a time, but such connections would be a silly waste of space in a visual communication book.

The three have all been appropriated, sampled, some would say plagiarized, by the American graphic designer and so-called street artist Shepard Fairey.

Born and raised in the historic Southern port city of Charleston, South Carolina, by not particularly artistic parents—his father, Frank, is a family medicine physician and his mother, Charlotte, a real estate agent—they nevertheless recognized Shepard's teenage creativity after he put his designs all over skateboards and T-shirts. As supportive, and fortunately wealthy, parents, they did what any loving couple would do for their son and shipped him across the country to an isolated boarding high school, Idyllwild Arts in the San Jacinto Mountains of California, that has an annual price tag of $52,000. After graduation, he moved back to the East Coast to attend Rhode Island School of Design, another private and pricey art school. After four years, Fairey graduated with a BFA in illustration in 1992.

Meanwhile, André the Giant, after an eventful, yet controversial career, died of heart failure in a Paris hotel room. Barack Obama graduated from Harvard Law School and became a lecturer at the University of Chicago. John Carpenter's 1998 horror movie, *They Live*, about aliens from outer space who try to take over the Earth, was released four days before George H.W. Bush was elected president. In *They Live* ordinary billboard advertisements are transformed into vehicles for subliminal messages, such as MARRY AND REPRODUCE, CONSUME, WATCH T.V., and OBEY, that can only be read through special sunglasses.

As an art project and to impress his skateboarder friends, Fairey's introduction into popular culture showed a close-up picture of Roussimoff with the phrase, "ANDRE THE GIANT HAS A POSSE" that was made into posters, stickers, and stencils mostly for viewing on public walls as a form of street art (Figure 12.1). But after Titan Sports, Inc., later renamed World Wrestling Entertainment, which trademarked the name "André the Giant" threatened to sue Fairey for infringement, he made a high-contrast illustration of the portrait and edited the words to just one—OBEY.

Figure 12.1 The ubiquitous nature of Shepard Fairey's "Obey" sticker is evident when it is seen attached to an electrical box on a college campus. The image comes from a likeness of the seven-foot, 500-pound wrestler and actor, André René Roussimoff, better known as André the Giant. *Photo courtesy of Paul Martin Lester.*

Fairey's replacement of the "Posse" message with "OBEY" proved to be commercial genius when the graphic became a wildly popular commentary on social customs, governmental regulations, and pseudo hipster anti-consumer aesthetics. Today, much of Fairey's business dealings have to do with administering his line of OBEY prints, stickers, collectables, books, and clothing merchandise.

The concept of copyright protection involves crediting authors or owners for their properties (intellectual or otherwise). One of the four tenets of the *fair use clause* as part of U.S. copyright laws is the purpose of the work—whether it substantially transforms or mimics the original. *Appropriation*, a term more often used in an art class or museum than in court, alludes to the act of taking a popular word, idea, image, or thing for the purpose of transforming it into something new. This new word/idea/image/thing might comment upon the original, demonstrate social patterns associated with the original, or through juxtaposition or comparison demonstrate an unexpected aspect of the original.

Most graphic designers are not geniuses suddenly inspired to produce a completely new style. Ideas are based upon previously created compositions, transformed by an artist's ability to transform or appropriate artifacts of her culture. For example, artist and critic Mark Vallen points out that Roy Lichtenstein made paintings based on comic book images as a commentary on American culture. Andy Warhol is famous for his use and transformation of commercial products. The British street artist Banksy is best known for a piece that is a composite of three popular culture icons—Ronald McDonald, Mickey Mouse, and the screaming Vietnam-era girl. When combined, the visual messages comment on the competing forces of consumerism, entertainment, and war (a juxtaposition results in an unexpected aspect or similarity between the original images). Lichtenstein, Warhol, and Banksy have escaped criticism largely because comic book characters, Brillo pads, Campbell soup cans, Marilyn Monroe, Disney characters, and other media icons are well known by members of the public who understand that the artists' messages constitute commentary. Conversely, the transformative nature of Fairey's images hides the source of the work from the casual viewer.

Fairey didn't help his argument that all's fair in art and appropriation in 2008 after he threatened to sue an Austin, Texas, artist, Baxter Orr, for a piece he called, "Protect Yourself—Obey," that used the OBEY GIANT picture covered with a white respiratory mask during a severe acute respiratory syndrome (SARS) outbreak (Figure 12.2). More

famously that same year, Fairey received negative press after he made a poster that featured a head-and-shoulders portrait of Barack Obama above the word "PROGRESS" and then "HOPE" from a photograph taken by Associated Press (AP) freelance photographer Manny Garcia in 2004. Garcia believed he should have been compensated for the work. Fairey argued that his appropriation was protected by the fair use clause of copyright law. In 2011 it was announced that the AP, Garcia, and Fairey settled out of court for an undisclosed sum. On the OBEY GIANT website Fairey writes, "I am pleased to have resolved the dispute with the Associated Press. I respect the work of photographers, as well as recognize the need to preserve opportunities for other artists to make fair use of photographic images. I often

Figure 12.2 Illustrator Baxter Orr's *Protect Yourself—Obey* piece is a parody of Shepard Fairey's *Obey* sticker. *Courtesy of Baxter Orr at baxterorr.com.*

collaborate with photographers in my work, and I look forward to working with photos provided by the AP's talented photographers."

Shepard Fairey's defenders often cite Pablo Picasso who famously said, "Good artists copy; great artists steal." In Mark Vallen's critique of Shepard in the "Art for a Change" website, he points out, "There's little doubt that Picasso was referring to the 'stealing' of aesthetic flourishes and stylings practiced by master artists, and not simply carting off their works and putting his signature to them." An artist who reproduces wholesale someone else's work without credit or compensation is engaging in plagiarism and courts legal problems.

The same is true for those creating code for websites. One of the most popular activities of those new to web programming is to pull down a browser's View Menu and study the page source for the website on display. Many learn how to manipulate HTML by copying and pasting the code and changing various parameters. Likewise, advanced computer developers have created numerous JavaScript and JQuery samples that are free to use as long as credit is given for the work. Credit and compensation are keys toward the ethical and legal use of web code. For example, Marc Andreessen and Eric Bina (see Chapter 1), the programmers for the first successful web browser, Mosaic, were rightly upset after the University of Illinois, through its commercial licensing partner, Spyglass Mosaic, sold their source code to the Microsoft Corporation as a basis for the Internet Explorer browser. Spyglass and the university were paid a fee plus a percentage of the royalties for the sale of the software. For their efforts, Andreessen and Bina received multiple entries on Wikipedia pages.

Nevertheless, not all programmers expect or want their code to be secretive or protected. Richard Stallman began the "free software movement" through his GNU Project founded in 1983 (Figure 12.3). A group of programmers in 1998, with a desire to share their software, formed the Open Source Initiative. Both were formed to enhance the development of new programs, creative applications, and to foster collaboration. The philosophy of openness inspired a similar movement in publishing in 2001 with Creative Commons, formulated to achieve a compromise between free and illegal access and strict copyright laws. With a *Creative Commons license*, a creator gets to choose how she can share her work legally while retaining attribution (credit). FLOSS (Free/Libre and Open Source Software) is a nonprofit foundation started in the Netherlands in 2006 to document how to use free software. Many designers learn to code using Adobe's Dreamweaver, but some use its open-source counterpart, Kompozer. The first edition of *Digital Foundations: Introduction to Media Design with Adobe Creative Suite* (co-authored by xtine burrough, the author of the exercises in this book) was translated for open-source software, including Kompozer, on Flossmanuals.net.

Figure 12.3 In 2010 Richard Stallman spoke to a group at the University of Pittsburgh on the nature of free software and copyright law. *Courtesy of Victor Powell.*

Many programmers and designers are willing to share snippets of code for discrete purposes. It is always proper to acknowledge (credit) the author of the code within your files using the comment tag. OBEY.

Practice

Citing Your Sources

Once you understand the basics of web coding with HTML and CSS, you will find that incorporating someone else's code can often be a helpful solution to a design problem. For this chapter we will create a gallery of images with Visual Lightbox (VL) and incorporate this gallery into a web page of our own. While we will modify some of the settings, our use of VL does not constitute appropriation—the transformative nature of our work will not change the concept of the original image gallery produced by the free software. Nonetheless, we will cite our source using comment tags.

Results of Chapter 12 Exercises

In the following exercises you will learn to use borrowed code in your own work. We will borrow *Visual Lightbox* in order to add a gallery of images on our web page (Figure 12.4). Adopting someone else's code requires great focus, file management, and patience.

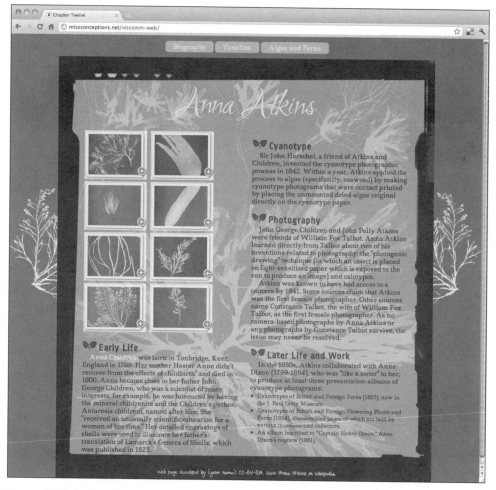

Figure 12.4 In the Chapter 12 exercises you will use Visual Lightbox to create JavaScript and additional style sheets to link to *index.html*.

Download Materials for Chapter 12 Exercises

We will modify the results files from Chapter 11 and Visual Lightbox to begin the exercises in this chapter. You can download Chapter 11 results files from the website. You will also need a few images to place in your gallery, which you can download from Wikipedia. [http://visuallightbox.com/index.html#download] [http://viscommontheweb.wordpress.com/downloads/]

Exercise 1: Downloading Visual Lightbox

1. As of this writing, you can download Visual Lightbox for free. [http://visuallightbox.com/index.html#download] This user-friendly application generates JavaScript and CSS code that creates a web gallery to display images selected from your hard drive. Before you begin, follow these steps:
   a. Download the application.
   b. **Set up your work folder:** Copy and paste the final Chapter 11 exercise files to a new folder named *chapter12*.
   c. Download eight digital reproductions of Anna Atkins' cyanotypes from the New York Public Library Flickr set. Create an "images" folder in your root directory (that is, inside the *chapter12* folder) that contains the eight image files saved with compression for the Web (Figure 12.5). [http://www.flickr.com/photos/nypl/sets/72157610898556889/]

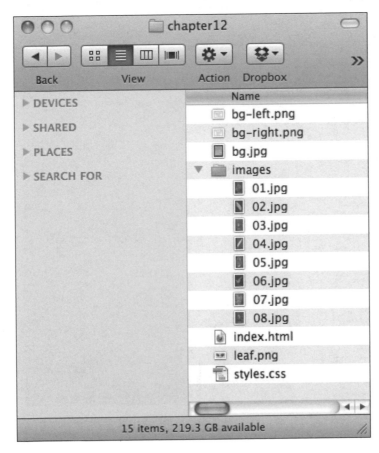

Figure 12.5 Chapter 12 work files include an images folder with eight digital photographs saved with JPG compression.

2. Open Visual Lightbox and then drag and drop your images into the application (Figure 12.6).

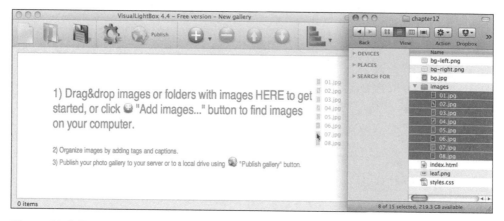

Figure 12.6 Drag the image files from the *images* folder to the Visual Lightbox application frame.

3. Click once on each image you dragged to the Visual Lightbox application and add a description (Figure 12.7). You will be able to modify descriptions later.
4. Choose Gallery > Properties to enable or disable properties of your gallery (such as enabling a slideshow, turning a zoom effect on or off, and so on). For instance, I turned off the "zoom" feature (Figure 12.8).
5. Click the Publish button. Select the Publish To Folder radio button and then browse to the folder on your hard drive where you are saving work files for

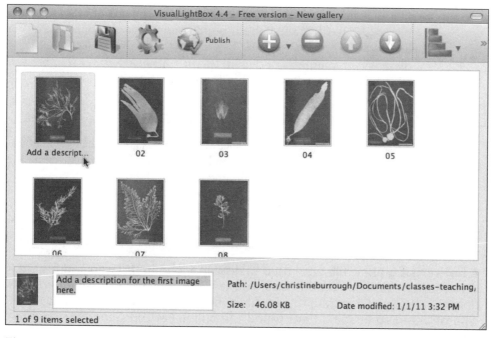

Figure 12.7 Add descriptions to each image.

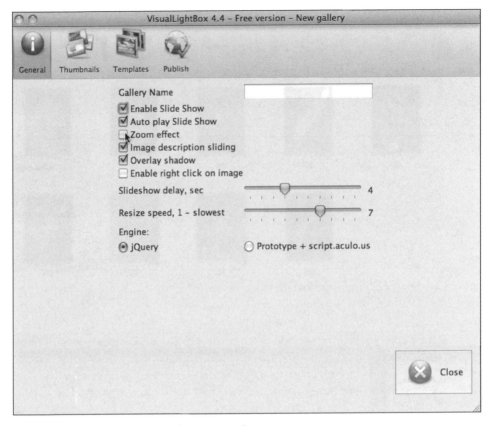

Figure 12.8 Select or deselect performance preferences.

Chapter 12. Name the new file *slideshow.html* so that you do not overwrite *index .html* (Figure 12.9). Click the Publish button once you are certain where your files will be saved.

6. View the gallery in your browser (Figure 12.10). Change the size of your browser window and notice how the gallery shrinks to fit into whatever space is available.

Exercise 2: Selecting and Pasting the Code into Your File

1. Look inside your *chapter12* folder (or your root directory) to see the new files that Visual Lightbox created for you. You should have new folders named "data" and "engine" as well as a *favicon.ico* file and *slideshow.html* (Figure 12.11).

Reference

A favicon is a graphic file (.ico) used to display a logo in the web address bar. If you search "favicon" on the Web, you will find easy-to-use online applications that help you generate the .ico file and the script required to display this type of branding image. I have found the online Favicon Generator easy to use. [http://www.favicon.cc/]

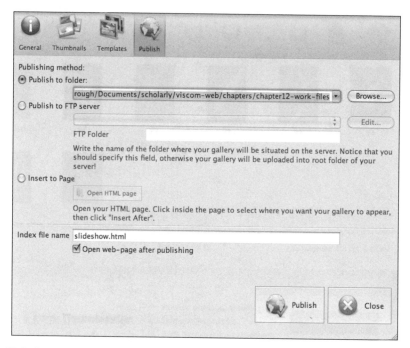

Figure 12.9 Pay attention to where you will publish the Visual Lightbox files (it should be saved in your root directory) and name it *slideshow.html* so as not to overwrite the index page.

Figure 12.10 Preview *slideshow.html* to see the gallery of images in a browser.

Figure 12.11 The root directory now contains subdirectories and a favicon file.

2. **Set up your workspace:** Open Dreamweaver and define or edit your site to point to the root directory, *chapter12.* Choose Window > Workspace Layout > Designer. Open *index.html* and change the title to read "Chapter Twelve."

3. Open *slideshow.html* and view the HTML code. In the **head** section of the document, the page links to two external CSS files, *vlightbox1.css* and *visuallightbox.css*, and three JavaScript files (stored in the *engine* folder). In the **body** section, there is one **<div>** named "vlightbox1." Notice how the image descriptions are added to the **title** attribution of the **a href** tag (Figure 12.12).

4. To insert the lightbox gallery into your page, copy and paste the scripts from the **head** section (between the comment tags "Start VisualLightBox.com HEAD section" and "End VisualLightBox.com HEAD section") of *slideshow.html* to the head section of *index.html*. Then copy all of the code from the **body** area of *slideshow.html*, including the open and close **div** tags, and paste it into the left column division in *index.html* above the **<h1>** tag and "Early Life" section. Be sure to cite your source. I added a comment tag just after **<div id="vlightbox1">**

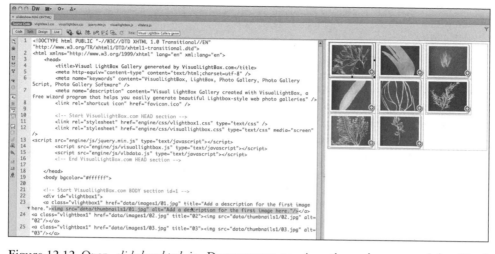

Figure 12.12 Open *slideshow.html* in Dreamweaver to view the code generated by Visual Lightbox.

to acknowledge that the code was generated by the Visual Lightbox application. Save your files and view the web page in a browser. If *index.html* seems to be functioning properly, you can close *slideshow.html*.

5. Notice all of the linked files next to where *source code* and *styles.css* appear across the top of the workspace window. Click *vlightbox1.css* to view this style sheet.

Copy and paste the specified code from the **head** section of *slideshow.html* to *index.html*

```
<title>Chapter Twelve</title>
<!--LINK HREF TO THE EXTERNAL STYLE SHEET AND GOOGLE FONTS
-->
<link href="styles.css" rel="stylesheet" type="text/css" />
<link
href='http://fonts.googleapis.com/css?family=Ropa+Sans|Ruthi
e|Ledger|Zeyada' rel='stylesheet' type='text/css'>
<!-- Start VisualLightBox.com HEAD section -->
<link rel="stylesheet" href="engine/css/vlightbox1.css"
type="text/css" />
<link rel="stylesheet" href="engine/css/visuallightbox.css"
type="text/css" media="screen" />
<script src="engine/js/jquery.min.js"
type="text/javascript"></script>
<script src="engine/js/visuallightbox.js"
type="text/javascript"></script>
<script src="engine/js/vlbdata.js"
type="text/javascript"></script>
<!-- End VisualLightBox.com HEAD section -->
</head>
```

Copy and paste the specified code from the **body** section of *slideshow.html* to *index.html*

```
<header>Anna Atkins</header>
<div class="leftcol"> <!--1ST HALF COLUMN DIV-->
<!-- Start VisualLightBox.com BODY section id=1 -->
<div id="vlightbox1">
<!--Code generated by Visual Lightbox, see
www.VisualLightbox.com -->
<a class="vlightbox1" href="data/images1/01.jpg" title="Add
a description for the first image here."><img
src="data/thumbnails1/01.jpg" alt="Add a description for
the first image here."/></a><a class="vlightbox1" href="data/
images1/02.jpg" title="02"><img src="data/thumbnails1/02.
jpg"
alt="02"/></a>
<a class="vlightbox1" href="data/images1/03.jpg"
title="03"><img src="data/thumbnails1/03.jpg"
alt="03"/></a>
<a class="vlightbox1" href="data/images1/04.jpg"
title="04"><img src="data/thumbnails1/04.jpg"
alt="04"/></a>
<a class="vlightbox1" href="data/images1/05.jpg"
title="05"><img src="data/thumbnails1/05.jpg"
alt="05"/></a>
<a class="vlightbox1" href="data/images1/06.jpg"
title="06"><img src="data/thumbnails1/06.jpg"
alt="06"/></a>
<a class="vlightbox1" href="data/images1/07.jpg"
title="07"><img src="data/thumbnails1/07.jpg"
alt="07"/></a>
<a class="vlightbox1" href="data/images1/08.jpg"
title="08"><img src="data/thumbnails1/08.jpg"
alt="08"/></a><a class="vlb" style="display:none"
href="http://visuallightbox.com">Photo Gallery Program by
VisualLightBox.com v4.4m</a>
</div>
<!-- End VisualLightBox.com BODY section -->
<h1>Early Life</h1>
```

6. The first selector is **#vlightbox1**. This is the id assigned to the **div** containing all of the images in the gallery. There are only two properties in the declaration block. You are familiar with the **width** property, but the **zoom** property is new. **Zoom** controls the display size. When the value is "1," the viewer experiences the content at 100 percent of its value. You can assign positive or negative values to the **zoom** property. Change the code to reduce the **zoom** value to .5, and then save your work and preview it in multiple browsers (Figure 12.13).

```
#vlightbox1 {
  width:100%;
  zoom:.5;
}
```

Figure 12.13 In Chrome the gallery appears smaller, but in Firefox the size of the gallery remains the same.

7. As of this writing, the **zoom** property is not supported in many browsers. For instance, the version of Chrome I use displays the change to the zoom setting, while the same set of images in Firefox appear at 100 percent of their original size. Set the **zoom** value back to 1 (the default value in all browsers) and save your work. Fortunately, we have designed the page so that the default value results in a balanced design.

Note

You can also control how many columns of thumbnails are produced in your gallery in the Visual Lightbox application. Select the Properties button (its icon looks like a gear) > Thumbnails, and you will see a pull-down list of choices for a number of columns as well as other editable thumbnail properties.

```
#vlightbox1 {
  width:100%;
  zoom:1;
}
```

8.   Finally, if you upload your work to a server, remember that you will need to upload all of the files and directories to your root directory, except *slideshow.html*, to see the page function "live" on the Web (Figures 12.14 and 12.15).

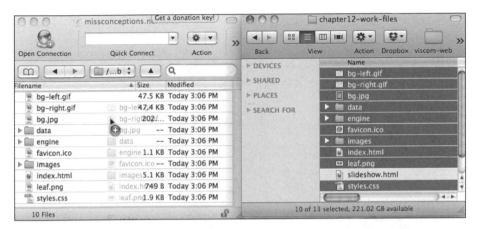

Figure 12.14 Upload all of the files and directories in your root folder to the server.

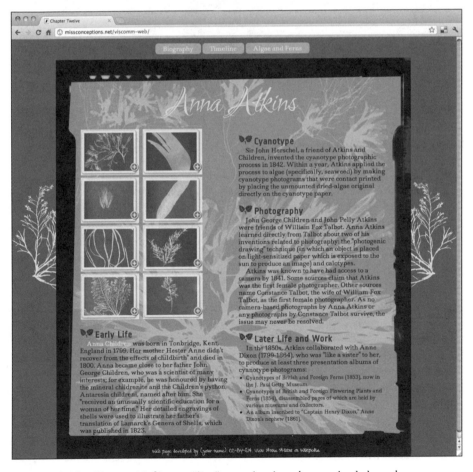

Figure 12.15 The Chapter 12 files are "live" once they have been uploaded to a browser.

Uploading Changes to the Code

If you need to make a change to your code, you will do that offline and then reupload the file to the server space. In this case, if you needed to change, for instance, the zoom property, which is in the *vlightbox1.css* file, you would modify the page in Dreamweaver and then upload the file to the directory where it is saved. That is, you would upload the file to the *css* folder that is stored inside the *engine* folder (or root directory > engine > css) (Figure 12.16).

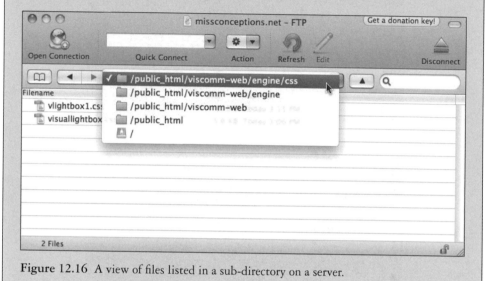

Figure 12.16 A view of files listed in a sub-directory on a server.

The Art and Craft of Code

In Jillian McDonald's 2005 *Screen Kiss* (Figures 12.17, 12.18, and 12.19), scenes from popular movies that feature Angelina Jolie kissing an assortment of actors are supplemented with McDonald's image and appropriated into a web project intended to render Billy Bob Thornton jealous. McDonald writes,

> *Me and Billy Bob*, a recent DVD and web project, takes as its subject a 'crush' I have on actor and musician Billy Bob Thornton. Unfortunately, Billy Bob has not responded, and I am ready to make him jealous. *Screen Kiss* features several popular actors including Daniel Day Lewis, Billy Crudup, Gary Oldman, Johnny Depp, and one actress, Billy Bob's former wife Angelina Jolie. In each case I insert myself into existing film scenes as stand-in for the actress or actor kissing these stars. I make eye contact with the camera, which functions as voyeur and Billy Bob's, presumably jealous, eye. [http://www.soilmedia.org/screenkiss/]

Create, Reflect, Critique

Now that the home page is almost complete, it is time to develop secondary pages. When designing a full website (or a multipage layout, such as a book or magazine), it is often helpful to create a tree diagram that expresses the levels of hierarchy among pages. For

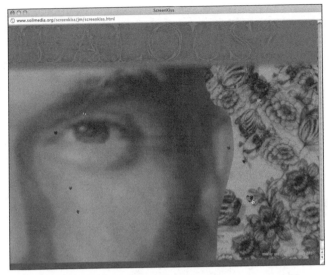

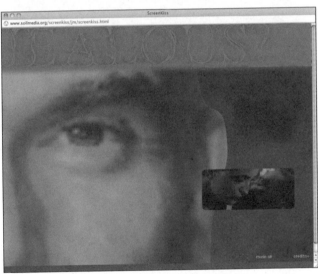

Figures 12.17 and 12.18 Screen shots from Jillian McDonald's *Screen Kiss*. *Courtesy of Jillian McDonald.*

Figure 12.19 Video still from McDonald's 11-minute single channel video. *Courtesy of Jillian McDonald.*

Figure 12.20 A simple tree diagram displays the hierarchy of our four-page website.

this website, the tree would be expressed by Figure 12.20. The home page, like the root directory, is at the top level. The design of each page should be set as follows: Pages that are common to a level should share the same layout. Sets of pages on different levels of the tree *could* display a slightly different design treatment. We created three navigation buttons for the categories "biography," "timeline," and "algae and ferns." Develop web pages for each of these categories, or change the wording of the navigation buttons and develop landing pages for them.

How similar should the new pages look to the home page? The gestalt law of similarity holds that readers perceive similar elements in a design as part of a whole group (or in this case, as part of a consistent visual message). Since the pages are connected via the top navigation tool, the user should see similar visual properties among them. However, you will also want to create contrast between the home page and the second-level pages.

Glossary Words

appropriation, Creative Commons license, fair use

13   ACCESSIBILITY

VIDEO
INTRODUCTION

Principles, History, Theory

Beyond Best Practices

If blind, is it possible for you to still see?

Yes and no.

One of the most enduring and recognizable songs ever written, one that has given strength to millions of persons to overcome obstacles, faith to prevail against impossible odds, and redemption since its publication in 1779, is "Amazing Grace." It has been estimated that the hymn is performed more than ten million times a year and is especially treasured by African American gospel singers, which is ironic because its songwriter, Anglo British John Newton, was a slave trader.

Newton's life reads like a man in need of salvation. Born in London in 1725, his mother died when he was seven. As his father was a ship captain for a private company, young John went on several voyages with him. When his father retired, John eventually joined a ship that delivered African slaves to England. After a falling out with the ship's crew, he was made a slave to an African duchess and treated cruelly. At one point he felt his life so hopeless that he thought of killing himself. Luckily, at the age of 23, he escaped. However, on the return to England off the coast of Ireland the ship almost sank in a storm. His near-death experience awakened religious fervor that would eventually lead him to become an Anglican priest and become active in the abolitionist movement.

Written in 1772, the first verse of "Amazing Grace" comes from the Gospel of John in which it is told that Jesus healed a blind man (Figure 13.1):

> Amazing grace! (how sweet the sound)
> That saved a wretch like me!
> I once was lost, but now am found,
> Was blind, but now I see.

For some, to be spiritually blind is one type of disability. Not able to physically see what may be in your way can also be a serious liability. In 2008, Volvo, the Swedish car maker in business since 1927, introduced an optional feature for its S40 sedan. If you paid extra, technicians would install tiny cameras below each side mirror that were a part of the appropriately named acronym BLIS, short for Blind Spot Information System. With more than half a million lane-change and merging accidents in the United States each year, blind spot detection devices are an important safety feature. They can be found in 2012 models such as the Audi A6, the Ford Taurus Limited and Fusion, the Lincoln MKZ, the Mazda 6, and the Volvo S60. Was blind, but now I see.

Religion and technology are two ways many are helped to see, but sometimes a government must step in to assure that aid is provided for all. Back when the U.S. Congress used

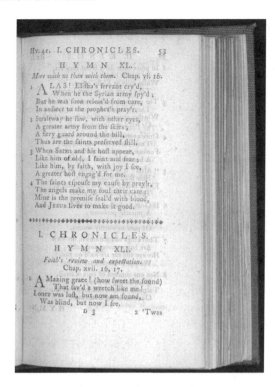

Figure 13.1 Page 53 of the 1779 publication *Olney Hymns* by John Newton and William Cowper contains a verse that would become the spiritual classic, "Amazing Grace." Printed materials during that time often used a "long s" that resembled the letter "f" whenever an "s" was at the start or in the middle of a word. Most famously, the spelling of "Congress" in the original "Bill of Rights" has a "long s." By 1810 its use was discontinued in America. *Courtesy of the Library of Congress.*

to pass significant legislation because members understood the art and need of compromise, the ***Americans with Disabilities Act (ADA)*** was passed. President George H. W. Bush, the elder, signed the ADA into law in 1990. The ruling was a major step in granting civil rights to those with disabilities. It regulated a wide range of social, architectural, and technical accommodations. The ADA allowed equal opportunities in hiring, mandated that public restrooms have features that aided those who use wheelchairs, and by implication, ***Section 508*** of the ADA required the addition of code as a part of websites so that disabled users could use text-to-speech and other devices.

And yet, someone without vision can only "see" a picture on the Web if a developer includes an alternative description (the **alt** attribute) in the website's code. If the description for an image that is displayed on a website is omitted or only minimally explanatory, the person with a disability remains disabled.

As much as the alternative band The White Stripes, the married-then-divorced Detroit couple Jack and Meg White were loved by their fans, imagine trying to use its website with your eyes closed. [http://www.whitestripes.com/home/home.html] With its use of a splash page, hot spot areas for links that are hidden from view, and without an "alt" explanation for its homepage's illustration, an intriguing combination of a skull, twin-lens reflex cameras, and likenesses of Jack and Meg as part of a red, white, and black color scheme, the content is lost (Figure 13.2). Was blind, but now I am still blind.

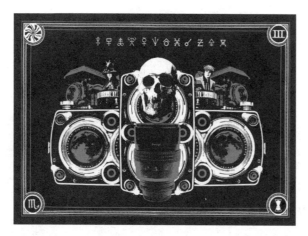

Figure 13.2 A musician in several underground bands in Detroit, Jack Gillis met bartender Meg White and was smitten. They married in 1996, and Jack took her surname. The partnership became more interesting after Meg learned to play the drums for Jack's innovative guitar and singing compositions—The White Stripes was formed. Although the two would divorce and dissolve the band, the website lives on. Like the music played by White, the site is a curious mix of visual and audio treats for the senses and old-school traditions in the form of HTML programming that uses a splash page, JavaScript, Flash and tables. *Courtesy of Rob Jones and WhiteStripes.com.*

Whether someone is spiritually lost, unsure of a lane change, or unaware of the visual treats the Web offers, not being able to see is a disability. At least for the Web, seeing is possible through a simple fix that provides access to more of what the Web offers. Accessibility is about communicating with all users. This means that when you develop code for a website, you should consider those with color deficiencies, low vision, or no vision who use text-to-speech or other adaptive technology devices. It's not just a good idea—it's the law.

You were blind, but now you see.

Amen.

Practice

Accessibility Standards

Certain elements, such as tables and image maps, may cause you to read through the W3's Web Content Accessibility Guidelines. [http://www.w3.org/TR/2008/REC-WCAG20-20081211/] We haven't added image maps or tables within our exercises (not because they are troublesome, but because they were not necessary for our project).

Whether you were aware of it or not, throughout this book we have been building our code, for the most part, to meet the best practices in accessibility design. We have provided alternate text for images by utilizing the **alt** attribute of the **img** tag. We are using a navigational tool that is based on an unordered list, which means that it can be "read" by a screen reader. Our design markup is saved in a style sheet. We have not used (at the time of this writing) deprecated tags. Our design supports legibility. We have even used new HTML5 elements that further enhance accessibility by descriptive naming (some would say, we have developed semantically consistent code). For instance, there is a tag named "nav" and one named "footer," which are helpful because the name of the tag indicates its function.

Nonetheless, there are still a few modifications we can make in order to meet accessibility standards.

Results of Chapter 13 Exercises

In the following exercises you will convert some of your design into a fluid layout. You will also validate all of the code you produced while working on the exercises in this book (Figure 13.3).

Figure 13.3 Changes made to the Anna Atkins website in Chapters 13 and 14 may not be immediately visible in your browser, but they will contribute to a more reliable set of code.

Download Materials for Chapter 13 Exercises

We will use the results files from Chapter 12 to begin the exercises in this chapter. You can download the Chapter 12 results file from the website. [http://viscommontheweb. wordpress.com/downloads/]

Exercise 1: Percentages and Elastic Measurements

In Chapter 7 we set parts of our typography in elastic measurements (ems). While pixels are familiar measurements, they are not always the best way to describe a "page" that ultimately is contained by measurements defined by the viewer (think about how often you expand a browser window to fit your needs). Pixels describe absolute properties. By contrast, elastic measurements (ems) and percentages (%) are fluid methods of defining measurements as relationships among objects on a page. We will convert parts of our page to percentages and ems in the following steps.

> **Note**
>
> Once you are familiar with ems and percentages, you may start the process of designing a web page using these units of measurement. For people who are brand new to designing for the Web, translating the familiar (pixels) into these new forms of measurement can be helpful in demonstrating how the new units of measurement relate to the old paradigm (pixels).

1. **Set up your workspace:** Copy your files from the *chapter12* folder to a new folder named *chapter13*. Open Dreamweaver and define or edit your site to point

to the root directory, *chapter13*. Choose Window > Workspace Layout > Designer. Open *index.html* and change the title to read, "Chapter Thirteen."

2. View *styles.css* to modify layout measurements in the CSS code. Instead of 400 pixels, try modifying the width of **.rightcol** and **.leftcol** to a value in percentages. You might be inclined to set each width property to a value of 50 percent, but if you do you will see that the right column falls beneath the left. Don't forget that you have to account for any padding or margin values when building the width of the box. I used 40 percent in my code.

Change the units of measurement in the width value from pixels to percentages

```
.leftcol {
text-align: left;
float: left;
width: 400px;
width: 40%;
padding: 0 15px 0 65px;
}

.rightcol {
text-align: left;
float: left;
width: 400px;
width: 40%;
padding: 0 65px 0 15px;
}
```

---

3. Assuming 1em is usually equal to 16 pixels, you can convert pixels to ems (see Chapter 7 for a longer description of this conversion). Our current font size is not set in the **body** or **p** selectors. Check the default settings by adding the font-size property, and set it to 1em (you will probably not notice a change in your layout). Reduce the size to .95em to see the type appear smaller.

Note

When using percentages you have to remember that the browser will read "40%" as "40% of ___" where the blank is filled in by the parent element. In the case of the half-columns, their widths are 40 percent of the total width of **#content**, or 960 pixels.

```
p {
        font-family: 'Ledger', Georgia, serif;
        line-height: 1.2em;
        text-indent: 1.2em;
        font-size: .95em;
}
```

Exercise 2: Validating HTML

Just when you think you are done, you should be aware that you are more than likely not

Note

If 1em is 16 pixels, then .95em is .95*16, or 15.2 pixels.

finished yet. However much time you budget for a project, give yourself about twice as much time. The same is usually true for CSS *validation*. One of the best things you can do for your files, both in terms of accessibility and all-around best practices, is validate your code. The W3C maintains an HTML and CSS validator. Dreamweaver has a built-in validator, which is easy enough to use from the menu File > Validate. Software changes rapidly, and though I don't believe these features will be discontinued in future versions of Dreamweaver, I will demonstrate HTML and CSS validation using the W3 website that has been published since 1994 (before the first version of Dreamweaver was released in 1997).

1. Search the Web for "HTML Validator" and you will find the tool currently available on validator.W3.org. [http://validator.W3.org] Using the W3C validator, select the second tab (to validate by uploading your file) and then click the Choose File button to select *index.html* from the *chapter13* folder from your hard drive (Figure 13.4). Click the Check button and hold your breath.

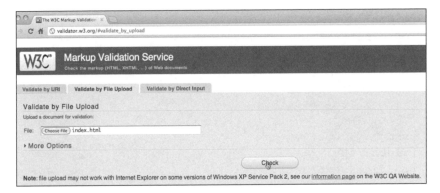

Figure 13.4 Validate the HTML file by uploading it to the W3 validator.

2. To my surprise (yes, even competent designers and developers expect to find errors), the document was successfully validated (Figure 13.5).

Figure 13.5 The HTML validator success screen is always nice to see.

Note

There is no shame in using the validator website repeatedly and for the same page. If your code did not validate successfully the first time, keep debugging. One of your goals should be a successful validation.

Exercise 3: Validating CSS

Validating your CSS file is similar to validating your HTML file. You should make no assumptions and always validate both files.

1. Go to the CSS Validator and choose the By File Upload tab. [http://jigsaw.w3.org/css-validator/] Click the Browse button and select your file. Before clicking the Check button, be sure to expand the More Options area and validate for CSS level 3, as we are using CSS3 in our document (Figure 13.6).

Figure 13.6 Validate the CSS file for CSS level-3 since we used CSS3 properties in the style sheet.

2. At first, it may seem that we are in a little trouble as the validator returned three errors and one warning. However, the three errors are actually the same error repeated three times, which is that the **border-radius** properties that are specific to certain browsers do not validate by W3C standards (Figure 13.7). This is fine, because the last line of code in the **nav li** declaration block uses the **border-radius** property, and this is validated. The second warning is in regard to what could potentially be an illegible situation: the background color

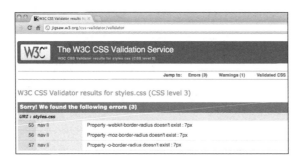

Figure 13.7 Error messages regarding the browser-specific CSS code in *styles.css* are unpleasant, but this time they do not indicate problems.

Additional Links and Resources

Figure 13.8 Accessibility tips from WebAIM. *Courtesy of WebAIM.org, see http://webaim.org/resources/designers/*

A really technical listing by the W3C
[http://www.w3.org/TR/WCAG10-HTML-TECHS/]
Web AIM
[http://www.webaim.org]
Alexa 100 Accessibility Errors
[http://webaim.org/blog/alexa-100-accessibility-errors/]
Section508.gov
[http://www.section508.gov]

of the content section (**#ccc** or gray) is the same as the color of text elements in the footer section (also **#ccc**). The validator does not know what we know: the footer section includes the dark cyan at the bottom of the background graphic. So what the validator interprets as a red-flag situation is in fact under control.

Exercise 4: Validating Web Accessibility

Once your HTML and CSS files are validated, it doesn't hurt to also check the files on WAVE (the web accessibility evaluation tool provided by WebAIM). [http://wave.webaim.org/]

1. Go to http://wave.webaim.org/ and upload the HTML file in your *Chapter13* folder. [http://www.webaim.org]
2. Receive your web accessibility report. WAVE detected no accessibility errors, but I can see that I should add descriptions (alternative text, via the **alt** attribute) to all of the image files I placed in the web gallery (Figure 13.9). This was a lazy oversight on my part when I was putting together the demonstration of the Visual Lightbox application.

Add alternative information to the **img** tags in *index.html* using the **alt** attribute

```
<img src="data/
thumbnails1/02.jpg"
alt="cyanotype of British
algae"/>
```

Note

You might notice that in some browsers if you hover over the image you will see the information coded into the **title** property of the **img src** tag. You should modify that area, too, for better communication with your users.

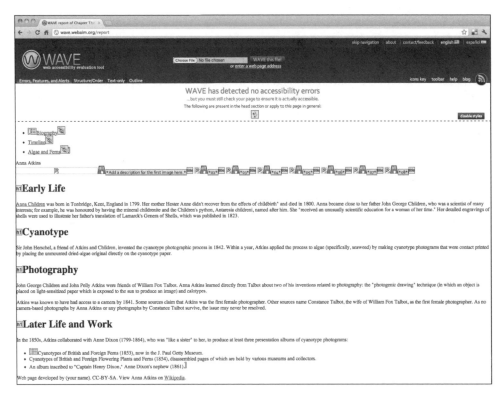

Figure 13.9 WAVE accessibility results.

The Art and Craft of Code

In Stephanie Rothenberg's ironic *School of Perpetual Training* online students are prepared for new entry-level jobs in the technology industry by the following actions performed in a webcam-enabled training module: waving arms, jumping up and down, or swinging rapidly from side to side (Figures 13.10 and 13.11). Just imagine a future of computing where you not only have to see and type, but wave your arms, jump up and down, or swing rapidly from side to side. If this were a viable training site for online jobs, even more accessibility issues would need to be addressed. [http://turbulence.org/Works/perpetualtraining/index.php]

Figures 13.10 and 13.11 *School of Perpetual Training* by Stephanie Rothenberg, 2009. *Courtesy of Stephanie Rothenberg*

Create, Reflect, Critique

After reading about appropriation in Chapter 12 and while thinking about accessibility features from the previous exercises, consider a curating project in which available public media is modified into a new visual message via the Web. Find media in the Library of Congress Flickr stream, the Wikimedia Commons website, or the Prelinger Film Archives. Curate a set of modified images or videos and then design a web page to exhibit your work. Be sure to validate your HTML and CSS code.

Reference

When I started to assign this project to students, I created a couple of examples based on some of my own remix projects: Balloons in the Library of Congress and Library of Congress Remixed. [http://missconceptions.net/loc/balloons/] [http://missconceptions.net/loc]

Glossary Words

Americans with Disabilities Act (ADA), Section 508 of the ADA, validation

14   BROWSER COMPATIBILITY

VIDEO
INTRODUCTION

Principles, History, Theory

Your Continuing Education

Can an Aries and a Virgo find lasting happiness?

According to the experts of eAstrolog.com, the answer is a resounding no.

The reason has something to do with a fire sign (Aries, the ram) not being a good match for an earth sign (Virgo, the virgin maiden). Because Aries is the first symbol of the Zodiac and controlled by the red planet of Mars, such a person is considered to be creative, impulsive, assertive, and perhaps rightly so, a bit arrogant. On the other hand, a Virgo, symbolized by a virgin maiden and governed by the planet Mercury, has a personality that is practical, careful, introverted, and humble—about as opposite as you can get (Figures 14.1 and 14.2).

Figures 14.1 and 14.2 From an 1825 set of cards called *Urania's Mirror*, these illustrations by the British etcher Sidney Hall show the constellations of Aries the Ram (with a fly) and Virgo the Virgin Maiden. She holds a lily, a symbol of purity, and a stalk of wheat, a symbol of the Earth's bounty. Users were meant to poke holes through the stars and line up each picture with the constellations in the sky. *Courtesy of the Library of Congress.*

According to the Western school of astrology (other forms of the art include Celtic, Chinese, financial, Indian, psychological, Tibetan, and more than 30 others), an Aries would do better with a Libra (fire and air need each other), while a Virgo should have a much better time with a Pisces (earth and water don't compete). Besides no doubt exhaustive and thorough personality profiles of successful and disastrous historical and current partnerships, with each member of the team compared with their birth signs by serious and learned astrologers from prestigious educational institutions throughout the four corners of the world, a simpler method of establishing compatibility was devised. Based on the magical and mysterious number 6 (see Chapter 7), when the 12 astrology signs are shown around a circle, its opposite is found by counting six signs around the wheel, or at its sextile, 60 degrees from the starting symbol (Figure 14.3).

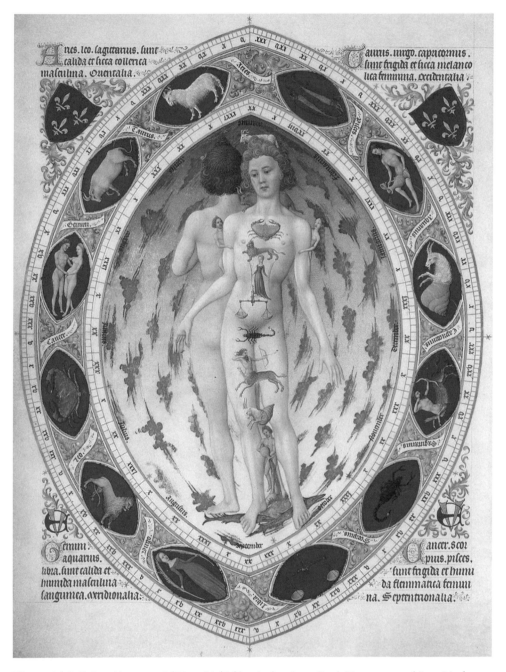

Figure 14.3 Painted between 1412 and 1416 by the brothers, Paul, Hermann, and Jean Limbourg for Jean, Duc de Berry, a wealthy patron of the arts in France, "Anatomical Man" from *Les Très Riches Heures* illustrates the connection between the astrological signs and the human body. *Courtesy of the U.S. National Library of Medicine.*

With this method it is reasonable to conclude that couples that have worked and/or lived together in mutually beneficial and satisfying ways should be born under signs that are 60 degrees of separation. To test this hypothesis, the following are six successful duos with their birth dates and astrological signs:

- Marie Sklodowska-Curie, born November 7, a Scorpio, and Pierre Curie, born May 15, a Taurus. Married couple that shared a Nobel Prize in physics for their work on radiology.
- Christo Vladimirov Javacheff and Jeanne-Claude Marie Denat de Guillebon, both born June 13, Gemini (and in the same year, 1935). Married couple known for their colorful environmental artistic displays.
- Martin Luther King, Jr., born January 15, a Capricorn, and Coretta Scott King, born April 27, a Taurus. Married couple that worked toward civil rights in the United States.
- Sir Elton Hercules John, born March 25, an Aries, and David James Furnish, born October 25, a Scorpio. The pop singer and filmmaker have been in a relationship since 1993 and civil partners since 2005.
- Steven Paul Jobs, born February 24, a Pisces, and Stephen Gary Wozniak, born August 11, a Leo. Co-founders of the Apple Computer Company.
- Sergey Brin, born August 21, a Leo, and Larry Page, born March 26, an Aries. Co-founders of Google, Inc.

Of the six couples listed, chosen for their important contributions in several different areas (art, entertainment, science, social justice, and technology), only one is well matched according to the sextile theory of astrological compatibility (you can find out which one on your own).

All of this goes to show that compatibility doesn't necessarily depend on where the sun was located or how the moon and planets were arranged at the time of your birth. Compatibility is two persons working together well because similarities and differences are, in equal measure, accepted and celebrated.

And what is true for people is also true for things. Apple, Google, and Microsoft with their Safari, Chrome, and Explorer or Bing browsers can all get along because through the software tips included with this chapter, they can be made compatible.

If you still hold a few doubts, be comforted by the fact that the co-authors of this textbook have lived and worked together in relationship, married, and professional bliss despite, or because, one is an Aries and the other a Virgo.

Practice

Quirky Browsers

One of the most challenging aspects of designing for interactive platforms is the quirks and differences among competing browsers. Internet Explorer seems to be the trickiest, while Firefox and Chrome usually update their browsers to support the most recent developments in HTML5 and CSS3 (at least, at the time of this writing—who knows, by the time you read this, maybe IE will be a favored browser). In the following exercises you will decide if you want to use *CSS reset code*, check for *browser compatibility* using Dreamweaver's tool, and learn to use Adobe BrowserLab.

Results of Chapter 14 Exercises

In the following exercises you will choose to add (or not to add) CSS reset code to your CSS document. Lastly, you will debug your HTML and CSS code for as many browsers as you would like to pursue using Adobe BrowserLab (Figure 14.4).

Figure 14.4 In the following exercises you will alter the code to see successful displays of your web page in multiple browsers.

Download Materials for Chapter 14 Exercises

We will modify the results file from Chapter 13 to begin the exercises in this chapter. You can download the Chapter 13 results file from the website. [http://viscommontheweb. wordpress.com/downloads/]

Exercise 1: Adding (or Not) Code for CSS Reset

In an effort to "wipe the slate clean" or trick the browser into behaving as we expect it to, many web designers and programmers add a block of code at the beginning of the CSS document to "reset" the web browser.

However, Steven Benner's article, "Reset Cascading Style Sheets Are Bad Practice," offers a strong argument against implementing CSS reset code. Benner writes, "Just about every browser has a default set of styles that it applies to pages. Ninety-nine percent of these quirks could be remedied by globally setting margin and padding to zero." [http://stevenbenner.com/2010/02/reset-cascading-style-sheets-are-bad-practice/] Our web page, thus far, is following Benner's advice and uses the universal selector to set margin and paddings to zero.

I don't think a block of reset code is necessary for this page design, but if you'd like to try adding it, feel free to copy/paste Eric Meyer's reset code or the YUI (Yahoo! User

Interface) reset code into the top of your CSS file. [http://meyerweb.com/eric/tools/css/reset/] [http://developer.yahoo.com/yui/reset/#code] Remember: Cascading starts at the top and trickles down. The last definitions for CSS properties on your page are the definitions that display in the browser. If you do use reset code, it should appear first in your style sheet.

> **Tip**
>
> Save a copy of your HTML file to use with a copy of your CSS file where you implement the reset code so you can compare the effects of both in the browser.

Exercise 2: Browser Compatibility

Some people check for browser compatibility before validating their code. Since validating often offers clues to errors, my method is to validate first and then check for browser compatibility (some browsers are more forgiving with certain types of errors). Since we validated our code in Chapter 13, now we will turn our efforts to creating code that is compatible with several browsers. There are two places to check—Dreamweaver's compatibility tool and Adobe's BrowserLab.

1. In Dreamweaver, view your source. Choose File > Check Page > Browser Compatibility.
2. You will see the Browser Compatibility panel open at the bottom of the screen where you would normally see the Properties panel. This panel opens in a tabbed interface that displays when selected from the File Menu (as we did earlier) or from Windows > Results. If your file is like mine, you should see that no issues are detected (Figure 14.5).

Figure 14.5   Detected issues are reported in the white space of the Browser Compatibility panel. You can re-test your file from within the panel as seen here, by using the pull-down menu in the top left corner.

Exercise 3: Comparing Views in Adobe BrowserLab

One of my favorite *free* Adobe services is BrowserLab. You can access it online or through the Dreamweaver interface. We will access it through Dreamweaver to see what our offline web page looks like in multiple browsers.

1. View the source code and then choose File > Preview In Browser > Adobe BrowserLab. Click OK through the Permission Settings dialog box to approve viewing your files on Adobe's server.

Note

You will need an Adobe ID to log in to BrowserLab. If you are not logged in, you will be directed to the log-in page, which doubles as a sign-up page.

2. BrowserLab will load in the primary browser where you usually view your work, on a website hosted by Adobe. You will need to log in with an Adobe ID.

Link

Learn more about Browser Lab on Adobe TV. [http://tv.adobe.com/watch/adobe-cs-live/browserlab-user-interface-tour]

Technical Difficulties?

I have occasionally experienced difficulty when accessing Browser-Lab online in the past. If you have a hard time entering BrowserLab, and you've signed in, verified your e-mail address, closed all other BrowserLab tabs in your browser(s), and cleared your cache, see if there might be updates available from Adobe. From the Dreamweaver Help Menu, select Updates. Install new updates and retry BrowserLab. If that doesn't work, find out if you can update your primary browser or your operating system.

3. If you have used BrowserLab before, you will see your page load in a test browser that you selected in the past. When I log in to BrowserLab, I immediately see a version of my web page as it would appear in Internet Explorer version 9 (IE9). As a Mac user, I have to be extra careful about how my page designs will appear when they are viewed on a PC. Since Internet Explorer is the most commonly used browser on the most commonly used platform (PC), this is where I begin. IE9 is a much more compatible browser than previous versions of Explorer, so I'm delighted when the page previews well in IE9 (Figure 14.6).

Figure 14.6 Preview the web page in Internet Explorer version 9 using BrowserLab.

Google Web Fonts in BrowserLab

The Google Web Fonts at use in the page design will not be displayed because BrowserLab is simply showing the offline file—it is not accessing the Google server. So we have to trust that those fonts are going to load in any browser because if a user is seeing your online page, then she has downloaded your content. This means she could also download the fonts from Google's site. In BrowserLab you will see a preview of what the font-face would look like in an offline environment, or if for some reason Google's service was unavailable.

4. No matter what loads when you first launch BrowserLab, let's create a new browser set and see a comparison of views. Click the Browser Sets button at the top of the screen. Select a couple of browsers to define your default browser set (Figure 14.7).

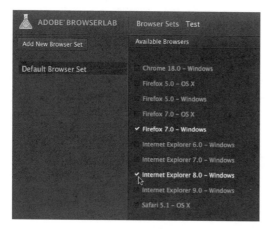

Figure 14.7 Select default browser sets.

5. Click the Test button. If you receive an error about not defining sets, try Step 4 again. Or, if it is possible, use the down arrow to select the default browser set. When the web pages load, select View > 2-up View from the top menu bar to see the two pages side by side (Figure 14.8). Our page looks fine on the Windows version of Firefox, but the IE8 version is not good.

Figure 14.8 Side-by-side views of the Anna Atkins web page in Internet Explorer 8 (IE8) and Firefox 7 for Windows displays the differences between these two browsers.

Exercise 4: Debugging for IE

Overall, this page is actually in pretty good shape. The main trouble that I see is that the navigation tool is rendering improperly in IE8.

1. **Analyze.** What part of the code is problematic? Is it the HTML or the CSS? The CSS on the navigation tool is pretty safe, meaning there is some CSS3 in use, but the structure of the navigation is an inline list with no style type. This validates at the "safe" CSS2 level. However, in the HTML document I did change my navigation tool from a division tag to the more semantically correct HTML5 **<nav>** element. This is probably where Explorer is having trouble. Internet Explorer (at least in versions prior to IE9) has been known to be late in updating the browser for new or progressive code. My options are to change the **nav** tag to a **div** tag and then change my CSS code, which would basically be coding for 2009 when I could be coding for 2013, or find a work-around specifically for versions of Internet Explorer prior to IE9.

2. **Search.** You will spend more time than you would like searching the Web for solutions. Fortunately, on a search for "HTML5" and "IE" I quickly found advice on Google Code {http://code.google.com/p/html5shiv/}, which prompted me to add a few new lines of code to the **head** section of *index.html*.

Tech Tip

I often find useful programming tips on Stack Overflow [http://www.stackoverflow.com] and both programming and conceptual ideas on A List Apart [http://www.alistapart.com].

---

3. **Experiment.** I added these lines of code in the **head** section of my document before the Visual Lightbox section.

Add the patch for IE versions prior to 9 to the **head** section of *index.html*

```
<!--LINK HREF TO THE EXTERNAL STYLE SHEET AND GOOGLE
FONTS -->
<link href="styles.css" rel="stylesheet" type="text/css"
/>
<link
href='http://fonts.googleapis.com/css?family=Ropa+Sans|Ru
thie|Ledger|Zeyada' rel='stylesheet' type='text/css'>
<!--[if lt IE 9]>
<script src="//html5shiv.googlecode.com/svn/trunk/html5.
js"></script>
<![endif]-->
<!-- Start VisualLightBox.com HEAD section -->
```

---

4. **Test.** Save the necessary files (in this case, just *index.html*) and refresh the view in BrowserLab. *Success!* (See Figure 14.9.) The script I pasted from Google Code references a JavaScript file that fixes HTML5 for Internet Explorer versions prior

to IE9. The JavaScript is embedded in a conditional comment (an *if* statement inside a comment tag) that is only seen by the Internet Explorer web browser. All other browsers disregard the script due to the comment tag surrounding it. Explorer was built to recognize conditional comments (perhaps Microsoft realized we would all be writing work-arounds to IE). Our comment basically reads, "For all versions of IE less than 9 run the following script." The script is essentially a patch, enabling prior versions of IE to recognize HTML5 elements. Now my **<nav>** element is recognized, so the CSS is applied to it and the layout displays as I intended.

Figure 14.9 Side-by-side views in which the navigation tool displays properly in IE8.

Reference

For more information on conditional comments, see the Microsoft Developer website. [http://msdn.microsoft.com/en-us/library/ie/hh801214(v=vs.85).aspx]

---

5. **Finish.** Versions of Internet Explorer prior to IE9 do not display many of the CSS3 properties that are now commonly used. For instance, the rounded borders on the navigation tool (that is, the **border-radius** property) are invisible to all versions of IE prior to IE9. You might also notice that the **rgba** property is not supported. Remember that we coded for this possibility as we thought about the design strategy of progressive enhancement in Chapter 10. Rounded borders are not essential to our design. They do appear softer on the page, above the harsh top line at the edge of the background cyanotype graphic, but communication is not limited by the lack of rounded edges in our navigation. The background

color on the navigation tool is also less assuming and more unified with our web page in browsers that do recognize the **rgba** property. Let's modify the background color of the navigation tool that appears before the **rgba** property to make the coloring of **nav li** elements a little less harsh. As I can see now in the IE8 display, the near-primary colors are too childish for Anna Atkins (as is the font-face that would appear if we were strictly offline) and the rest of the layout. Modify the **nav li** selector in *styles.css*. Save your files and retest the page (Figure 14.10).

Modify the `nav li` selector for graceful degradation

```
nav li {
      display: inline;
      padding:3px 20px 3px 20px;
      list-style-type: none;
      background-color: #69F;
      background-color: #b2b2cb;
      background: rgba(255, 255, 255, .5);
      -webkit-border-radius: 7px;
      -moz-border-radius: 7px;
      -o-border-radius: 7px;
      border-radius: 7px;
}
```

Figure 14.10 View the completed web page debugged for proper display in IE8.

Tip

To find the six-digit background color that would most closely mimic the results of our **RGBa** property I took a screen shot of the navigation area of the page in a browser where **RGBa** displayed properly (I also magnified the browser for a close view). Then I opened the screen shot in Photoshop. There I used the Eyedropper tool to sample the color. I was able to find the red, green, and blue values of the foreground color chip properties in the Color sliders set to Web Color Sliders (Figure 14.11). I also could have viewed these properties in the Color Picker.

Figure 14.11 Use the Eyedropper tool in Photoshop to find the RGB color values for the 50% black background when it is set on top of the background color of the website.

6. **Check for further compatibility.** It is a good idea to check for compatibility in as many browsers as you can. Most of the current browsers, including IE9, will display HTML5 and CSS3 pretty well. Older browsers are the most concerning. If you have the luxury of working with a programmer, you will probably be able to pass off design files that display properly in IE8, IE9, and in other current browsers. Only you can decide how accurate you want your site to be among so many browsers. Our page gets a bit goofy in the footer area in prior versions to IE8—it centers in a wider space than the 960 pixels defined in the declaration block (Figure 14.12). I have a feeling the footer can be fixed in those earlier versions of Internet Explorer.

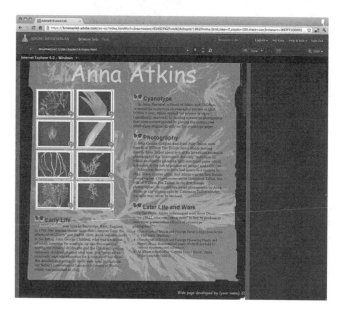

Figure 14.12 Previewing the web page in prior versions of Internet Explorer yields a footer that expands outside the bounds of the container division.

Reference

According to Net Market Share at the time of this writing, approximately 12 percent of the viewing population would experience an off-centered footer in IE6 or IE7. You can generate a report on browser usage any time on NetMarketShare.com. [http://netmarketshare.com/browser-market-share.aspx?qprid=2&qpcustomd=0]

Your Turn!

Repeat steps 1 through 5 to try to debug the footer. Hint: I found a solution on StackOverflow.com. [http://stackoverflow.com/] (At least try to debug for a couple of hours on your own before giving up. You can certainly view my final resulting file for the fix to our last bug). When you are finished, you should be able to load an accurate display of the Anna Atkins web page in BrowserLab for IE6 (Figure 14.13).

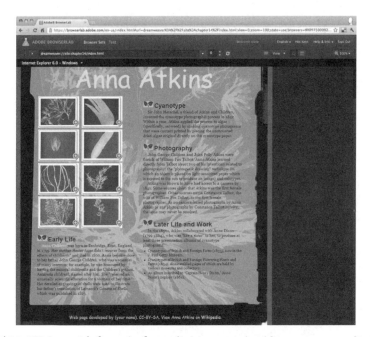

Figure 14.13 With a quick fix to the footer division, you should see an accurate display of the Anna Atkins web page in BrowserLab for IE6.

Note

PNG files will not display transparency in IE6 without the hassle of a work-around. If you are super determined to make the leaf images transparent, you can check out Drew McClellan's 24 Ways article from 2007, "Transparent PNGS in Internet Explorer 6." [http://24ways.org/2007/supersleight-transparent-png-in-ie6] Read it all the way to the end, as you'll likely find SuperSleight to be easier to deal with than some of his beginning ideas.

The Art and Craft of Code

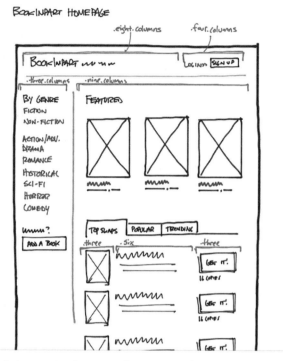

Figure 14.14 A hand-drawn plan for the *Book Impart* interface to be assembled using *Foundations*. *Courtesy of ZURB.*

A List Apart is an e-mag "for people who make websites." It is a beautifully designed site where programmers and designers contribute articles about contemporary trends in website design and development. In Jonathan Smiley's April 10, 2012, article, "Dive into Responsive Prototyping with Foundation," Smiley demonstrates how to use the Zurb framework foundation for creating a prototype of a faux interactive book-sharing project, *BookImpart* (Figure 14.14). [http://www.alistapart.com/articles/dive-into-responsive-prototyping-with-foundation/] This framework is basically a template that you can modify for your own designs. The free package includes CSS style sheets, JavaScript files, images, and a single *index.html* document that displays all of the features. You can download Foundation from Foundation.Zurb.com for further exploration. [http://foundation.zurb.com]

Create, Reflect, Critique

Revisit the secondary pages you created for the Anna Atkins website. Do they validate for HTML5/CSS3? Do they pass the WAVE accessibility test? Do they preview accurately in BrowserLab? (*Really? In all browsers?*) Continue to keep in mind the design principles Dr. Lester wrote about in the introductions to each chapter—contrast, unity, hierarchy, and so on, while completing your version of the website. What elements can you add to the page to break the grid? How does the structure of the division tag help you achieve unity? What properties can you use in the typographic declarations to create contrast? As you complete this website, know that you can always borrow the code for future projects. Add comments to new lines of code as reminders of their functionality.

And when Internet Explorer has you tearing your hair out, remember this: It was so much harder in the 1990s, when we walked backwards, uphill, through ice and snow, just to make an animated GIF for our under-construction websites.

Glossary Words

browser compatibility, CSS reset code

BIBLIOGRAPHY

Chapter 1

Tim Berners-Lee, Robert Cailliau, and the World Wide Web (n.d.). Retrieved from: http://www
.livinginternet.com/w/wi_lee.htm.

Cerf, V. (2009). *Nature*. The day the internet age began. Vol. 461.

DARPA History (n.d.). Retrieved from: http://www.darpa.mil/About/History/History.aspx.

JODI Website (n.d.). Retrieved from: http://www.jodi.org.

Metcalfe, B. (August 21, 1995). *InfoWorld*, Vol. 17, Issue 34.

Quinn, M. (August 15, 2007). Andreessen casts a wide net. *Los Angeles Times*.

Quittner, J. (March 29, 1999). Tim Berners Lee—Time 100 people of the century. *Time Magazine*.

Web's inventor gets a knighthood (December 31, 2003). Retrieved from: http://news.bbc.co.uk/2/
hi/technology/3357073.stm.

Webmonkey Staff. (February 15, 2010). HTML cheatsheet. *Webmonkey.com*. Retrieved from: http://
www.webmonkey.com/2010/02/html_cheatsheet/.

The World Wide Web hall of fame (n.d.). *Best of the web* (2012). Retrieved from: http://botw
.org/1994/awards/fame.html.

Chapter 2

Atkins, Anna. (n.d.). Retrieved from: http://en.wikipedia.org/wiki/Anna_Atkins.

Arnheim, R. (1969). *Visual thinking*. Berkeley: University of California Press.

Brainy Quote. (2012). Retrieved from: http://www.brainyquote.com/quotes/quotes/j/
johannwolf169653.html.

Dingbats > Nature. (n.d.). *Dafont.com*. Retrieved from: http://www.dafont.com/theme.php?cat=712.

Erbez, J. M. (January 21, 2001). Origins of the swastika flag (Third Reich, Germany). Retrieved
from: http://www.crwflags.com/fotw/flags/de%7Dns_or.html.

Fox, M. (June 14, 2007). Rudolf Arnheim, 102, psychologist and scholar of art and ideas, dies.
The New York Times.

Google Labs. (n.d). Browser size. Retrieved from: http://browsersize.googlelabs.com.

Kane, C. HTML color codes. *Rhizome*. Retrieved from: http://archive.rhizome.org/exhibition/
html_color_codes/.

Image Alpha. (n.d.). Retrieved from: http://pngmini.com.

List of displays by pixel density (n.d.). *Wikipedia*. Retrieved from: http://en.wikipedia.org/wiki/
List_of_displays_by_pixel_density.

Vennell, A. (2009). *Color field television*. Retrieved from: http://andrewvenell.com/color-field-
television/.

W3Schools. (n.d.). Browser display statistics. Retrieved from: http://www.w3schools.com/
browsers/browsers_display.asp.

Chapter 3

Frank, A. (2005). *Dontclickit*. Retrieved from: http://dontclick.it/.

Future Exploration Network. (n.d.). Retrieved from: http://futureexploration.net/.

HTML color picker. (n.d.). *W3schools*. Retrieved from: http://www.w3schools.com/tags/ref_colorpicker.asp.

HTML links. (n.d.). *Echoecho.com*. Retrieved from: http://www.echoecho.com/htmllinks.htm.

Lester, P. M. (2013). *Visual communication images with messages, 6th Edition*. Boston: Cengage Learning.

Newspapers: 400 years young! *World Association of Newspapers*. Retrieved from: http://www.wan-press.org/article6476.html 2004.

PDF King website. (n.d.). Retrieved from: http://www.pdfking.com.

Russell, M. C. (2005). Hotspots and hyperlinks: Using eye-tracking to supplement. *Usability Testing*. Vol. 7, Issue 2, pp. 1–11.

Chapter 4

2010 Whitney biennial online Twitter tour. (2010). Retrieved from: http://whitney.org/Events/2010BiennialTwitterTour.

Casey, W. (2009). *Firsts: Origins of everyday things that changed the world*. New York: Penguin.

Free themes directory. (n.d.). *Wordpress.org*. Retrieved from: http://wordpress.org/extend/themes/.

Jorn Barger weblog. (n.d.). Retrieved from: http://www.robotwisdom.com/.

Kalina, N. (n.d.). *Everyday*. Retrieved from: http://www.youtube.com/watch?v=6B26asyGKDo.

Les Liens Invisibles. *A fake is a fake*. Retrieved from: http://fake.isafake.org/.

Noah Kalina website (n.d.). Retrieved from: http://www.noahkalina.com/.

Pepys, S. (n.d.). *The diary of samuel pepys*. Retrieved from: http://www.pepysdiary.com/.

Weschler, L. (1996). *Mr. Wilson's cabinet of wonder: Pronged ants, horned humans, mice on toast, and other marvels of jurassic technology*. New York: Vintage.

WordPress.com (n.d.). Retrieved from: http://www.wordpress.com.

Chapter 5

CSS saga, the. (n.d.). Retrieved from: http://www.w3.org/Style/LieBos2e/history/.

Fu, R. (n.d.). *Dark rose website*. Retrieved from: http://www.csszengarden.com/?cssfile=194/194.css.

Hustwit, G. (2007). *Helvetica*. Gary Hustwit, Swiss Dots, and Veer. Trailer Retrieved from: http://youtu.be/wkoX0pEwSCw.

Lie, H. W. and B. Bos. (1999). *Cascading style sheets, designing for the web*. Harlow: Addison Wesley.

Lester, P. M., op. cit.

Shea, D. (n.d.). *CSS Zen garden website*. Retrieved from: http://www.csszengarden.com/.

Starr, C. G. (1974). *A History of the ancient world, 2nd Edition*. Oxford: Oxford University Press.

Stoltz, E. (n.d.). *Under the sea! website*. Retrieved from: http://www.csszengarden.com/?cssfile=213/213.css.

Tan, J. (n.d.). *Leggo my ego website*. Retrieved from: http://www.csszengarden.com/?cssfile=193/193.css.

Chapter 6

Bhushan, A. K. (n.d.). Retrieved from: www.soton.ac.uk/~auk1w07/files/iitk50profiles.pdf.

Cyberduck. (n.d.). Retrieved from: www.cyberduck.ch.

Firefox. (n.d.). *Add-ons for Firefox*. Retrieved from: https://addons.mozilla.org/en-US/firefox/.

FireFTP. (n.d.). *FireFTP*. Retrieved from: http://fireftp.mozdev.org/.

Free Art and Technology Lab (F.A.T.) (n.d.). *Occupy internet*. Retrieved from: http://occupyinter.net/.

Instructables website. (n.d.). Retrieved from: http://www.Instructables.com.

Lester, P. M., op. cit.

Livingston, J. (2008). *Founders at work: Stories of startups' early days*. New York: Apress.

Make. (n.d.). Retrieved from: http://www. makezine.com.

Chapter 7

Font Squirrel website. (n.d.). Retrieved from: http://www.fontsquirrel.com/.

Google Web Fonts. (n.d.). Retrieved from: http://www.google.com/webfonts.

Kinetic website. (n.d.). *Not just a fanzine.* Issue 1. Retrieved from: http://www.kinetic.com.sg/main.html.

Lester, P. M. op. cit.

Pagels, E. (2012). *Revelations: Visions, prophecy, and politics in the book of revelation.* Viking Adult.

Santa Maria, J. (November 17, 2009). On web typography. *A List Apart.* Retrieved from: http://www.alistapart.com/articles/on-web-typography/.

Way, J. (Februrary 19, 2010). Quick tip: How to work with @Font-face. *Nettutsplus.com.* Retrieved from: http://net.tutsplus.com/tutorials/design-tutorials/quick-tip-how-to-work-with-font-face/.

Chapter 8

Biography of Vincent Flanders (2012). Retrieved from: http://www.webpagesthatsuck.com/vincent-flanders.html.

Chapman, C. (September 29, 2007). 80+ Free 2-column website templates. *Mashable.* Retrieved from: http://mashable.com/2007/09/29/2-column-website-templates/.

Cronin, M. (February 4, 2009). 50 Beautiful and user-friendly navigation menus. *Smashing Books.* Retrieved from: http://www.smashingmagazine.com/2009/02/04/50-beautiful-and-user-friendly-navigation-menus/.

Holt, C. (November 1, 2010). Readability: The optimal line length. Retrieved from: http://baymard.com/blog/line-length-readability.

Lester, P. M. (1993). Looks are deceiving: The portraits of Christopher Columbus. In *Visual anthropology.* Vol. 5, pp. 211–227.

____. (2009). *On floods and photo ops: How Herbert Hoover and George W. Bush exploited catastrophes.* Mississippi: University Press of Mississippi.

Listamatic website. (n.d.). Retrieved from: http://css.maxdesign.com.au/listamatic/.

Livingstone, D. (n.d.). Basic box model demo. *Tstme.* Retrieved from: http://www.redmelon.net/tstme/box_model/.

W3C. (June 7, 2011). Recommendation: Box model. Retrieved from: http://www.w3.org/TR/CSS21/box.html.

Where are they now? Roy Riegels worst football blunder (n.d.). Retrieved from: http://www.trivia-library.com/a/where-are-they-now-roy-riegels-worst-football-blunder.htm.

Young-Hae Chang Heavy Industries. (2007). *Resumé I?* Retrieved from: http://www.yhchang.com/RESUMAY_I.html.

Chapter 9

Knight, K. (June 2, 2009). Fixed vs. fluid vs. elastic layout: What's the right one for you? *Smashing Magazine.* Retrieved from: http://coding.smashingmagazine.com/2009/06/02/fixed-vs-fluid-vs-elastic-layout-whats-the-right-one-for-you/.

Lester, P. M. *Visual communication.* op. cit.

Smalley, T. (2011). *Vector drawings.* Retrieved from: http://www.travesssmalley.com/vector_drawings/.

W3C. (Last updated November 20, 2011). CSS/Properties/background. Retrieved from: http://www.w3.org/wiki/CSS/Properties/background.

Writer's almanac, the. (September 26, 2008). Retrieved from: http://writersalmanac.publicradio.org/index.php?date=2008/09/26.

Chapter 10

Bijani, J. (n.d.). *Border radius.* Retrieved from: http://border-radius.com/.

Broms-Engblom, J. (2011). *It's all about the lighting.* Retrieved from: http://www.likeneveralways.com/itsallaboutthelighting/.

___. (2009). *Playing in the surf.* Retrieved from: http://www.likeneveralways.com/playinginthesurf/.

Cornelius, J. (2011). *IsHTML5ReadyYet?* Retrieved from: http://ishtml5readyyet.com/.

Coyier, C. (July 8, 2009). All about floats. *CSS-Tricks.* Retrieved from: http://css-tricks.com/all-about-floats.

CSS3 previews. (n.d.). *CSS3.info.* Retrieved from: http://www.css3.info/preview/.

DanceDanceRevolution Wii (n.d.). Retrieved from: http://www.konami.com/games/ddr/.

Guttmann, A. and L. Thompson. (1979). *Japanese sports: A history.* Hawaii: University of Hawai'i Press.

HTML5 differences from HTML4. (March 29, 2012). *W3C.* Retrieved from: http://www.w3.org/TR/html5-diff/.

Harris, H. A. (1972). *Sport in Greece and Rome.* New York: Cornell University Press.

Lawson, B. and R. Sharp. (2011). *Introducing HTML5.* Berkeley: New Riders.

Lennartz, S. (April 8, 2008). Footers in modern web design: Creative examples and ideas. Retrieved from: http://www.smashingmagazine.com/2008/04/08/footers-in-modern-web-design-creative-examples-and-ideas/.

McNall, G. (January 19, 2011). Football soccer history & development. Retrieved from: http://www.livestrong.com/article/360994-football-soccer-history-development/.

Paulo Taneda website (n.d.). Retrieved from: http://www.paulotaneda.com.br/.

Progressive enhacement: Core principles (n.d.). *Wikipedia.* Retrieved from: http://en.wikipedia.org/wiki/Progressive_enhancement#Core_principles.

Totilo, S. (January 25, 2006). *West Virginia adds Dance Dance Revolution to gym class.* Retrieved from: http://www.mtv.com/news/articles/1521605/dance-dance-revolution-added-gym-classes.jhtml?headlines=true.

Chapter 11

burrough, x. (2011). *On the web—original version.* Retrieved from: http://www.missconceptions.net/on-the-web/index-otw-original.html.

___. (2012). *On the web homepage.* Retrieved from: http://www.missconceptions.net/on-the-web.

Cairns, M. (2010). *New CSS sticky footer.* Retrieved from: http://www.cssstickyfooter.com/.

Fait, R. (2012). *A CSS sticky footer.* Retrieved from: http://ryanfait.com/sticky-footer/.

Font designer—Howard Kettler (2012). Retrieved from: http://www.linotype.com/3315/howardkettler.html.

Font designer—William Caslon (2012). Retrieved from: http://www.linotype.com/348/williamcaslon.html.

History of columns (n.d.). Retrieved from: http://www.columns.net/column_history.php 2010.

Lester, P. M. *Visual communication.* Op. cit.

Macmillan, N. (2006). *An A-Z of type designers.* New Haven: Yale University Press.

Roberts, W. (1992). *Jacques-Louis David, revolutionary artist: Art, politics, and the french revolution.* North Carolina: The University of North Carolina Press.

Schom, A. (1998). *Napoleon Bonaparte: A life.* New York: Harper Perennial.

Chapter 12

Animal. (April 8, 2008). Shepard Fairey threatens to sue artist for OBEY giant parody *ANIMALNewYork.* Retrieved from: http://animalnewyork.com/2008/04/shepard-fairey-threatens-to-sue-artist-for-obey-giant-parody/.

Banksy website (n.d.). Retrieved from: http://www.banksy.co.uk/.

Favicon.ico generator website (n.d.). Retrieved from: http://www.favicon.cc/.

Free/Libre/Open source software (2012). *Worldwide impact study.* Retrieved from: http://www.flossworld.org/.

Kleber, J. E. (1992). Carpenter, John Howard. In *The Kentucky encyclopedia.* Thomas D. Clark, Lowell H. Harrison, and James C. Klotter (eds). Kentucky: The University Press of Kentucky.

Krugman, M. (2009). *André the giant: A legendary life.* New York: Pocket Books.

McDonald, J. (2005). *Screen kiss.* Retrieved from: http://www.soilmedia.org/screenkiss/.

New York Public Library (December 9, 2008). Cyanotype of British algae by Anna Atkins. In *Flickr .com website*. Retrieved from: http://www.flickr.com/photos/nypl/sets/72157610898556889/.

Ng, D. (October 16, 2009). Shepard Fairey admits to wrongdoing in Associated Press lawsuit. *Los Angeles Times*. Entertainment. Retrieved from: http://latimesblogs.latimes.com/culturemonster/2009/10/shepard-fairey-admits-to-wrongdoing-in-associated-press-lawsuit.html.

Open Source Initiative website (n.d.). Retrieved from: http://www.opensource.org/.

President Barack Obama (2008). *The white house*. Retrieved from: http://www.whitehouse.gov/administration/president-obama.

Shepard Fairey website (n.d.). *Obey*. Retrieved from: http://obeygiant.com/headlines/obama.

Smith-Miles, C. (January 17, 2009). *Independent mail*. Local woman's grandson behind the Obama "Hope" poster. Retrieved from: http://www.independentmail.com/news/2009/jan/17/local-womans-grandson-behind-obama-hope-poster/?partner=RSS.

Vallen, M. (n.d.). *Whatever happened to the future!* Retrieved from: http://art-for-a-change.com/blog/2006/04/whatever-happened-to-future.html.

Visual Lightbox Application. (Last updated November 15, 2011). Retrieved from: http://visuallightbox.com/index.html#download.

Chapter 13

ADA website. (2012). U.S. Department of Justice. Retrieved from: http://www.ada.gov/.

Aitken, J. (2007). *John Newton: From disgrace to amazing grace*. New York: Crossway Books.

Amazing Grace with Bill Moyers (1990). *Public Affairs Television, Inc*. Retrieved from: http://en.wikipedia.org/wiki/Amazing_Grace - cite_ref-moyers_2-4.

burrough, x. (2012). *Balloons in the Library of Congress*. Retrieved from: http://missconceptions.net/loc/balloons/.

____. (2010). *The Library of Congress remixed*. Retrieved from: http://missconceptions.net/loc.

Hanlon, M. (2012). Volvo launches blind spot information system (BLIS). *Gizmag*. Retrieved from: http://www.gizmag.com/go/2937/.

Rothenberg, S. (2009). *School of perpetual training*. Retrieved from: http://turbulence.org/Works/perpetualtraining/index.php.

Section 508 website. (n.d.). Retrieved from: http://www.section508.gov/.

Smith, J. (December 6, 2011). Alexa 100 accessibility errors. *WebAIM website*. Retrieved from: http://webaim.org/blog/alexa-100-accessibility-errors/.

W3C (1994, 2009). *CSS validation service*. Retrieved from: http://jigsaw.w3.org/css-validator/.

W3C (November 6, 2000). HTML techniques for web content accessibility guidelines 1.0. Retrieved from: http://www.w3.org/TR/WCAG10-HTML-TECHS/.

W3C (1994, 2012). *Markup validation service*. Retrieved from: http://validator.W3C.org.

W3C (December 11, 2008). *Web content accessibility guidelines*. Retrieved from: http://www.w3.org/TR/2008/REC-WCAG20-20081211/.

WAVE (2012). *Web accessibility evaluation tool*. Retrieved from: http://wave.webaim.org/.

Web accessibility in mind website. (1999, 2012). Retrieved from: http://webaim.org/.

White Stripes website. (n.d.). Retrieved from: http://www.whitestripes.com/.

Chapter 14

Adobe BrowserLab website. (2011). Retrieved from: https://browserlab.adobe.com/en-us/index.html.

Benner, S. (February 20, 2010). Reset cascading style sheets are bad practice. *Steven Benner's Blog*. Retrieved from: http://stevenbenner.com/2010/02/reset-cascading-style-sheets-are-bad-practice/.

Campion, N. (2009). *A history of western astrology: The ancient and classical worlds*. New York: Continuum.

Foundation. (n.d.). Retrieved from: http://foundation.zurb.com.

Google Code. (n.d.). Html5shiv: HTML5 IE enabling script. *Google Code*. Retrieved from: http://code.google.com/p/html5shiv/.

Horoscopes. (n.d.). *eAstrolog.* Retrieved from: eAstrolog.com.

MSDN. (n.d.). About conditional comments. *MSDN website.* Retrieved from: http://msdn.microsoft
.com/en-us/library/ms537512(v=vs.85).aspx#syntax.

McLellan, D. (December 2007). Transparent PNGs in Internet Explorer 6. *24 Ways.* Retrieved
from: http://24ways.org/2007/supersleight-transparent-png-in-ie6.

Meyer, E. (n.d.). CSS tools: Reset CSS. *Meyerweb.com.* Retrieved from: http://meyerweb.com/eric/
tools/css/reset/.

NetMarketShare. (April 2012). Desktop browser version market share. Retrieved from: http://
netmarketshare.com/browser-market-share.aspx?qprid=2&qpcustomd=0.

Smiley, J. (April 10, 2012). Dive into responsive prototyping with Foundation. *A List Apart.*
Retrieved from: http://www.alistapart.com/articles/dive-into-responsive-prototyping-with-
foundation/.

Stack Overflow website. (n.d.). http://www.stackoverflow.com.

Watters, J. (2003). *Astrology for today.* New York: Carroll & Brown.

Yahoo! (2012). YUI 2: Reset CSS. *Yahoo! Developer Network.* Retrieved from: http://developer
.yahoo.com/yui/reset/#code.

Zeldman, J. L. (Ed.). (1998, 2012). *A List Apart.* Retrieved from: http://www.alistapart.com.

GLOSSARY

<a> represents a hyperlink. It is commonly used with an attribute such as **<a href>** or **<a name>**.

<a href> is the **a** tag with the **href** attribute, used to establish a hyperlink.

<a name> is the **a** tag with the **name** attribute, used to establish an anchor on a page.

Absolute positioning Used to remove an element from the normal flow of the page and place it according to an offset value (top, right, bottom, or left) from the edges of its first (relative or fixed) positioned ancestor element.

Add-ons See *Browser add-ons*.

Americans with Disabilities Act (ADA) An act passed into law in 1990 granting civil rights, including Section 508, which accounted for accessible technologies, to those with disabilities.

Anchor In HTML, an anchor is an invisible placeholder that can be used for linking to a specific location on a page.

Appropriation The act of taking a popular word, idea, image, or thing for the purpose of transforming it into something new. This new word/idea/image/thing might comment upon the original, demonstrate social patterns associated with the original, or through juxtaposition or comparison, present an unexpected aspect of the original.

ARPA The Advanced Research Projects Agency (U.S.) is partly responsible for the invention of the Internet during the Cold War era.

Bauhaus style Stemming from the Bauhaus architectural school, this design style includes an organized grid approach where balance and alignment are keys in producing layouts for print and screen media.

body is the second of two areas in an HTML document. **<body>** is the tag used to denote where the content of the web page begins. All of the content ends just before the closing tag, **</body>**.

Blackletter An ornate and decorative typeface originally used by scribes in monasteries for handwritten works.

Blogging

    Categories Unlike tags, which can be used to establish the taxonomy of a single post, categories are used to establish the taxonomy of an entire blog.

    Dashboard The main portal to content management when a user is logged in to her WordPress blog.

    Header The area at the top of the blog that often includes a banner-sized image and/or a caption.

    Post A single article or scheduled communication.

    Sidebar A section of the blog devoted to widgets such as a calendar, list of links (Blogroll), meta information, and so on.

Theme The graphic design template for the blog.

Widget A graphical user interface that visually organizes information.

Browser add-ons Downloadable files that extend or modify the way a browser functions.

Browser compatibility Code that displays similarly in multiple web browsers.

Class selector This variable selector is not limited to an HTML tag and can be given any name and referenced multiple times in the HTML page.

Comments Code that is hidden or skipped by the browser, most often used to write messages to other coders, hints, or reminders about the code.

Container div A division used to wrap the contents of a page, usually with the CSS properties of automatic left and right margins and a defined width.

Contrast A break in visual harmony.

Creative Commons license An alternative to the traditional U.S. copyright license that allows the author to share her work and retain attribution.

CSS Cascading Style Sheets contain the code that controls how content in the browser should be displayed. A CSS file is often saved in the root directory and referenced in the **head** section of the HTML document in order to separate the display (or form) from the content.

CSS

Declaration A set of properties and values ascribed to a selector (there can be more than one declaration for a selector).

Declaration block A series of properties and values inserted between (and including) an open and closed curly bracket.

Reset code A snippet of code that is placed at the top of a style sheet in order to control the browser default settings.

Rule or rule set Defines how to display an element on an HTML page and includes both a selector and its declaration block.

Selector Indicates which element in the HTML document will be affected by the rule set, and can be a tag, class, ID, or "compound" (such as a class and particular children tags).

Deprecated tag An HTML tag that is no longer supported by current browsers. For instance, the center tag, <center>, was once widely used to center-align elements in HTML. Now the preferred method of declaring alignment is with the text-align CSS property.

<div> is an HTML tag used to separate content into divisions on the page. Surrounds content with the open and close tag, **<div>** and **</div>**.

Domain See *Web domain*.

Elastic layout A web page layout defined by elastic measurements (ems).

Elastic measurement (em) Determined by the user. 1em is a user-defined preference based on the default type size setting. If a user does not modify the default type size setting in a browser, 1em is equivalent to 16 pixels.

External style sheets Saved in a .css file and linked to the HTML document via the **link** tag in the **head** section of the file.

Eye-tracking A method of following where users or readers look within the confines of a viewport.

Fair use A clause in the U.S. copyright laws that allows artists and authors to transform existing copyright-protected works into new works.

Fixed layout A web page layout defined by pixel dimensions.

Fixed positioning Displays an element according to values measured from the top, right, bottom, or left edge of the browser window.

Float A CSS property used to align HTML elements.

Fluid layout A web page layout defined by percentages so the content fills the space of the browser.

Footer A (usually) horizontal strip of information and links at the bottom of a web page.

FTP File Transfer Protocol is a method of passing files from one computer connected to a network to another connected computer.

Freeform artistic styles Includes art nouveau, Dada, art deco, pop art, punk, new wave, and hip-hop; and are noted for a playful placement of text and graphic elements within a design's frame.

Gestalt theory of visual perception Accounts for perception of unity through the cohesiveness of an entire presentation.

GIF (Graphics Interchange Format) A file format used to compress line art, vector art, or graphics with absolute transparency using only eight bits of color data.

Grid An organizational structure that can lead to a seemingly objective or unemotional approach to creative stylings.

head is the first of two areas in an HTML document. This area contains information about the document, also known as meta-information, and it is indicated by the opening and closing tags, **<head>** and **</head>**.

Hosting See *Web hosting*.

HTML Hypertext Markup Language is the programming language recognized by browsers. Using HTML, you can direct a browser to display content on a web page.

HTML5 The fifth version of HTML in which new tags are named according to the types of functions they perform.

<html> is a tag used to open an HTML page. Close the page with **</html>**.

Hyperlink A media element that refers to another set of data via a mouse click (commonly known as a "link").

ID selector A name given to a declaration block that will be referenced only one time in the HTML document.

<img> is the HTML image tag. It is most often accompanied by the attributes **src** (source) and **alt** (alternative text).

Inline CSS styles Saved on a single line of HTML code in the **body** section utilizing the **style** attribute of an HTML tag.

Internal CSS styles Saved in the **head** section of the HTML document between the **<style>** and **</style>** tags.

JPG (Joint Photographic Experts Group) A file format used to compress photographic images, or images with a continuous tonal range, for viewing in a browser with 24 bits of color data.

<li> is an HTML tag used to create list items. Surround the listed item with the open and close tag, **<li>** and **</li>**.

<link> is a tag used to connect external files to an HTML document. This tag should be placed in the **head** section of the HTML file.

Local files Saved on a user's hard drive. Local files are not necessarily networked.

Lossless compression A form of data compression in which the saved information can be selected by the user.

Lossy compression A form of data compression in which the saved file loses information with little user input.

Miscellaneous typeface Also known as display type, the style is too expressive and ornate to be used in body copy, and draws attention to itself when it is used in headlines.

Modular design Text and images are placed within a layout in rectangular shapes called modules.

Mosaic The first web browser created by Marc Andreessen and Eric Bina.

`<ol>` is an HTML tag used to create an ordered list. Surround each set of listed items in the ordered list with the open and close tag, **`<ol>`** and **`</ol>`**.

`<p>` is the tag used at the beginning of a paragraph of body copy in the HTML document. The close p tag, **`</p>`**, should be used at the end of the paragraph.

Parents and children (in HTML or CSS) Parent elements contain (or surround) children elements.

Perception The process from the eye to the brain.

Perceiving This is reserved for the mind where understanding and meaning happen.

PNG (Portable Network Graphics) A file format used to compress line art, vector art, or graphics with some degree of transparency for viewing in a browser with 24 bits of color data.

Progressive enhancement Steven Champeon's terminology for programming a web page in such a way that the newer elements will be displayed in browsers that support them while also including older elements for browsers that are not updated.

Proportion A visual relationship in regard to scale.

Resolution The number of dots (for ink-related media) or pixels (for screen media) per inch of output.

RGBa A color model used in CSS style sheets that recognizes the full red, green, and blue spectrum, as well as an alpha channel for transparency.

Relative positioning Used to offset an element by values (top, right, bottom, or left) relating to where the element would have been placed according to the normal page flow.

Roman typeface The most commonly used typeface today, with gently curved serifs that create easy-to-read lines.

Root directory The first-level directory on a server or the first-level folder on your hard drive where, for instance, you save all of the files you will use to create a website.

Sans serif A modern typeface that lacks serifs and is generally easier than a serif typeface to read on a screen where light is projected from behind the text to the viewer's eye.

Script typeface A type family designed to mimic the handwriting of ordinary people.

Section 508 of the ADA The part of the Americans with Disabilities Act of 1990 that specifically accounts for creating accessible technologies, including code for websites.

Server A networked hard drive that is able to facilitate communication between clients.

Square serif A typeface characterized by its awkward, blocky appearance.

Static positioning The default position value when no other value is declared. Static positioning follows the regular page flow.

Tag selector An HTML tag that is used to define a CSS rule.

Taxonomy The science of classifying organisms.

`<title>` is the tag used to indicate the title of the web page, which can be viewed in the tab area of the browser. Use the close title tag, **`</title>`**, to surround the word or phrase you want to use as the title of your web page.

Tool tip In Dreamweaver, tool tips assist you when you are working in code view.

`<ul>` is an HTML tag used to create an unordered list. Surround each set of listed items in the unordered list with the open and close tag, **`<ul>`** and **`</ul>`**.

Unity In visual communication, this is a presentational concept in which separate elements are seen as a consistent whole.

Universal selector A CSS selector that can be used to represent (or add declarations to) any element, indicated by the asterisk (*).

Validation (in code) Checking your code to ensure proper usage.

Viewport Any location where a user is interacting with media, usually on a screen and through a browser.

Visual constructivism A theory of visual communication in which users perceive images via an active state of collecting in their brains a series of short-term memory bursts that work together to produce a visual array.

Visual cues The four major categories of visual perception—color, form, depth, and movement—comprise the visual cues.

Web domain A unique Internet Protocol address translated into the name of a website.

Web hosting A storage service for files you want to display or share on the Web.

xtine A nickname for Christine, silly.

z-index is a CSS property that controls the visual stacking order of overlapping elements.

INDEX